The Mystery of Scripture

Volume 1

Larry D. Harper

The Elijah Project

— Mesquite, Texas —

The Mystery of Scripture, Volume 1
Copyright © 1994, 2005 by The Elijah Project
Mesquite, Texas

ISBN 1-880761-04-1 (*The Mystery of Scripture* Series)
ISBN 1-880761-05-X (*The Mystery of Scripture*, Volume 1)

Unless otherwise indicated, Scripture taken from the NEW AMERICAN STARDARD BIBLE, © Copyright 1960, 1962, 1963, 1968, 1971, 1972, 1973, 1975, 1977, 1987, 1988, The Lockman Foundation. Used by permission. Boldfaced segments of scriptural passages represent the emphasis of the author.

World rights reserved. No part of the new matter in this publication may be stored in a retrieval system, reproduced, or transmitted in any way by any means—electronic, mechanical, photocopy, photograph, magnetic recording, or any other—without the prior written permission of the publisher.

Address all correspondence to:
The Elijah Project
P.O. Box 870153
Mesquite, Texas 75187

Printed in the United States by Morris Publishing
3212 East Highway 30
Kearney, NE 68847
1-800-650-7888

Preface

As many of you are aware, this first volume of *The Mystery of Scripture* is more than a decade late. For that, I sincerely apologize to those who have been patiently waiting for so long. When research on the project began in 1992, I envisioned the publication as nothing more than a 60-page booklet. As work progressed, however, what I had initially viewed as just a small booklet first grew into a 283-page book and eventually into what is currently on track to be a set of at least three volumes. Therefore, some—but by no means all—of the delay in publishing this book was the result of the expanded nature of the work itself.

Although the initial postponement in publication was not due to things over which I had total control, the project has been stymied for the past seven or eight years because I could never figure out why the work did not "feel right" when I tried to complete the final edits. Needless to say, I needed someone to help me get past a fairly serious case of "writer's block." So if you profit from what you read here, please let Faye Chandler know you appreciate the contributions she has made to both The Elijah Project and *The Voice of Elijah* over the years. Earlier this year, she not only pointed out what was wrong with the original manuscript; she also told me how to fix it. Words are not sufficient to express my gratitude. The impending publication of this book has already alleviated a good deal of the "psychological dysfunction" I have felt for several years now.

My sincere thanks also go out to Faye's daughter, Janet Lohman, and to Marcia Woody, both of whom, together with Faye, picked up the editing of *The Mystery of Scripture* project after the death of Susan Clay on March 28, 2000. Without the advantage of their knowledge and willingness to help, I would still be trying to decide where to put punctuation—and why. Working together, these three women have continued to maintain the incredibly high standard of editorial excellence that Susan set during her brief run as editor. From the zeal and dedication that Susan brought to her own work, I can only imagine she is, even now, enthusiastically cheering them on (Heb. 12:1).

August 15, 2005

CONTENTS

INTRODUCTION

In any academic inquiry, regardless of the area of study, scholars conduct research under the assumption that there is but one truth to be discovered. The premise of investigation into everything from anthropology to zoology is exactly the same: Truth is truth; error is error. Truth must be sought out and shown to be such by rational means. If two theories concerning relevant evidence contradict each other, those involved in the inquiry immediately understand they must reject one or both of those theories as erroneous.

Yet, if one accepts conventional wisdom, the assumption of one truth does not hold true for any inquiry concerning God. Oh sure, everybody pays lip service to the idea, but in practice, there is a tacit understanding that *the Truth* about God is impossible to obtain. There is also the underlying supposition that an accurate understanding of God's plan and purpose for this Creation—if indeed it is even allowed that He created it—is not all that important, so why quibble over a few minor details?

The more accommodating among us believe God must be like Rome, as in the old saw "all roads lead to Rome." That being the case, it doesn't matter all that much what religious beliefs one holds. It is only important that one believes there is a god.[1] Obviously, those who believe that lie have no interest in seeking the Truth concerning the *Living* God. They are perfectly content to construct elaborate theological theories which they then present for the admiration and approval of others. Unfortunately, such people have long been the majority. As a result, theological truth has long since become nothing more than a matter of numbers. The more who believe a particular theory, the more comfortable its adherents are in believing it to be true. But they forget what Jesus said about the many who follow the broad road that leads to destruction.[2]

The difficulty one faces in any inquiry concerning God is an apparent lack of hard evidence. No one has ever seen Him. Therefore, it is rather difficult to determine what is and is not true when the subject of the discussion may or may not even exist. That is why, in the opinion of most, the issue of God and His supposed existence has rightly been relegated to the realm of philosophy. As everybody knows, there is no truth or error in philosophy. There is only the "sophisticated" demonstration of mental prowess and impressive elocution on the part of the philosopher. The foremost consideration in philosophical studies over the past couple of centuries has not been, "Is it true or false?" It has increasingly become, "Are we sufficiently impressed?"

The consignment of the discussion of God's existence to philosophers as their exclusive domain toward the end of the nineteenth century was a direct result of the publication and widespread acceptance of the thesis presented in Charles Darwin's *Origin of Species*.[3] Darwin's theory of evolution had an extremely detrimental effect on Christianity. It drove wedges

---

[1] I have demonstrated the fallacy of that position in these two articles: "The Demons Also Believe (Poor Devils!)" and "Do You Believe the Gospel of Jesus Christ?" *The Voice of Elijah*, October 1991.

[2] Matthew 7:13.

[3] See "Do You Believe the Gospel of Jesus Christ?" *The Voice of Elijah*, October 1991.

between three areas of discussion which had been inseparably linked in orthodox Christian theology up to that time:

The Hebrew/Greek Scriptures

Christianity

The God of the Old Testament

After the publication of Darwin's *Origin of Species*, for many the Bible became nothing more than ancient literature, Christianity just another religion, and the existence of the God of the Old Testament an issue for philosophical discussion.

To their credit, some segments of Christendom have continued to defend the historic Christian beliefs that the Bible is revelation, Christianity is the only true religion, and the God of the Old Testament is the author of salvation through the death and resurrection of Jesus Christ. During the early part of the twentieth century, the Fundamentalist Movement even made the delineation of these truths its primary focus. Some Evangelicals have continued the same campaign down to our own day, although most now seem to have rejected the Old Testament (and historic Christian) concept of a vengeful God of wrath in favor of the loving, all-forgiving god of grace that liberal theologians concocted in the late nineteenth century.[4]

Lately, the conservative defense of the historic tenets of Christianity has devolved into a demand that "scientific creationism" be taught in public schools and "abortion on demand" be outlawed.[5] That is unfortunate inasmuch as it diverts the True Believer's attention from the primary issue at stake: What do we know about God?

---

[4] See "Oh, So Many Four-Letter Words!" and "On Fairy Tales and Holy Hell," *The Voice of Elijah*, July 1992.

[5] I have discussed some of the reasons for the conservative focus on social issues in "Protestants All Agree on This: Somebody Laid an Egg!" *The Voice of Elijah*, January 1994.

The Apostolic Teaching

The Apostles founded Christianity on the single, unified, divinely revealed plan of salvation recorded in the Hebrew Scriptures—that is, in the Old Testament. The Prophets who wrote those Scriptures claim the God of Abraham, Isaac, and Jacob, whom they repeatedly describe as a God of wrath, revealed that Truth to them.[6] In the historic Christian view, Jesus Christ revealed that same Truth to the Apostles, who proclaimed it to the world as the Gospel message of Jesus Christ.[7] So, for the past eighteen hundred years, Christians have contended that the twenty-seven books of the New Testament contain a written record of that revealed Gospel.

---

[6] See "Did You Mean That Literally?" *The Voice of Elijah*, January 1993 and "Some People Will Make Light of Anything," *The Voice of Elijah*, April 1994.

[7] Early Christians sometimes called their understanding of the Old Testament message *The Teaching*, as the Apostle Paul does in his letter to the church at Rome:

> Now I urge you, brethren, keep your eye on those who cause dissensions and hindrances contrary to **the teaching** which you learned, and turn away from them.
> (Romans 16:17)

Paul used the same terminology in a letter to his disciple Titus:

> For the overseer must be above reproach as God's steward, not self-willed, not quick-tempered, not addicted to wine, not pugnacious, not fond of sordid gain, but hospitable, loving what is good, sensible, just, devout, self-controlled, holding fast the faithful word which is in accordance with **the teaching**, that he may be able both to exhort in sound doctrine and to refute those who contradict.
> (Titus 1:7–9)

The Apostle John uses more or less the same expression:

> Anyone who goes too far and does not abide in **the teaching of Christ**, does not have God; the one who abides in **the teaching**, he has both the Father and the Son.
> (2 John 9)

I have already mentioned why the apostolic understanding of the Old Testament message was called *The Teaching*. See "Where Are Jesus' Disciples?" *The Voice of Elijah*, April 1991 and *Not All Israel Is Israel* (Mesquite, Texas: The Elijah Project, 1991), p. 92, fn. 14, et al.

The Apostles firmly believed the Gospel they preached could be found in the Hebrew Scriptures. Moreover, they and the Early Church Fathers up until the time of Clement of Alexandria (ca. A.D. 185) vehemently rejected the suggestion that there might be more than one way to understand the message of the Old Testament. In his letter to the Galatians, the Apostle Paul agrees. He denounces those false teachers who were infiltrating the Church and preaching a "different gospel," that is, a message contrary to the Gospel message he insisted he and the other Apostles preached—in perfect agreement. He writes this:

> *I am amazed that you are so quickly deserting Him who called you by the grace of Christ, for **a different gospel**; which is {really} not another; only there are some who are disturbing you, and want to distort the gospel of Christ. But **even though we, or an angel from heaven, should preach to you a gospel contrary to that which we have preached to you, let him be accursed**. As we have said before, so I say again now, **if any man is preaching to you a gospel contrary to that which you received, let him be accursed**.*
> *(Galatians 1:6–9)*

Paul says he rejected "a different gospel" because he had not derived the Gospel he preached by studying the Hebrew Scriptures or from theological discussion with others. He obtained it directly from Jesus Christ by revelation:

> *For I would have you know, brethren, that the gospel which was preached by me is not according to man. For **I neither received it from man, nor was I taught it, but {I received it} through a revelation of Jesus Christ**.*
> *(Galatians 1:11–12)*

Paul also contends that the Gospel Jesus Christ revealed to him was exactly the same Gospel that Peter and the other Apostles preached. He makes that point a bit later in his letter to the Galatians. He says he went up to Jerusalem fourteen years after God called him for the specific purpose of submitting the content of his Gospel for the inspection and approval of the other Apostles:

*Then after an interval of fourteen years I went up again to Jerusalem with Barnabas, taking Titus along also. And it was because of a revelation that I went up; and I **submitted to them the gospel which I preach among the Gentiles**, but {I did so} in private to those who were of reputation, **for fear that I might be running, or had run, in vain**.*
(Galatians 2:1–2)

During that visit, the Apostles who lived in Jerusalem acknowledged that Jesus Christ had indeed given Paul the same insight into the Old Testament Gospel message that He had granted them during the forty-day interval between His resurrection and His ascension:[8]

*But from those who were of high reputation (what they were makes no difference to me; God shows no partiality)—well, those who were of reputation contributed nothing to me. **But on the contrary, seeing that I had been entrusted with the gospel to the uncircumcised**, just as Peter {had been} to the circumcised (for He who effectually worked for Peter in {his} apostleship to the circumcised effectually worked for me also to the Gentiles), and **recognizing the grace that had been given to me**, James and Cephas and John, who were reputed to be pillars, gave to me and Barnabas the right hand of fellowship, that we {might go} to the Gentiles, and they to the circumcised. {They} only {asked} us to remember the poor—the very thing I also was eager to do.*
(Galatians 2:6–10)

The Apostle Peter went even further in his rejection of any Gospel message other than that preached by him and the other Apostles. He flatly dismissed the notion that an understanding of the Hebrew Scriptures could ever be the product of "one's own interpretation," contending instead that a knowledge of the Truth could come only from the Holy Spirit Who had spoken through the Prophets:[9]

---

[8] Acts 1:1–3. For a discussion of Jesus' revelation of *The Mystery* to His disciples after His resurrection, see "Jesus Talks About The Mystery," *The Voice of Elijah*, January 1991 and "Where Are Jesus' Disciples?" *The Voice of Elijah*, April 1991.

[9] See "On Fairy Tales and Holy Hell," *The Voice of Elijah*, July 1992.

*For we did not follow cleverly devised tales when we made known to you the power and coming of our Lord Jesus Christ, but we were eye-witnesses of His majesty. For when He received honor and glory from God the Father, such an utterance as this was made to Him by the Majestic Glory, "This is My beloved Son with whom I am well-pleased"—and we ourselves heard this utterance made from heaven when we were with Him on the holy mountain. And {so} we have the prophetic word {made} more sure, to which you do well to pay attention as to a lamp shining in a dark place, until the day dawns and the morning star arises in your hearts. **But know this first of all, that no prophecy of Scripture is {a matter} of one's own interpretation, for no prophecy was ever made by an act of human will, but men moved by the Holy Spirit spoke from God.***
(2 Peter 1:16–21)

No reasonable person can dispute the fact that Peter and Paul believed there was only one valid understanding of the message of the Hebrew Scriptures. They were absolutely convinced Jesus Christ had given them insight into that message by revelation. Yet the vehemence with which they denounced any understanding of the Old Testament other than the one Jesus Christ revealed to them has long since fallen into disfavor among theologians. After all, how can anyone expect them to reject the discussion of various theological viewpoints when that practice provides the very basis for their profession?

Among Protestant scholars at least, the consensus of opinion is that Christians must magnanimously "agree to disagree." Their unstated assumption is, the Hebrew and Greek Scriptures have no one *true meaning*. There is instead a wide range of *unobjectionable meanings*—a sort of theological smorgasbord from which one can pick and choose various *acceptable* interpretations. Nobody who engages in such theological waffling, governed as it is by this unstated premise, would dare consider the possibility they might be guilty of preaching what the Apostle Paul calls "a different gospel." They are guilty, nonetheless.

The Mystery of Scripture

The currency of thought among "Christians" of all persuasions is that it is best to ignore anyone naïve enough to believe that there is only one true *meaning* to the Scriptures. Furthermore, anyone who claims to understand that one true *meaning* must be "dogmatic," "parochial," "unsophisticated" and certainly, by their standards at least, "heretical." Some even go so far as to contend that any group who claims knowledge of the one true *meaning* of the Scriptures is, by definition, a "cult." That is because, for most in the Church today, the Scriptures are not meant for the Believer's accurate understanding and edification. They are instead intended only for theological investigation and discussion. Unfortunately for those who believe that nonsense, the fallacy of such arrogant disregard for the Truth the Prophets hid in the Hebrew Scriptures is now being seen by many for what it is.[10]

Contrary to conventional wisdom, there is only one true *meaning* to the message of the Scriptures, just as there is but one truth in every other area of study.[11] Furthermore, that one true *meaning* is a detailed explanation of the Gospel of Jesus Christ—the *complete* Gospel of Jesus Christ, not the "maybe this, maybe that" hash dished out for popular consumption today. Although biblical scholars will scoff at the notion, the Prophets who wrote the Hebrew Scriptures securely *hid* the Gospel of

---

[10] The first volume in The Resurrection Theology Series, *Not All Israel Is Israel*, is the first of four volumes that will eventually tear down the façade behind which Protestant Scholastics have hidden for so long. In so doing, those four volumes will also disclose the ridiculous fabrications of theologians for what they are—vain imaginations.

[11] I have explained the basics of how the Early Church lost *The Apostolic Teaching*. (See "The Protestant Confession: The Church Lost The Teaching," *The Voice of Elijah*, January 1992 and "Did You Mean That Literally?" and "The Origen of Folly," *The Voice of Elijah*, January 1993.) In *The Mystery of Scripture*, I plan to give a detailed account of the history of *The Teaching* from the time God revealed it to Moses down to the time of its final loss around A.D. 200.

Jesus Christ in their writings as *objective revelation.*[12] Consequently, the *complete* Gospel message that explains God's purpose in the Person and work of Jesus Christ is to be found in the Old Testament, not the New.[13] The New Testament contains

---

[12] I am using *objective revelation* to refer to the Scriptures produced by the divinely inspired Prophets and Apostles. That revelation is *objective* in the sense that we may investigate it as an *object* to verify its credibility. The *objective* nature of such revelation contrasts markedly with the *subjective revelation* the Prophets and Apostles *received* directly from God. The men who were the direct *subjects* of divine revelation have long since died. Hence, the validity of their *subjective revelation* can only be verified on the basis of the *objective revelation* they left in the literature they wrote.

God revealed *The Mystery* to Moses and the other Prophets as *subjective revelation.* They subsequently recorded much of what they understood concerning *The Mystery* in an *objective* form, thus creating the divinely inspired Hebrew Scriptures—the Old Testament. Jesus Christ in turn revealed the *meaning* of this *objective revelation—The Mystery* hidden in the Hebrew Scriptures—to His disciples after His resurrection, thus providing them *subjective revelation* that was in no way inferior to that *delivered* to the Prophets.

The Apostles also recorded some of what they understood concerning *The Mystery* in an *objective* form, thus creating the divinely inspired Greek Scriptures—the New Testament. The Hebrew and Greek Scriptures together are *objective revelation* on which subsequent generations have been forced to rely for their understanding of the Truth because the leaders of the Early Church lost the insight into the *meaning* of the *objective revelation* of the Hebrew Scriptures that Jesus Christ *delivered* to the Apostles. Since that time, every attempt at recovering an understanding of that Truth has been unsuccessful. (See "Protestants All Agree on This: Somebody Laid an Egg!" *The Voice of Elijah,* January 1994.)

The seven *parabolic* seals that have sealed the *meaning* of the Hebrew Scriptures down through the centuries are now being removed by Jesus Christ, the Lamb of God (Rev. 5–10). Therefore, *subjective revelation* of *The Mystery* the Prophets hid in the Hebrew Scriptures is no longer necessary. (See "Did Jesus Leave a Will?" *The Voice of Elijah,* July 1991.) Such *subjective revelation* was required only as long as the Scriptures remained sealed. After the seven seals the Prophets placed on the Hebrew Scriptures have been removed one by one, *The Mystery* will once again be understood by "the Many" as *The (restored) Apostolic Teaching* (Dan. 12:1–10).

[13] To Paul and the other Apostles, "the Scriptures" were the Old Testament. The New Testament had not yet been written, much less canonized.

nothing more than a few bits and pieces of that Gospel, which is in many ways completely different than what the Church teaches today, yet contradicts little of *significance* in the Protestant Reformers' understanding of the Gospel.

The fundamental truths of the Gospel message are the heritage of Protestant Christians only because some of the men who labored to understand the one *true meaning* of the Hebrew and Greek Scriptures during the Protestant Reformation were apparently called of God to *restore* that Truth to the Church. They fulfilled their calling by thoroughly examining the New Testament Scriptures and the writings of the Church Fathers. Consequently, the authority of the Scriptures, the priesthood of the Believer, and salvation by faith are all more or less accurately understood truths of the Scriptures.[14]

Beyond these few truths, however, the Old Testament Gospel of Jesus Christ has a much greater content. But that content can only be understood by an accurate reading of the Hebrew Scriptures, just as Paul states in his letter to the Romans:

> *Now to Him who is able to establish you **according to my gospel and the preaching of Jesus Christ**, according to the revelation of the* **mystery**[15] ***which has been kept secret for long ages past, but now is manifested, and by the Scriptures of the prophets**, according to the commandment of the eternal God, has been made known to all the nations, {leading} to obedience of faith; to the only wise God, through Jesus Christ, be the glory forever. Amen.*
> *(Romans 16:25–27)*

---

[14] See "The Authority of Scripture," *The Voice of Elijah*, January 1991 and "A Long and Checkered History," *The Voice of Elijah*, October 1991.

[15] The history of *The Mystery* is the primary subject of discussion in this series; it is not my purpose to explain the content. I have already begun that process in the first volume of The Resurrection Theology Series—*Not All Israel Is Israel* and will continue that explanation in future volumes. In this series, I seek only to explain what happened to create the current circumstance wherein *The Mystery* hidden in the Hebrew Scriptures must be explained once more before Christ returns.

"The Mystery" that Paul mentions in that passage is the Old Testament Gospel of Jesus Christ—which is explained in the seven *parabolic* messages that the Prophets of Israel intentionally hid in the Hebrew Scriptures. Paul's point is, Jesus Christ revealed *The Mystery of Scripture* to the Apostles so that they could explain the *meaning* of the Hebrew Scriptures to others as *The Apostolic Teaching.*

Immediate disbelief will be the reaction of most on hearing the claim that the Prophets intentionally hid the Gospel of Jesus Christ in the Hebrew Scriptures. Some who might otherwise consider that a possibility would not dare do so for fear of faulting God for hiding the Truth. "God wouldn't do that," they say. Or, "That's not fair!"

Those seemingly pious beliefs regarding the unconditionally benevolent nature of God undoubtedly provide them the temporary comfort of a deception. But history itself indicates the Truth is somewhat other. Until a century and a half ago, Christians were well aware of the fact that the God of Abraham, Isaac, and Jacob—the Father of Jesus Christ—is a God of unmitigated wrath, a God Who holds a deep burning hatred for those who hate Him. Moreover, as the Early Church Fathers explain,[16] these seriously misguided souls fail to lay blame where blame is due. God is not responsible for the current unhappy state of affairs; it is the fault of sinful man alone.

The Mystery that lies hidden in the Hebrew Scriptures began as *The Teaching of Moses.* Through Moses, God revealed the Gospel of Jesus Christ to the sons of Israel some thirty-five hundred years ago. Although Moses told the sons of Israel to *hand down* their understanding of *The Teaching* to their children as *"The Way* of the Lord," they failed to do that.[17] Consequently, they soon lost an accurate understanding of what Moses had taught them, and thus the Truth of *The Teaching of Moses* became

---

[16] See Irenæus, *Against Heresies,* xxvi, 2, and Larry D. Harper, *The Advent of Christ and AntiChrist* (Mesquite, Texas: The Elijah Project, 2nd ed., 2005), p. 66.

[17] See *The Way, The Truth, The Life.*

hidden in the written account he left them. That is how *The Teaching of Moses* became *The Mystery of Scripture*. Men, not God, turned Moses' understanding of the Gospel of Jesus Christ into a message hidden in the Pentateuch—that is, the first five books of the Hebrew Scriptures that Moses wrote.

What was God to do after the sons of Israel abandoned *The Teaching of Moses*? Explain it over and over again to every subsequent generation? Certainly not! But to His credit, He tried. He repeatedly revealed *The Teaching of Moses* to the Prophets of Israel, and sent them one right after the other to explain it to the sons of Israel. But the people would not listen to *The Teaching of the Prophets*. Therefore, God told His Prophets to write down an explanation of *The Teaching of Moses*, but to speak in terms of an obscure *parabolic imagery* that even the most learned people of their own day could not understand! Eventually, He quit sending His Prophets altogether, leaving only the Hebrew Scriptures as cryptic testimony against a people who adamantly refused to listen to and believe the Truth.

Mankind once again attained an understanding of *The Mystery of Scripture* through *The Teaching of Jesus Christ*. Like Moses, who had taught the sons of Israel the *meaning* of the *parabolic imagery* of *The Teaching*, Jesus taught His disciples what Moses and the Prophets *meant* by what they wrote. After His resurrection, He continued to explain *The Teaching* to them over a period of forty days, just as God had explained it to Moses on the Mountain of God.[18] Finally, Jesus told His disciples to *hand down The Teaching* to the next generation exactly as they had *received* it from Him:

> *"All authority has been given to Me in heaven and on earth. Go therefore and **make disciples of all the nations**, baptizing them in the name of the Father and the Son and the Holy Spirit, **teaching them** to observe all that I commanded you; and lo, I am with you always, even to the end of the age."*
> *(Matthew 28:18b–20)*

---

[18] Exodus 24:18; Acts 1:1–3.

Although most people no longer grasp what Jesus *meant* when He said "make disciples,"[19] the Apostles would have understood. Discipling was a common practice at that time, a practice whereby one generation sought to preserve the teaching of a deceased master teacher by *delivering* it to the next generation *orally* just as they had *received* it from the generation that preceded them.

Unfortunately, just as the sons of Israel had failed to *hand down The Teaching of Moses*, the leaders of the Early Church also failed to do as Jesus commanded His disciples. During the second century A.D., the Church gradually lost its understanding of *The Apostolic Teaching* as one Christian leader after another failed to *hand down* his understanding of *The Mystery of Scripture* to the next generation of disciples. So, for many

---

[19] The *meaning* of Jesus' command is not clearly understood today. The *significance* of the Great Commission (Matt. 28:18–20) lies in the fact that when Jesus told *His disciples* to *make disciples*, He was indicating they should take His *Teaching* and *deliver* it to others as an *oral tradition*. (See "Where Are Jesus' Disciples?" *The Voice of Elijah*, April 1991 and "Some People Will Make Light of Anything," *The Voice of Elijah*, April 1994.)

Jesus and the Apostles were not alone in the practice of *discipling*, that is, teaching their *disciples* an *oral tradition* they expected them to preserve and teach, just as they had been taught. The Pharisees and John the Baptist had disciples as well (Mark 2:18). To understand New Testament allusions to the discipling process followed by the Apostolic Church, however, it is necessary first of all to understand Greek terminology that refers to the transmission of an *oral tradition*. I have discussed some of those terms as they relate to *The Apostolic Teaching* in "Some People Will Make Light of Anything," *The Voice of Elijah*, April 1994.

The Pharisees were definitely concerned with the preservation of an *oral tradition*. The very foundation of modern Judaism is based on the Pharisaic premise that God *delivered* to Moses an *oral torah* which He expected the sons of Israel to *hand down orally* from one generation to the next. Jesus alluded to the Pharisees' claim concerning the source of their *oral torah* by saying they had "seated themselves in the chair of Moses" (Matt. 23:2). John also alludes to the fact that they considered themselves *disciples* of Moses when he records their boast: "You are His disciple, but we are disciples of Moses" (John 9:28).

Church leaders who had not been fully trained, *The Apostolic Teaching* once again became *The Mystery*, well hidden in the Hebrew Scriptures—fully but cryptically explained in the writings of Moses and the other Prophets of Israel.

Around A.D. 200, leaders of the orthodox Church turned away completely from all but the remnants of *The Apostolic Teaching*. At the urging of two Church Fathers—Clement of Alexandria and Origen—they turned to Stoic philosophy for an allegorical method of interpreting the Scriptures that many Church leaders believed would unlock the Gospel message they understood the Prophets had hidden in the Hebrew Scriptures.[20]

What was God to do this time? Should He send more Prophets to explain *The Teaching* to each new generation of Christians? Why should He? He had already done that with the sons of Israel, and they had not listened. That is why, after Christian leaders proved to be just as treacherous as the sons of Israel had been, God remained silent, making no further attempt to *restore The Teaching*. Instead, He has waited patiently for the End of the Age—the time when the firm belief of the "saints" of God will be vindicated by the Second Coming of Jesus Christ.

The Apostles and Prophets tell us the Second Coming will be heralded by a "period of restoration of all things."[21] That "period of restoration" has finally arrived, and you can be certain that the "time of distress" mentioned by the Prophet Daniel is following hard on its heels:[22]

*"Now **at that time** Michael, the great prince who stands {guard} over the sons of your people, will arise. And **there will be a time of distress such as never occurred since there was a nation until that time; and at that time your people, everyone who is found written in the book, will be rescued.** And many of those who sleep in the dust of the ground*

---

[20] See "The Origen of Folly," *The Voice of Elijah*, January 1993.

[21] Malachi 4:5–6; Matthew 17:10–11; Acts 3:20–21.

[22] See "One Train. One Track. Two Rails." *The Voice of Elijah*, January 1992.

*will awake, these to everlasting life, but the others to disgrace {and} ever-lasting contempt. **And those who have insight will shine brightly like the brightness of the expanse of heaven, and those who lead the many to righteousness, like the stars forever and ever. But as for you, Daniel, conceal these words and seal up the book until the end of time;** many will go back and forth, and knowledge will increase." Then I, Daniel, looked and behold, two others were standing, one on this bank of the river, and the other on that bank of the river. And one said to the man dressed in linen, who was above the waters of the river, "How long {will it be} until the end of {these} wonders?" And I heard the man dressed in linen, who was above the waters of the river, as he raised his right hand and his left toward heaven, and swore by Him who lives forever that it would be for a time, times, and half {a time}; and as soon as they finish shattering the power of the holy people, all these {events} will be com-pleted. As for me, I heard but could not understand; so I said, "My lord, what {will be} the outcome of these {events}?" And he said, "**Go {your way}, Daniel, for {these} words are concealed and sealed up until the end time. Many will be purged, purified and refined; but the wicked will act wickedly, and none of the wicked will understand, but those who have insight will understand.***
(Daniel 12:1–10)*

Isn't that interesting? The messenger of the Lord told the Prophet Daniel that "the Many" living at "the end time" will once again have "insight" into the message that has been "con-cealed and sealed up" in his writings. Daniel doesn't mention it, but the same holds true for the writings of Moses and the other Prophets of Israel. Isaiah, for example, mentions the fact that God told him to seal up his work as well.[23] But from what Daniel says here, we know that God intends for His people to understand *The Teaching* one final time before Jesus Christ returns. And just as Daniel says, "none of the wicked will understand, but those who have insight will understand." What will "those who have insight" understand? They will understand *The Mystery of Scripture*—the Old Testament Gospel of Jesus Christ. And through their insight into that Truth, "the

---

[23] Isaiah 29:9–14.

many" will prepare themselves for the appearance of the Antichrist[24] and the soon Return of Jesus Christ.

Don't be deceived, however. Daniel clearly says, "None of the wicked will understand." The wicked won't understand because they have no "love of the truth"[25] and will refuse to believe it. Furthermore, they will consider anyone who does believe the Truth to be naïve. How do I know that? Because history has always had a way of repeating itself, and it will do so once again. The scribes and Pharisees in the time of Christ rejected *The Teaching of Jesus Christ* and *The Apostolic Teaching* because it did not agree with the lies embodied in their own *oral tradition*. So also today most "Christians" will reject the Truth of *The (restored) Apostolic Teaching* because it contradicts some *oral tradition* they hold dear.

If you are seeking Truth, you must understand that all is not as it appears to be in the Church. Most "Christians" have no interest at all in hearing any explanation of *The Mystery of Scripture* because they have never been born again. They are nothing more than Pretenders who take mental comfort in the confusion created by the plethora of conflicting beliefs they find in the Church. That confusion allows them to believe whatever they choose to believe and continue to do as they please, all the while proudly claiming to be Christian, thinking they stand completely in God's favor. Their pretense is nothing but a lie.[26]

Pretenders will either vehemently reject or casually dismiss the Truth of *The Mystery of Scripture* because they are not interested in the Truth. They take refuge in the confusion and uncertainty created by the lies they have chosen to believe.

---

[24] See L. Harper, *The AntiChrist* and *The Advent of Christ and AntiChrist.*

[25] 2 Thessalonians 2:10.

[26] I have dealt with the issue of Pretenders in the Church in various articles I have written for *The Voice of Elijah*. See "Mystics, Meatballs, and the Marvelous Works of God," and "Watching Ducks Sashaying 'Round the CornerStone," *The Voice of Elijah*, April 1993. Check the articles referenced in those two works for additional information.

They are nothing more than liars living a lie, securely garbed in their own hypocrisy. However, it is a foregone conclusion that, just as God's messenger told Daniel so long ago, those who want to know the Truth will see that *The (restored) Apostolic Teaching* is true.[27] They will accept it as true because, as Jesus said, *The Teaching* contains its own means of verification within those who serve the *Living* God:[28]

> *But when it was now the midst of the feast Jesus went up into the temple, and {began to} teach. The Jews therefore were marveling, saying, "How has this man become learned, having never been educated?" Jesus therefore answered them, and said,* **"My teaching is not Mine, but His who sent Me. If any man is willing to do His will, he shall know of the teaching, whether it is of God, or {whether} I speak from Myself."**
> *(John 7:14–17)*

A Biblical Theology

The Apostle Paul alludes to *The Mystery of Scripture* when he says this:

> *To me, the very least of all saints, this grace was given, to preach to the Gentiles the unfathomable riches of Christ, and to bring to light what is the administration of* **the mystery which for ages has been hidden in God**, *who created all things; in order that the manifold wisdom of God might now be made known through the church to the rulers and the authorities in the heavenly {places}.*
> *(Ephesians 3:8–10)*

In addition to that brief mention of *The Mystery of Scripture* as something hidden in the *Living* Word of God, there is other evidence in the New Testament that indicates *The Mystery* has also been hidden in the Hebrew Scriptures. Jesus plainly told the Jews that an explanation of His Person and

---

[27] Daniel 12:10.

[28] See "Mystics, Meatballs, and the Marvelous Works of God," *The Voice of Elijah*, April 1993 for a cursory explanation of how the Holy Spirit provides an internal witness to True Believers concerning the Truth.

work could be found in the writings of Moses, that is, in the first five books of the Old Testament—the Pentateuch. Pay close attention to what He says:

> *"You search the Scriptures, because you think that in them you have eternal life; and it is these that bear witness of Me; and you are unwilling to come to Me, that you may have life. I do not receive glory from men; but I know you, that you do not have the love of God in yourselves. I have come in My Father's name, and you do not receive Me; if another shall come in his own name, you will receive him. How can you believe, when you receive glory from one another, and you do not seek the glory that is from the {one and} only God? Do not think that I will accuse you before the Father; the one who accuses you is Moses, in whom you have set your hope. For if you believed Moses, you would believe Me; for he wrote of Me. But if you do not believe his writings, how will you believe My words?"*
> (John 5:39–47)

If Moses wrote about Jesus Christ, describing Him in any detail at all, the *meaning* of what he wrote must somehow be veiled from sight. That is precisely the argument the Apostle Paul uses to explain why the Jews did not accept Jesus Christ as their Messiah when He came in the flesh:

> *Having therefore such a hope, we use great boldness in {our} speech, and {are} not as Moses, {who} used to put a veil over his face that the sons of Israel might not look intently at the end of what was fading away. But their minds were hardened; for until this very day at the reading of the old covenant the same veil remains unlifted, because it is removed in Christ. But to this day whenever Moses is read, a veil lies over their heart; but whenever a man turns to the Lord, the veil is taken away. Now the Lord is the Spirit; and where the Spirit of the Lord is, {there} is liberty. But we all, with unveiled face beholding as in a mirror the glory of the Lord, are being transformed into the same image from glory to glory, just as from the Lord, the Spirit. Therefore, since we have this ministry, as we received mercy, we do not lose heart, but we have renounced the things hidden because of shame, not walking in craftiness or adulterating the word of God, but by the manifestation of truth commending ourselves to every man's conscience in the sight of God. And even if our gospel is veiled, it is veiled to those who are*

perishing, in whose case the god of this world has blinded the minds of the unbelieving, that they might not see the light of the gospel of the glory of Christ, who is the image of God.
(2 *Corinthians 3:12–4:4*)

Scholars will deny that the Prophets hid anything at all in the Hebrew Scriptures. Yet, as Paul explained, they do that because a "veil" covers the Old Testament Gospel message. That is, the Prophets did not write the Hebrew Scriptures so that they could be easily understood. They wrote in a sort of *parabolic* "code." However, Paul also says a "veil" covers the unregenerate mind ("heart") so that the unbeliever has no hope of ever understanding what the Prophets wrote. He will not be able to understand even when someone openly explains the *meaning* of the Hebrew Scriptures to him and thereby pulls back the "veil" on the Scriptures.

Most theologians agree with Paul, not in the fact that they are unregenerate or that Moses concealed the *meaning* of what he wrote, but in the fact that they can see only a vague, *symbolic* reference to Jesus Christ in the Pentateuch.[29] But they fail to comprehend that they cannot understand because they refuse to "turn to the Lord" so that the "veil" covering their "heart" (mind) might be "taken away."

Not only did Jesus Christ tell His disciples that "Moses wrote of" Him, He also tells them the Prophets had done exactly the same thing:

*And He took the twelve aside and said to them, "Behold, we are going up to Jerusalem, and **all things which are written through the***

---

[29] I have already pulled back the "veil" from the Scriptures somewhat in explaining how the Pentateuch contains an amazingly detailed *parabolic* explanation of the Person and work of Jesus Christ. (See "The Passover Parable," *The Voice of Elijah*, July 1991.) Unfortunately, not everyone is willing (or able) to accept my explanation of the biblical text. That is possible only for those who have, as Paul said, "turned to the Lord" in total repentance and had "the veil" removed from their minds. Pretenders will vehemently deny that. That is to be expected. Those who don't know, don't know that they don't know.

*prophets about the Son of Man will be accomplished. For He will be
delivered to the Gentiles, and will be mocked and mistreated and spit
upon, and after they have scourged Him, they will kill Him; and **the
third day**[30] He will rise again." And **they understood none of these
things, and this saying was hidden from them, and they did not
comprehend the things that were said.**
(Luke 18:31–34)*

In saying that, Luke confirms that the *meaning* of the
Hebrew Scriptures must have been hidden. That is why the
disciples of Jesus did not understand even after He explained
the Prophets' detailed message concerning His death and resurrection. If the Old Testament Gospel message had not been
hidden, why would Jesus have found it necessary to explain it
to His disciples? And if their minds were not unregenerate,
why would they have found it impossible to understand?

Again, not many of the statements of the Prophets
appear to have any obvious reference to Jesus Christ. That is
only because a *parabolic* "veil" covers the message of the
Hebrew Scriptures, just as Paul said it did. If it were not for
statements in the New Testament that refer to specific passages in the Prophets, Christians would have no idea that
those passages even refer to Jesus Christ. Therefore, it should
be obvious to anyone but the staunchest of traditionalists and
the more contentious Pretenders among us that the Church
has long since lost an accurate understanding of the Old Testament.

One has only to do a superficial survey of academic
research in the field of Old Testament theology to come away
absolutely amazed at the contradictory and conflicting views
held by experts in that area of study. As one scholar who has
worked in the field for years has so aptly put it:

---

[30] Jesus' reference to "the third day" is an allusion to Hosea 6:2. Yet how can
that prophetic passage be shown to refer to Him when it clearly refers to
Israel? If you have believed what you read in *Not All Israel Is Israel*, you
already know the answer to that question.

The final aim of OT theology is to demonstrate whether or not there is an inner unity that binds together the various theologies and longitudinal themes, concepts, and motifs. This is an extremely difficult undertaking which contains many dangers. If there is behind the experience of those who left us the OT Scriptures a unique divine reality, then it would seem that behind all variegation and diversity of theological reflection there is a hidden inner unity which has also drawn together the OT writings. The ultimate object of a theology is then to draw the inner hidden unity out of its concealment as much as possible and make it transparent.[31]

That is a fairly succinct summary of the current status of scholarly investigation into the unified, coherent message of the Hebrew Scriptures (if indeed there is one, as Jesus and the Apostles claimed). Coming as it does from a leading scholar in the field of Old Testament theology, that frank admission does not bode well for those who irrationally dispute what has long been a generally accepted fact among Christian scholars and many laypeople: The Church no longer understands the *meaning* or *significance* of the Old Testament.

What Do You Think?

Since God does not think *The Way* we think, the Prophets did not put His explanation of *The Mystery* in a form that could easily be understood. The Prophet Isaiah succinctly states the case this way:

Seek the LORD while He may be found;
Call upon Him while He is near.
Let the wicked forsake his way,
And the unrighteous man his thoughts;
And let him return to the LORD,
And He will have compassion on him;
And to our God, For He will abundantly pardon.
"For My thoughts are not your thoughts,
Neither are your ways My ways," *declares the LORD.*

---

[31] Gerhard Hasel, *Old Testament Theology: Basic Issues in the Current Debate* (Grand Rapids: Eerdmans, 1972), p. 93.

"For {as} the heavens are higher than the earth,
So are My ways higher than your ways,
And My thoughts than your thoughts."
(Isaiah 55:6–9)

Consider this: Over the eighteen hundred years since the Church lost *The Apostolic Teaching*, the approach of Christian theologians has not been to search the Hebrew Scriptures for the Gospel message of Jesus Christ. It has been to look first at the New Testament writers' explanation of the Old Testament message and then try to read that message back into the Old Testament passages those men quoted, all the while trying to figure out what they understood the text to *mean*. That is not the most logical tack, nor is it even intellectually honest.

The Truth is, there is only one way anyone will ever be able to come to an understanding of *The Mystery of Scripture*, which is a detailed account of God's plan of salvation for His people. That is by somehow gaining the ability to understand God's Own explanation of it. That process is called "regeneration." Some call it the "new birth." It goes like this: When Jesus revealed *The Mystery of Scripture* to His disciples shortly after His resurrection, He first "opened their minds to understand the Scriptures."[32] Then He explained the Old Testament Gospel message to them.[33] The same methodology applies today; but for those who want to strike out on their own, here are a few pointers.

One cannot logically expect to understand the *meaning* and *significance* of the Hebrew Scriptures just by reading a translation of the original biblical text because, to a large extent, every translation is an inaccurate *interpretation*. That is, it contains glosses that conceal idiomatic Hebrew expressions the translator himself did not accurately understand. Consequently, he was forced to resort to a "best guess" and thereby leave the Truth hidden behind an inaccurate translation, a

---

[32] Luke 24:45.
[33] Acts 1:3.

simple transliteration of a Hebrew word or phrase,[34] or in a literal translation of an idiomatic expression.[35]

To gain insight into what Moses and the Prophets wrote, *the reader must begin with a precise understanding of the exact Hebrew words and phrases the Prophets used.* Only then can he go on to determine the precise *meaning* and *significance* of those words and phrases. Although the exact *meaning* of many of the words and idiomatic expressions in the Hebrew Scriptures are no longer understood, even by learned scholars, one can often confirm their *meaning* on the basis of epigraphic evidence found in the Hebrew text itself and in other ancient Near Eastern texts.

After determining the *meaning* of key Hebrew words and idiomatic expressions, the reader must then use his or her insight into that information to ascertain what the ancient Hebrew mind-set was in regard to those words and phrases. Ultimately, *to understand* The Mystery of Scripture, *the reader must learn to think in terms of the same mental imagery the ancients*

---

[34] The Hebrew words for "heaven" and "hell" are excellent examples of that fact. The Hebrew word *translated* as both "heavens" and "heaven" (*shemayim*) is actually a compound word composed of the Egyptian word *she* ("sea" or "lake") and the Semitic word *mayim* ("waters"). The word *literally means* "sea of waters" because the ancients thought Heaven above was an ocean. (See A. J. Wensinck, *The Ocean in the Literature of the Western Semites* [Wiesbaden: 1968].)

In like manner, the Hebrew word for "hell" has been *transliterated* into English as *Sheol* because translators have no clear understanding of that term either. However, it, too, is a compound word composed of the Egyptian word *she* ("sea" or "lake") and another Semitic word, the proper noun *El.* (See W. Wifall, "The Sea of Reeds as Sheol," *Zeitschrift fur die alttestamentliche Wissenschaft* 92 [1980], pp. 326–331.) The discrepancy in the spelling is due to the fact that the Rabbis began to vocalize the proper name for God with an *o* (*ol*) instead of an *e* (*El*) after they lost a clear understanding of *The Teaching of Moses.*

[35] Three good examples are the Hebrew idioms "build a house," "raise up a seed," and "make a name." These three idioms all *mean* exactly the same thing—"engender a son." That is clear from Genesis 38:1–11, Deuteronomy 25:5–10, and Ruth 4:1–12.

visualized when they heard the ancient Hebrew words and phrases used.[36] That involves a fairly good understanding of their culture and religion, especially of their religious rituals and symbols.

Finally, *the reader must learn to think in terms of the message that God delivered to these ancient people through His Prophets.* That involves an accurate understanding of the *meaning* and *significance* of the Hebrew idioms and theological symbols that Moses and the Prophets of Israel used to convey God's message.

For those of you who are a bit intimidated by the thought of striking out on your own, there is a better "way." Moses and the other Prophets of Israel called it "*The Way* of the Lord." All you have to do to gain insight into *The Mystery* the Prophets hid in their writings is *listen.* That is, you need only adhere to the pattern that Jesus established when He *handed down The Teaching* to His disciples. Find a *Teacher* that you believe God has called to explain the Truth in regard to the message of the

---

[36] Over the last two centuries, archaeologists and peasant Arabs alike have uncovered a vast treasure of written documents at various sites throughout the Near East. These documents range all the way from the Greek papyri of the Nag Hammadi texts to the Ugaritic clay tablets recovered at Ras Shamra. By far the most important of these epigraphic sources for our purposes in validating the *meaning* of the Hebrew idioms, however, are the *multiplied thousands* of clay tablets discovered in Mesopotamia. The ancient scribes wrote these texts in Akkadian cuneiform.

Much of the work of verifying the *meaning* of the Semitic idioms found in the Hebrew Scriptures has already been done by scholars at the Oriental Institute of Chicago. They compiled the evidence for Akkadian word usage that is now contained in *The Assyrian Dictionary of the Oriental Institute of the University of Chicago* (Chicago: various volumes, 1956 to the present). However, additional sleuthing into the *meaning* of specific Hebrew idioms comes to light from time to time in the publication of articles and monographs written by individual scholars. See, for example, Jacob Milgrom, *Studies in Levitical Terminology, 1: The Encroacher and the Levite, The Term 'Abodah* (Berkeley: University of California Press, 1970) and John D. Currid, "Why Did God Harden Pharaoh's Heart?" *Bible Review* (December 1993), pp. 47–52.

Hebrew Scriptures and then *listen* to, and learn from, him. The Apostle Paul put it this way:

> But what does it say? "THE WORD IS NEAR YOU, IN YOUR MOUTH AND IN YOUR HEART"—that is, the word of faith which we are preaching, that if you confess with your mouth Jesus {as} Lord, and believe in your heart that God raised Him from the dead, you shall be saved; for with the heart man believes, resulting in righteousness, and with the mouth he confesses, resulting in salvation. For the Scripture says, "WHOEVER BELIEVES IN HIM WILL NOT BE DISAPPOINTED." For there is no distinction between Jew and Greek; for the same {Lord} is Lord of all, abounding in riches for all who call upon Him; "WHOEVER WILL CALL UPON THE NAME OF THE LORD WILL BE SAVED." **How then shall they call upon Him in whom they have not believed? And how shall they believe in Him whom they have not heard? And how shall they hear without a preacher? And how shall they preach unless they are sent?** Just as it is written, "HOW BEAUTIFUL ARE THE FEET OF THOSE WHO BRING GLAD TIDINGS OF GOOD THINGS!" (Romans 10:8–15)

The basic difficulty you face in gaining an understanding of the Truth is this: There are a lot of people who claim God called them to preach, but not many are telling the Truth. That is nothing new. The Prophet Jeremiah faced exactly the same circumstance:

> "I did not send {these} prophets,
> But they ran.
> I did not speak to them,
> But they prophesied."
> (Jeremiah 23:21)

Where To From Here?

My purpose in the book *Not All Israel Is Israel* and the other volumes in The Resurrection Theology Series is to provide some of the information necessary for you, the reader, to develop the mind-set required for understanding *The Mystery of Scripture*. By contrast, in this and the other volumes in this series I seek only to explain those things that bear directly on

God's revelation of *The Teaching* to Moses and the other Prophets of Israel. They will also shed some light on the subsequent loss of insight into the *meaning* and *significance* of the things these men wrote.

The Mystery of Scripture courses through the entirety of the Hebrew/Greek Scriptures, from Genesis to Revelation. However, in this volume I will consider only Israel's Exodus from Egypt under the leadership of Moses, since Moses was the first and most important of the Prophets of Israel through whom God communicated *The Teaching*. Since God also spoke through Prophets other than Moses, in the second volume I will explain some of the things they say, since they are equally important witnesses. I will also show how the Prophets reveal they were instructed to "seal up" the *meaning* of their writings, as the Prophets Isaiah and Daniel clearly state.[37] Consequently, by the time prophecy ended, the Prophets had placed seven symbolic "seals" on their explanation of *The Teaching*.[38] That left the *meaning* of the Hebrew Scriptures well beyond the reach of human inquiry.

The Greek Scriptures—that is, the New Testament—indicate Jesus Christ revealed the *meaning* of the Hebrew Scriptures to the Apostles shortly after His resurrection.[39] Those men then recorded their understanding of *The Teaching* in various works that were subsequently collected and canonized as the New Testament. Thus, *The Mystery of Scripture* series will also investigate those apostolic writings before concluding with a look at the writings of the Early Church Fathers that disclose how the second-century Church lost *The Apostolic Teaching*.

In the New Testament literature, the Apostles provide a summary glimpse into their understanding of the intricately

---

[37] Isaiah 8:16; Daniel 12:4.

[38] See "Did Jesus Leave a Will?" *The Voice of Elijah*, July 1991 and "That's Why He's Called AntiChrist!" *The Voice of Elijah*, April 1992. The last article has been reprinted with additional comments in *The Advent of Christ and AntiChrist*, pp. 109–135, esp. pp. 120–23.

[39] Luke 24:45; Acts 1:3.

detailed Gospel message that lies hidden in the Hebrew Scriptures. Their writings add a more easily understood addendum to the divinely inspired Hebrew Scriptures, thus completing the *objective revelation* of the Scriptures.[40] Although the Apostles did not seal this addendum in the same way the Prophets sealed the Hebrew Scriptures, they may just as well have.

After the Church lost *The Apostolic Teaching*—which explained *The Mystery of Scripture* hidden in the Hebrew Scriptures—around A.D. 200, Christian leaders found it all but impossible to understand even the *parabolic statements* of the Apostles. That is not surprising. Without an under-

---

[40] The Scriptures were written in Hebrew, Aramaic, and Greek. A working knowledge of these three languages is essential to anyone who proposes to undertake any serious biblical study. Otherwise, one is left to rely on the assumptions and presuppositions of the individuals whose translations he utilizes in his study.

Besides these three languages, however, one also needs competency in the Ugaritic and Akkadian languages, inasmuch as these two languages provide much-needed confirmation as to the *meaning* of Hebrew words and idioms at many points. In addition to these basic tools, the investigator must also begin with a solid knowledge of the biblical account. Beyond that, an acquaintance with the history, culture, and religion of the following peoples is essential as well: Sumerians, Babylonians, Assyrians, Amorites, Hittites, Egyptians, Canaanites (Phoenicians), Minoans, Greeks, and Persians.

Anyone without this basic background can hardly be considered equipped to understand the message of the Hebrew Scriptures within its historical/cultural setting—*even after the Scriptures have been unsealed.* One final prerequisite is absolutely essential for anyone who seeks insight into the message of the Hebrew Scriptures (or even learn from what I write): A valid born-again experience with God and a willingness to reconsider the preconceptions and assumptions that inhere in every existing Christian tradition.

Notice I said "preconceptions and assumptions." I did not say "doctrines." Most of the historic Christian doctrines recovered by the leaders of the Protestant Reformation are accurate reflections of Early Church beliefs the Roman Catholic Church somehow managed to lose or distort down through the centuries. By contrast, many widely believed notions in the Christian Church today, as well as much recently contrived theological goofiness, have little in common with the historic Christian doctrines of the Early Church.

standing of the Old Testament message, many of the things stated in the New Testament *appear* to be nothing more than metaphorical comments based on religious symbolism prevalent in their time. In this case, appearances are certainly deceiving.

The statements of the Apostles are *precise parabolic state-ments* that speak in terms of *specific parabolic imagery,* which is fully explained by the Hebrew idioms and mythological symbols the Prophets used to conceal the Truth in the Hebrew Scriptures. Consequently, there is no way anyone can fully understand WHAT the Apostles wrote without first understanding WHAT the Prophets concealed in the Hebrew Scriptures. A goodly portion of the Hebrew Scriptures has already been unsealed[41] and is even now waiting to be understood by anyone who honestly wants to know the Truth and has the tools appropriate to the task. But it might be helpful to keep in mind what the Apostle Paul said about *The Mystery*: Not everyone is capable of understanding it:

> *Yet we do speak wisdom among those who are mature; a wisdom, how-ever, not of this age, nor of the rulers of this age, who are passing away;* **but we speak God's wisdom in a mystery, the hidden {wisdom}, which God predestined before the ages to our glory; {the wisdom} which none of the rulers of this age has understood; for if they had understood it, they would not have crucified the Lord of glory;** *but just as it is written,*
> "THINGS WHICH EYE HAS NOT SEEN
> AND EAR HAS NOT HEARD,
> AND {*which*} HAVE NOT ENTERED THE HEART OF MAN,
> ALL THAT GOD HAS PREPARED
> FOR THOSE WHO LOVE HIM."
> **For to us God revealed {them} through the Spirit; for the Spirit searches all things, even the depths of God.** *For who among men knows the {thoughts} of a man except the spirit of the man, which is in him? Even so the {thoughts} of God no one knows except the Spirit of God. Now we have received, not the spirit of the world, but the Spirit who*

---

[41] See "It's Going to Get Worse!" *The Voice of Elijah Update*, August 1992.

is from God, that we might know the things freely given to us by God, which things we also speak, not in words taught by human wisdom, but in those taught by the Spirit, combining spiritual {thoughts} with spiritual {words}. **But a natural man does not accept the things of the Spirit of God; for they are foolishness to him, and he cannot understand them, because they are spiritually appraised.** *But he who is spiritual appraises all things, yet he himself is appraised by no man. For* WHO HAS KNOWN THE MIND OF THE LORD, THAT HE SHOULD INSTRUCT HIM? *But we have the mind of Christ.*
(1 Corinthians 2:6–16)

What was true in Paul's day remains just as true today. *The Mystery of Scripture* may not be easy to master, yet those who have been born again will be able to do just that. However, that makes no difference at all to the "natural man."[42] He will arbitrarily choose to believe that the Truth the Prophets of Israel hid in the Hebrew Scriptures is sheer foolishness.[43]

---

[42] See "The Natural Man Is an Idiot (When It Comes to the Truth)" *The Voice of Elijah*, October 1993.

[43] I have been called to publish an explanation of the message of the Hebrew Scriptures—*The (restored) Apostolic Teaching*—so that it is available to anyone who wants to understand. I will do that over the next several years. When I have accomplished the task for which I was called, anyone who has ears to hear may read and understand *The Mystery of Scripture*.

What I have just stated concerning my calling will undoubtedly be ridiculed as foolishness by those scholars who have been (and still are) working in the field of Old Testament theology. That is to be expected. It makes light of the incredible difficulties they have faced in trying to sort out and understand the Truth the Prophets hid in the Hebrew Scriptures. It also challenges their mastery of what they have long considered their personal fiefdom. Yet in spite of their remarkable erudition, it is true nonetheless.

If what I claim appears to reflect extreme arrogance or pride on my part, so be it. I did not choose to do what I am doing; God called me to accomplish an extremely specific task before the Second Coming of Jesus Christ. I intend to do exactly what God called me to do. So if you consider my assertion to be the declaration of a fool, I willingly plead guilty. Your opinion, or the opinions of others like you, are of absolutely no concern to me. To my mind, it is far better to be thought a fool for Christ now than to discover in that Great Day that I was nothing more than Satan's "sophisticated" pawn. Besides, no one is forcing you to read what I have written.

CHAPTER 1:

THE *TESTIMONIES*

Two of the world's most influential religions—Judaism, and Christianity—trace their origins to events that occurred over 3000 years ago in the barren wilderness of the Sinai Peninsula. At the foot of a mountain in that vast desert, a solitary figure stood as mediator between God and man, offering a ragtag band of Egyptian slaves the opportunity to become God's Own people. When the sons of Israel accepted the terms of the covenant relationship God offered, they forever altered the course of human history.

Although the Hebrew Scriptures purportedly contain a historical record of what happened at that time, the *meaning* and *significance*[1] of the biblical account has long since been obscured by theological speculation. Over the past eighteen hundred years since the leaders of the Early Church lost their understanding of *The Apostolic Teaching*, several basic questions have never been adequately addressed. Consequently, their *significance* has not been even remotely understood. The single most important question is this: What did Moses, the author of

---

[1] See my discussion of these two terms in *Not All Israel Is Israel*, pp. 112 ff., and in *The Way, The Truth, The Life,* pp. 171 ff.

the Pentateuch, intend for us to understand about those events? He says God "cut a covenant"[2] with "all Israel" at Mt. Sinai, and that covenant has since become known as the "Mosaic Covenant"[3] to distinguish it from all other covenants that God made with men. But what was God's purpose in ratifying that covenant with the sons of Israel, and what did He demand of them in return for the benefits He promised?

When the sons of Israel accepted God's offer of a covenant relationship under the terms of the Mosaic Covenant, they quite obviously obligated themselves to adhere to the terms of that agreement. While that may appear to be a simple matter of "do this" and "don't do that," the reality of what they agreed to lies much deeper, completely hidden in the terminology Moses uses to explain the terms of the covenant. Consequently, insight into what God set out to accomplish through the Mosaic Covenant depends in large part on an accurate understanding of the terminology that refers to the various *commandments* that God gave the sons of Israel through His "mouth"—the Prophet Moses.

The Prophets who wrote the Hebrew Scriptures use a variety of terms to describe the legal stipulations God issued through Moses. The Prophet who wrote Psalm 119 provides the most complete vocabulary of such terminology. However, Moses uses only five of the terms the Prophet uses in that psalm. Those five terms are the following:

---

[2] Exodus 34:10. The Hebrew idiom "cut a covenant" (*karath berith*) carries a nuance of *meaning* that points to the death of the sacrifice that was eaten at a communal meal by the parties ratifying the agreement. The intricately intertwined *parabolic imagery* surrounding the ratification of the Mosaic Covenant indicates the sacrifice that provided the "meat" for the covenant meal was Corporate Israel—"all Israel," the Firstborn Son of God. See "The Passover Parable," and "Did Jesus Leave a Will?" *The Voice of Elijah*, July 1991; and "As Hot as Hell (And Every Bit as Certain)" *The Voice of Elijah Update*, September 1993.

[3] I have already discussed the basic purpose of the Mosaic Covenant in *Not All Israel Is Israel*.

ENGLISH	HEBREW
TESTIMONIES	'EDÔT
STATUTES	CHUQQÎM/CHUQQÔT
JUDGMENTS	MISHPATÎM
LAWS	TORÔT
COMMANDMENTS	MITZVÔT

Of these five terms, only the first three refer to specific types of covenant stipulations. Those three terms are:

ENGLISH	HEBREW
TESTIMONIES	'EDÔT
STATUTES	CHUQQÎM/CHUQQÔT
JUDGMENTS	MISHPATÎM

Moses uses these three Hebrew words in the Pentateuch with specific *meaning*. That is, each of them has an extremely specific referent and thereby denotes one of three completely different kinds of covenant stipulations. Their use in that regard contrasts markedly with that of the last two terms on the list, both of which have a *specific* as well as a *general* usage. Those two terms are:

ENGLISH	HEBREW
LAWS	TORÔT
COMMANDMENTS	MITZVÔT

The general *meaning* of these last two terms sometimes encompasses every one of the legal stipulations denoted by the first three. That is, both of the Hebrew terms translated "*laws*" and "*commandments*," when used in a general sense, refer to the *testimonies, statutes,* and *judgments* of God. However, their specific *meaning* points to something completely other than the *testimonies, statutes,* and *judgments* themselves. If that is not somewhat confusing, it should be. Moses used confusing terminology to conceal *The Mystery of Scripture* from the view of prying eyes. That is why it is essential to understand the *meaning* and *significance* of these five terms.

Only then is it possible to comprehend the responsibility the sons of Israel assumed under the terms of the covenant they ratified at Mt. Sinai. Here is a quick survey of the *meaning* of the first three terms.

The first term—*'edôt*—is normally translated as either "testimony" or "testimonies" because the legal stipulations to which it refers function as a "witness" to provide "testimony" concerning Israel's adherence to the terms of the covenant. However, the word itself denotes the writing inscribed on the two stone tablets Moses *received* on the Mountain of God. That is, it refers to the Ten Commandments.

The second term—*mishpatîm*—is perhaps the most important term for our purposes in this investigation. It refers to regulations known as *judgments* and denotes the civil/criminal type of law known today as *case law.* The various *judgments* mentioned in the Hebrew Scriptures all require the judicial decision of a judge. Therefore, the term *judgment* sometimes denotes the legal process as well as the recorded precept.

The third term—*chuqqîm/chuqqôt*—designates the legal prescriptions known as *statutes.* It refers to any codified legislation that "mandates limits" for some fundamental order of existence.

In this chapter, I will explain only Moses' use of the term *'edôt* ("testimonies"). We will look at the *meaning* and *significance* of the other two terms in Chapter 2.

The Tablets of the Testimonies

Before one can understand why the "ten words"[4] we normally call the "Ten Commandments" are the *testimonies,* it is necessary to correct a mistaken notion the Jews have long held concerning the text of the Hebrew Scriptures. Their error stems from the fact that the sons of Israel wrote ancient Hebrew without vowels. That this is true in regard to the bib-

---

[4] This is what the Hebrew text actually says.

lical text has been confirmed by the Dead Sea Scrolls.[5] Since the copies of the Hebrew Scriptures found among the Dead Sea Scrolls have only a consonantal Hebrew text, they provide a definite date (ca. 160 B.C.) before which the Hebrew text of the Scriptures was copied without vowels. The only question is, when did the Jews add vowels to the biblical text? The answer might surprise you.

The Jewish Masoretes "pointed"—that is, added vowels to—the consonantal Hebrew text sometime around A.D. 600 as an aid to the reading of the Hebrew Scriptures in the synagogue. That means the Jews added vowels to the biblical text long after they lost an understanding of *The Teaching* that Moses and the other Prophets of Israel hid there.[6] Consequently, since the Jews had already lost the insight their ancestors once had into the *meaning* and *significance* of the biblical text, the vowels of the Masoretic Text should be taken as nothing more than suggestions. In many cases, they quite obviously stand in need of some correction.

During the Renaissance, Christian scholars accepted the Masoretic vocalization of the consonantal Hebrew text[7] as

---

[5] The Dead Sea Scrolls consist of Old Testament texts as well as various sectarian texts that many scholars believe were written by a Jewish sect known as the Essenes. These scrolls were discovered in 1947, hidden in several caves in the cliffs overlooking the western shore of the Dead Sea. Paleographic studies have shown the scrolls were written ca. 150–50 B.C. Whether or not the scrolls containing sectarian texts were actually composed at that time or are copies of an earlier original cannot be determined with certainty. In the case of the biblical scrolls, the accepted view is they are copies of an earlier text. Despite uncertainties as to their origin, the Dead Sea Scrolls have contributed greatly to the study of the biblical text and the history of the Jews during the Intertestamental Period.

[6] It can be shown the Jews had already lost an understanding of *The Mystery of Scripture* before the copies of the Hebrew Scriptures found among the Dead Sea Scrolls were made. I will do that later in this series.

[7] With the exception of a few notable standouts such as Jerome (A.D. 347–420), Christians more or less ignored the Hebrew Scriptures until the rise of Scholasticism (ca. A.D. 1270).

very little less than divinely inspired. Consequently, few Christian scholars have tried to correct what are fairly obvious errors in the Masoretic vocalization, even over the past half century since the discovery of the "unpointed" Ugaritic texts at Ras Shamra.[8] Yet correction of Masoretic mistakes is absolutely essential if one ever hopes to attain an accurate understanding of *The Teaching* that Moses and the other Prophets of Israel hid in the Hebrew Scriptures. That should become clear from the Masoretic error under discussion here.

---

[8] The Ugaritic texts discovered at Ras Shamra since 1929 were written in a cuneiform script on clay tablets. Although some exhibit the logographic and syllabic cuneiform of the Akkadian (Babylonian-Assyrian) language, others were written in the alphabetic cuneiform script of the Northwest Semitic language spoken at Ugarit. With the exception of the consonantal "aleph," which occurs in three forms depending on its accompanying vowel, the Ugaritic texts were written with only unvocalized consonants.

The consonantal script of the Ugaritic (Canaanite) texts from Ras Shamra has proven to be a Semitic dialectic (sister language) having much in common with Biblical Hebrew. For that reason, they can be especially valuable to anyone studying the Hebrew text of the Scriptures. The similarity of the Ugaritic language to Biblical Hebrew has led a few scholars to critique the Masoretic pointing of the consonantal text of the Bible. A leading advocate of the use of Ugaritic philology to correct errors in the Masoretic pointing has been Mitchell Dahood. He forthrightly states:

> *The study of the Psalter within the wider ambience of Northwest Semitic so frequently vindicates the consonantal text against its ancient translators and its medieval reworking by the Masoretes that one must concede its primacy. To be sure, in the majority of cases in the Psalter, the consonantal text and the Masoretic pointing are in happy agreement, but where the Masoretic punctuation cannot be coaxed into yielding sense, the textual critic should cut free and chart a course on the linguistic map of Northwest Semitic. The numerous new grammatical and lexical details supplied by the Ras Shamra texts and Phoenician inscriptions enhance the possibility of reaching a clear and coherent translation and exegesis with the consonantal text intact.*
> (Mitchell Dahood, Psalms II [Garden City: Doubleday & Company, 1968], p. xvii.)

Because of Dahood's willingness to question tradition, he has taken flack from all sides, especially from hidebound traditionalists who cannot see the incongruence of scholarly inquiry and their own blind acceptance of the Masoretic tradition.

In the Masoretic text of the Hebrew Scriptures,[9] the word that is normally translated "testimonies" is the plural form *'edôt*. That form, as it occurs in the consonantal Hebrew text (without vowels), is always written either *'dt* or *'dwt*. In spite of the fact that the Masoretes vocalized the word *'edôt* as a plural, they claim the singular form of the word never occurs in the Hebrew Scriptures. The Truth is, the singular form of the plural *'edôt* (*'dt*/*'dwt*) does occur. Its singular form is the Hebrew word *'edah* (*'dh*), a term that is usually translated "assembly." In Chapter 7, I will show you how that term is used.[10]

Another Hebrew word in the Masoretic Text has exactly the same consonantal form (*'dt*/*'dwt*) as the form they vocalize

---

[9] Lest anyone think I am advocating tampering with the divinely inspired text of the Hebrew Scriptures, I should point out that the original text is not the issue. The only issue is the accuracy of the vowels added by the Masoretes. The Masoretes were Jewish scholars who added not only vowels to the biblical text, but also various other "aids to reading." They did so several centuries after the crucifixion of Jesus Christ, but most likely no earlier than A.D. 600. The things I explain in the volumes of this series should reveal why it is not wise to uncritically accept any Jewish tradition that purports to explain what the Hebrew text does or does not say.

If sufficient evidence indicates a change in vocalization is valid, and the change contributes to a better understanding of the text, academic concern for truth demands that a change be made. However, the difficulty facing those who correct the Masoretic vocalization of the Hebrew text inheres not only in the resistance posed by the inertial force of traditional ways of thinking; it also resides in the sometimes monumental task of proving that a specific noun or verbal construct occurs in some other Semitic language.

Not many are willing to set out against the strong current of academic tradition and take on such a hazardous undertaking unless the evidence against the Masoretic vocalization is overwhelming and the academic gain substantial. Since I have no academic reputation to lay on the line, I see no reason to shrink from changing a Masoretic vowel here or there. However, you will discover in this and future publications that a single Masoretic vowel can often make a substantial difference in *meaning*.

[10] See below, p. 212, fn. 30.

as *'edôt*. Yet the Masoretes arbitrarily vocalized this form with a "*u*" vowel instead of an "*o*" vowel. Therefore, it appears in the Masoretic Text as *'edût* rather than *'edôt*. According to the Masoretes, the form they vocalized as *'edût* is always singular as opposed to the form they vocalized as *'edôt*, which they claim is always plural.[11] That is why the term they vocalized *'edût* is normally translated as "testimony" and the one they vocalized *'edôt* as "testimonies," as shown here:

CONSONANTAL HEBREW TEXT	MASORETIC VOCALIZATION	ENGLISH TRANSLATION
'dwt/'dt	*'edôt*	testimonies
'dwt/'dt	*'edût*	testimony

From the Masoretic point of view, there would appear to be two entirely different words in the Hebrew Scriptures—one plural, the other singular—even though both have

---

[11] The Masoretes obviously imposed an artificial system of vocalization on the forms *'dwt/'dt.* They indicate the form *'edôt* (with an *o* vowel) occurs only in Deuteronomy, and the form *'edût* (with a *u* vowel) occurs only in Exodus, Leviticus, and Numbers. Moreover, they have vocalized every other biblical occurrence of the two forms *'dwt* and *'dt* with either an *o* or a *u*, depending on whether it follows the pattern of usage evidenced by one or the other of the two supposedly different Pentateuchal forms.

The Septuagint—a Greek translation of the Hebrew Scriptures completed about 250 B.C.—is much earlier, perhaps as much as 850 years earlier, than the Masoretic vocalization of the Hebrew text. That Greek translation flatly contradicts the Masoretes' contrived system. It often has a plural form where the Masoretes have indicated a singular (Ex. 30:6, 36; Lev. 16:13; Num. 17:10, and Ps. 119:88; 132:12). In addition, in the two parallel passages of 2 Kings 11:12 and 2 Chron. 23:11, the Septuagint has translated one of the two as a plural (2 Chron. 23:11) and the other as a singular (2 Kings 11:12). The Masoretic text has both vocalized as the singular *'edût*.

The Greek Septuagint and the Masoretic vocalization both agree that, for obvious reasons, the Jews have long had a tendency to think of the *testimonies* as a *singular collective*. That view arose because the *testimonies*—that is, the Ten Commandments—are an easily identified *collective* set. However, the consonantal forms *'dwt* and *'dt* should never be considered as a singular form, not even as a collective noun.

exactly the same consonantal form (*'dt/'dwt*) and the same basic *meaning*.

Unfortunately, the Masoretic vocalization of the consonantal forms *'dt/'dwt* is completely in error. Since the Jews had long since lost *The Teaching of Moses*, the Masoretes did not understand why Moses elevated the entire covenant code to the status of *Torah* in the Book of Deuteronomy.[12] Therefore, they made an entirely artificial, and totally unwarranted, distinction between the two consonantal forms *'dwt/'dt* by vocalizing some of the forms with an "*o*" vowel and others with a "*u*."

The Masoretic error is understandable. The "*w*" in the consonantal form *'dwt* is a Hebrew vowel indicator for both "*o*" and "*u*." But in truth, all occurrences of the consonantal forms *'dwt/'dt* are plural forms of the singular *'dh*.[13] All should be vocalized as *'edôt*, and all should be translated "testimonies,"[14] as shown in the following table:

CONSONANTAL HEBREW TEXT	CORRECTED VOCALIZATION	ENGLISH TRANSLATION
'dwt/'dt	*'edôt*	testimonies

That settles the issue of how these two consonantal Hebrew forms should be vocalized and translated. It will also make it possible for you to understand why the Ten Commandments are the "testimonies" (*'edôt*) to which the Hebrew text so

---

[12] See below, pp. 138 ff.

[13] I agree completely with the conclusion of the venerable Hebrew lexicon known as "BDB" which says "M(asoretic) T(ext) pointing (is) artificial." See Brown, Driver, Briggs, *A Hebrew and English Lexicon of the Old Testament* (Oxford: Clarendon Press, 1907), p. 730. However, I disagree with the authors of that lexicon concerning the root form of the noun. They hold it to be the singular form *'edût*, whereas, as I mentioned above, all occurrences are plural forms of the singular noun *'edah*.

[14] I actually prefer the translation "witnesses" over "testimonies." However, in deference to convention, I will continue to use a term the English reader will most likely encounter in the translations. I will explain the *significance* of the "witness" provided by the *testimonies* below.

often refers. However, since English translators of the Hebrew text have uncritically accepted the Masoretic error in vocalizing the forms *'dwt/'dt* with a "*u*" vowel instead of an "*o*" vowel, they translate them as "testimony" (singular) in Exodus, Leviticus, and Numbers rather than "testimonies" (plural).[15] That makes it impossible for the English reader to see the Truth. Therefore, I will provide you my translation of the relevant texts from those three books.

First of all, the tabernacle tent is often called "the tent of the testimonies":[16]

> *On the day the tabernacle was raised up, the cloud covered the tabernacle,* **the tent of the testimonies**, *and in the evening it would be over the tabernacle as a manifestation of fire until morning.*
> *(Numbers 9:15) —my translation*

> *Then His Majesty said to Aaron, "You and your sons, and the house of your father with you, will bear the iniquity of the tabernacle; but you and your sons with you will bear the iniquity of your priesthood. So also bring with you your brothers, the tribe of Levi, the tribe of your father, so that they are joined with you, so that they serve you. But you and your sons with you {will serve} in front of* **the tent of the testimonies**.*"*
> *(Numbers 18:1–2) —my translation*

Likewise, the tabernacle compound is sometimes called "the tabernacle of the testimonies":[17]

> *"These are the assigned {responsibilities} of the tabernacle—***the tabernacle of the testimonies***—which were assigned according to the mouth of Moses—the transportation work of the Levites—in the hand of Ithamar, the son of Aaron the priest."*
> *(Exodus 38:21) —my translation*

> *"You must appoint the Levites over* **the tabernacle of the testimonies**, *and over all its furnishings, and over all that pertains to it. They will carry the tabernacle and all its furnishings, and they will service it, and*

---

[15] The boldfaced phrase in each passage is a translation of the consonantal forms *'dwt/'dt*.

[16] See also Numbers 17:7–8; 2 Chronicles 24:6.

[17] See also Numbers 10:11.

*they will camp around the tabernacle. When the tabernacle is to set out, the Levites will take it down; and when the tabernacle is to camp, the Levites will raise it up. But the stranger who comes near must be put to death. The sons of Israel will camp, each according to his camp, and each according to his standard, according to their hosts; but the Levites will camp around **the tabernacle of the testimonies**. There will be no wrath on the assembly of the sons of Israel, because the Levites will guard **the tabernacle of the testimonies**." And the sons of Israel did according to all that His Majesty commanded Moses. Thus they did.*
(Numbers 1:50–54) —my translation

It should be fairly obvious why Moses called the tabernacle tent "the tent of the testimonies" and the entire tabernacle compound "the tabernacle of the testimonies." It was because the tent/tabernacle housed "the ark of the testimonies":[18]

*"Then you must make a veil of blue and purple and scarlet, and fine twisted linen—a work of an artisan. He must make it with cherubim. Then you must put it on four pillars of acacia overlaid with gold, and their hooks with gold, on four pedestals of silver. Then you must put the veil under the clasps, and you must bring in there, within the veil, **the ark of the testimonies**; and the veil will make a distinction for you between the holy and the holy of holies. Then you must put the mercy seat on **the ark of the testimonies** in the holy of holies. Then you must set the table outside the veil, and the lampstand opposite the table on the south side of the tabernacle; but you must put the table on the north side."*
(Exodus 26:31–35) —my translation

*"But as for Me, look! I have given him Oholiab, the son of Ahisamach, of the tribe of Dan. And in the heart of all who are wise of heart I have put wisdom; and they will do all that I have commanded you: the tent of meeting, and **the ark for the testimonies**, and the mercy seat that is on it, and all the furnishings of the tent."*
(Exodus 31:6–7) —my translation

Since "the ark of the testimonies" resided behind a veil inside "the tent/tabernacle of the testimonies," that veil was,

---

[18] See also Exodus 25:22; 30:6; 39:35; 40:3, 5, 21; Numbers 4:5; 7:89; and Joshua 4:16.

for obvious reasons, called not only "the veil that is before the testimonies" but also "the veil of the testimonies":

> *"But you must command the sons of Israel to acquire for you pure oil of finely crushed olives for the light, to make a lamp burn continuously in the tent of meeting, outside* **the veil that is before the testimonies**. *Aaron and his sons must maintain it from evening until morning before His Majesty—as a statute of* **'olam** *for their generations of the sons of Israel."*
> *(Exodus 27:20–21) —my translation*

> *Then His Majesty spoke to Moses saying, "Command the sons of Israel to acquire for you pure oil of finely crushed olives for the light, to make a lamp burn continuously outside* **the veil of the testimonies** *in the tent of meeting. Aaron must maintain it from evening until morning before His Majesty continuously as a statute of* **'olam** *for your generations."*
> *(Leviticus 24:1–3) —my translation*

Inside the "tent/tabernacle of the testimonies," behind the "veil of the testimonies," and inside the "ark of the testimonies," Moses was told to place the two stone tablets on which He had written the Ten Commandments. Therefore, it is not surprising to find those two tablets called "the two tablets of the testimonies." The biblical text specifically states God had written something on both sides of those two tablets:

> *Then, when He finished speaking with him on Mount Sinai, He gave Moses* **the two tablets of the testimonies**, *tablets of stone, written by the finger of God.*
> *(Exodus 31:18) —my translation*

> *Then Moses turned and went down from the mountain with* **the two tablets of the testimonies** *in his hand—tablets that were written on both sides (they were written on one and the other). Now the tablets were the work of God, and the writing that was engraved on the tablets was the writing of God.*
> *(Exodus 32:15–16) —my translation*

When Moses learned the sons of Israel had sinned, he angrily threw down "the two tablets of the testimonies" and broke them:

And it came about, as soon as Moses came near the camp, that he saw the calf and {the} dancing; and Moses' anger burned, and he threw the tablets from his hands and shattered them at the foot of the mountain.
(Exodus 32:19)

Later on, God helped Moses replace the two tablets he had broken by writing the same words on two new tablets, which He required Moses to carve out of stone himself. The biblical text explicitly states that the writing on the two new tablets was exactly the same words that God had written on the former tablets:

*Now the LORD said to Moses, "Cut out for yourself two stone tablets like the former ones, and **I will write on the tablets the words that were on the former tablets** which you shattered."*
(Exodus 34:1)

Consequently, the two stone tablets that Moses placed inside "the ark of the testimonies" behind "the veil of the testimonies" inside "the tent/tabernacle of the testimonies" were still called "the two tablets of the testimonies":

*When Moses came down from Mount Sinai (now **the two tablets of the testimonies** were in Moses' hand when he came down from the mountain, and Moses did not know the skin of his face was shining because of Him speaking with him), Aaron and all the sons of Israel saw Moses. But look! The skin of his face was shining; so they were afraid to come near him.*
(Exodus 34:29–30) —my translation

All of those passages indicate the *testimonies* were something specific. But the text does not explicitly tell us what the *testimonies* were. They could not have been the two stone tablets because those two tablets are never specifically referred to as "the *testimonies;*" they are instead called "*the two tablets of the testimonies.*" They would not have been called that if the tablets were themselves the *testimonies*. Therefore, the *testimonies* must have been "the words" that God wrote on the tablets while Moses was on the Mountain of God. That would stand to reason since a "testimony" is normally something either spoken or written.

All of the passages quoted above lead to the logical conclusion that the *testimonies* were the "ten words" that God wrote on the two stone tablets Moses brought down from the Mountain of God. The Hebrew Scriptures even tell us what the "ten words" that God wrote on the two stone tablets were. They were what we call "the Ten Commandments":

> Then the LORD said to Moses, "Write down these words,[19] for in accordance with these words I have made a covenant with you and with Israel." So he was there with the LORD forty days and forty nights; he did not eat bread or drink water. And **he wrote on the tablets the words of the covenant, the Ten Commandments.**[20]
> (Exodus 34:27–28)

In what he says to the sons of Israel beyond the Jordan, Moses confirms that the *testimonies*—that is, the Ten Commandments—were the only things written on the two stone tablets. Therefore, the Ten Commandments must have been what Moses called "the *testimonies*":

> "At that time the LORD said to me, 'Cut out for yourself two tablets of stone like the former ones, and come up to Me on the mountain, and make an ark of wood for yourself. And **I will write on the tablets the words that were on the former tablets which you shattered, and you shall put them in the ark.**' So I made an ark of acacia wood and cut out two tablets of stone like the former ones, and went up on the mountain with the two tablets in my hand. And **He wrote on the tablets, like the former writing, the Ten Commandments which the LORD had spoken to you on the mountain from the midst of the**

---

[19] Note the apparent discrepancy between the two verses quoted (Ex. 34:1 and 34:28) as to whether God wrote on the second set of tablets or whether Moses did that himself. Deuteronomy 10:4 resolves the conflict and confirms that the text means God wrote the Ten Commandments on the second set of tablets as well. Therefore, God must have meant for Moses to "write down these words" on a papyrus scroll.

[20] The Hebrew here translated "the Ten Commandments" says, *literally*, "the ten words."

fire on the day of the assembly; and the LORD *gave them to me. Then I turned and came down from the mountain, and put the tablets in the ark which I had made; and there they are, as the* LORD *commanded me."*
(Deuteronomy 10:1–5)

Since Moses makes it clear that the Ten Commandments were all that was written on "the two tablets of the *testimonies*,"[21] the text of the Hebrew Scriptures identifies the two stone tablets so closely with the *testimonies* written on them that both together are sometimes called "the *testimonies*":

> *"Then you must put into the ark **the testimonies** that I will give you."*
> *(Exodus 25:16) —my translation*

> *"Then you must put the mercy seat on top of the ark, and into the ark you must put **the testimonies** that I will give to you."*
> *(Exodus 25:21) —my translation*

> *Then Moses raised up the tabernacle—fixed its pedestals, set its boards, fixed its bars, and raised up its pillars. And he spread out the tent over the tabernacle and set the covering of the tent on top of it, just as His Majesty commanded Moses. Then he took and put **the testimonies** into the ark, and set the poles on the ark, and put the mercy seat on top of the ark. Then he brought the ark into the tabernacle, and set the veil of the screen, and screened off **the ark of the testimonies** just as His Majesty commanded Moses.*
> *(Exodus 40:18–21) —my translation*

The evidence is fairly convincing; the *testimonies* were the Ten Commandments—that is, the "ten words" that God wrote on the two stone tablets. However, Moses also indicates the "ten words"—the Ten Commandments—were the essence of the covenant God made with the sons of Israel:

> *"{Remember} the day you stood before the* LORD *your God at Horeb, when the* LORD *said to me, 'Assemble the people to Me, that I may let them hear My words so they may learn to fear Me all the days they live on the earth, and that they may teach their children.' And you came near and stood at the foot of the mountain, and the mountain burned with fire to the {very} heart of the heavens: darkness, cloud and thick*

---

[21] Deuteronomy 4:13; 5:22; and 10:4.

gloom. Then the LORD *spoke to you from the midst of the fire; you heard the sound of words, but you saw no form—only a voice. So **He declared to you His covenant which He commanded you to perform, {that is,} the Ten Commandments; and He wrote them on two tablets of stone**. And the* LORD *commanded me at that time to teach you statutes and judgments, that you might perform them in the land where you are going over to possess it."*
(Deuteronomy 4:10–14)

From the foregoing, you should be able to see why the Jews would have reason to think of the Ten Commandments as a singular—a collective set of laws, which they called "the *testimony*"—when the two stone tablets were in view. Yet they would still have thought of them as plural, "the *testimonies*," when the emphasis was on their own adherence to God's commands. That may well have been the sort of thinking that led the Masoretes to incorrectly vocalize some of the forms *'dt/'dwt* as singular. Unfortunately, by the time the Masoretes added vowels to the consonantal Hebrew text, the Jews had long since lost sight of the fact that "the *testimonies*" were not just a pair of stone tablets,[22] they were instead the "ten words" written on those tablets.

The Witness of the Testimonies

The question is, Why were the Ten Commandments called "the *testimonies*"? Better yet, what defining characteristic of the Ten Commandments is indicated by the use of this particular terminology? One must accurately answer these two questions to fully understand the *significance* of the term translated "testimonies." The answers can be found in statements Moses made at the conclusion of the covenant renewal ceremony described

---

[22] J. Milgrom, *The JPS Torah Commentary: Numbers*. His comment on the phrase "ark of the testimonies" in Numbers 7:89 (p. 59) reflects the common view:

> Hebrew *'aron ha-'edut*. *"The Pact," with the definite article, can only mean the two tablets of the Decalogue that were deposited in the Ark (Ex. 25:10–16).*

in the Book of Deuteronomy. Moses tells us that after he finished writing the "law" (*Torah*) in a book—that is, on a scroll—he gave the priests instruction concerning the role that scroll should play thereafter as a *witness* to the covenant that God made with the sons of Israel at Mt. Sinai:

> *And it came about, when Moses finished writing the words of this law in a book until they were complete, that Moses commanded the Levites who carried the ark of the covenant of the LORD, saying, "**Take this book of the law and place it beside the ark of the covenant of the LORD your God, that it may remain there as a witness against you.** For I know your rebellion and your stubbornness; behold, while I am still alive with you today, you have been rebellious against the LORD; how much more, then, after my death? Assemble to me all the elders of your tribes and your officers, that I may speak these words in their hearing and call the heavens and the earth to witness against them. For I know that after my death you will act corruptly and turn from the way which I have commanded you; and evil will befall you in the latter days, for you will do that which is evil in the sight of the LORD, provoking Him to anger with the work of your hands."*
> *(Deuteronomy 31:24–29)*

Moses' actions will probably seem strange to the modern Western mind-set, but in his own day it was customary to establish an abiding *witness* of some sort at the conclusion of a covenant ceremony. For example, Joshua set up a single large stone as a witness to the covenant the people ratified at Shechem:[23]

> *Then Joshua said to the people, "You will not be able to serve the LORD, for He is a holy God. He is a jealous God; He will not forgive your transgression or your sins. If you forsake the LORD and serve foreign gods, then He will turn and do you harm and consume you after He has done good to you." And the people said to Joshua, "No, but we will serve the LORD." And Joshua said to the people, "You are witnesses against yourselves that you have chosen for yourselves the LORD, to serve Him." And they said,*

---

[23] In this instance, the people were witnesses against themselves. That concept is inherent also in the covenant Israel made at Mt. Sinai. See p. 212, fn. 30 for a discussion of the *meaning* of the Hebrew term *'edah*.

*"We are witnesses." "Now therefore, put away the foreign gods which are in your midst, and incline your hearts to the LORD, the God of Israel." And the people said to Joshua, "We will serve the LORD our God and we will obey His voice." So Joshua made a covenant with the people that day, and made for them a statute and an ordinance in Shechem. **And Joshua wrote these words in the book of the law of God; and he took a large stone and set it up there under the oak** that was by the sanctuary of the LORD. And Joshua said to all the people, "Behold, **this stone shall be for a witness against us, for it has heard all the words of the LORD which He spoke to us; thus it shall be for a witness against you, lest you deny your God."** [24]*

(Joshua 24:19–27)

By contrast, when Jacob and Laban made a covenant, the "witnesses" they chose were a heap of stones along with a separate stone "pillar":

*Then Laban answered and said to Jacob, "The daughters are my daughters, and the children are my children, and the flocks are my flocks, and all that you see is mine. But what can I do this day to these my daughters or to their children whom they have borne? So now come, let us make a covenant, you and I, and let it be a witness between you and me." Then **Jacob took a stone and set it up {as} a pillar.** And Jacob said to his kinsmen, "Gather stones." So **they took stones and made a heap**, and they ate there by the heap. Now Laban called it Jegar-sahadutha, but Jacob called it Galeed. And Laban said, "**This heap is a witness between you and me this day.**" Therefore it was named Galeed; and Mizpah, for he said, "May the LORD watch between you and me when we are absent one from the other. If you mistreat my daughters, or if you take wives besides my daughters, {although} no man is with us, see, **God is witness between you and me.**" And Laban said to Jacob, "**Behold this heap and behold the pillar which I have set between you and me. This heap is a witness, and the pillar is a witness,** that I will not pass by this heap to you for harm, and you will not pass by this heap and this pillar to me, for harm. The God of Abraham and the God of Nahor, the God of their father, judge between us." So Jacob swore by the fear of his father Isaac. Then*

---

[24] Pay close attention to the fact that Joshua wrote the "words" of the covenant on a scroll and made a single stone the "witness" of the covenant renewal ceremony. That will become important later on.

Jacob offered a sacrifice on the mountain, and called his kinsmen to the
meal; and they ate the meal and spent the night on the mountain.
(Genesis 31:43–54)[25]

These last two accounts[26] disclose the importance the
ancients sometimes attached to stones whose primary function was that of silent *witnesses* to a covenant ratification ceremony. However, in Deuteronomy 31:24–29 above we saw that
the writing on a scroll could function in exactly the same way.
Therefore, it is not difficult to see how the *witness*, that is, the
testimony, provided by the two stone tablets on which God
wrote the Ten Commandments is a logical combination of
these two concepts. The two tablets served as stone "scrolls"
on which God wrote the "ten words"—that is, the Ten Commandments—so that they would stand as "*witnesses.*" That
means not only the stone tablets but also the words written
on them must have functioned as *witnesses* against Israel.[27]

---

[25] It is not altogether implausible that the "pillar" mentioned in this passage
may have been the most prominent stone in the heap of stones. In other
words, there may be more to the account than meets the eye. The Hebrew
word for "pillar" in this passage is *massebah*. The ancient Canaanites
thought deceased spirits inhabited such stones. See, as an example, Jeremiah 2:27. God used that ancient notion for His Own purposes in revealing
the Old Testament Gospel of Jesus Christ to the sons of Israel.

Jesus gave Simon the name Cephas, which means "stone" (John 1:42)
and immediately told him he would "build" His *ekklesia* on a rock (Matt.
16:18). It is impossible to grasp the *significance* of that *parabolic* statement
without an understanding of the role of the *massebah* in the ancient Near
East. God took a foolish notion from ancient Near Eastern mythology and,
by combining it with the Hebrew idiom "build a house," crafted it into a
parabolic message that details the Person and work of Jesus Christ—the
Stone which the builders rejected only to find He had become the chief
cornerstone (Matt. 21:42). See "Watching Ducks Sashaying 'Round the
CornerStone," *The Voice of Elijah,* April 1993.

[26] Genesis 31:43–54 and Joshua 24:19–27.

[27] The same combination of writing on a stone can be found in Joshua 8:30–
32, where Joshua builds an altar of uncut stones on which he writes the
entire Law of Moses.

There is additional confirmation that the function of the writing on the tablets was to provide *testimony* concerning Israel's adherence to the terms of the Mosaic Covenant. That evidence comes from the *meaning* of the Hebrew term *'edôt*, which is routinely translated "testimonies." It is not obvious to the English reader, but that Hebrew term is a feminine plural form of the feminine singular *'edah*.[28] That feminine form, in turn, corresponds to the masculine form *'ed*.

You have already seen the masculine form *'ed* translated as "witness" in the passages quoted above. Knowing that, you should be able to understand how the "tablets of the testimonies," on which the *testimonies* were written, were supposed to be *witnesses* to the covenant Israel made with God at Sinai. Their specific purpose was to provide written *testimony* to confirm the fact that a covenant based on those "ten words" existed between God and Israel. If the sons of Israel ever broke the terms of the covenant (which they did), the "ten words" written on the two stone tablets would stand as silent *witnesses* against them, with every one of the Ten Commandments providing explicit *testimony* concerning their sin.[29]

An accurate understanding of the *significance* of the term *'edôt*—"testimonies"—provides insight into yet another passage of Scripture where that term occurs in connection with the ratification of a covenant. The Hebrew Scriptures describe how Athaliah, upon the death of Ahaziah, usurped the throne and ruled Judah for six years. In 2 Kings 11:4–8, when the chief priest Jehoiada moved to restore a legitimate ruler to the throne, the biblical account indicates *testimonies* had an obviously important, although unstated, role in that process. First,

---

[28] The suffix *-ah* in Hebrew indicates the feminine singular.

[29] God placed an extreme importance on the preservation of these two stone tablets and the writing etched on them. He considered them so important, in fact, that He charged all Israel with their protection, and even instituted a sacrificial cult focused on their presence in the Ark of the Covenant that resided in the Holy of Holies behind the veil in the tabernacle.

the text explains that Jehoiada made a covenant with a group of loyal bodyguards whose role was to protect the legitimate heir to the throne:

> Now in the seventh year Jehoiada sent and brought the captains of hundreds of the Carites and of the guard, and brought them to him in the house of the LORD. **Then he made a covenant with them and put them under oath in the house of the LORD,** and showed them the king's son. And he commanded them, saying, "This is the thing that you shall do: one third of you, who come in on the sabbath and keep watch over the king's house (one third also {shall be} at the gate Sur, and one third at the gate behind the guards), shall keep watch over the house for defense. And two parts of you, {even} all who go out on the sabbath, shall also keep watch over the house of the LORD for the king. Then you shall surround the king, each with his weapons in his hand; and whoever comes within the ranks shall be put to death. And be with the king when he goes out and when he comes in."
> (2 Kings 11:4–8)

Having arranged these things to his satisfaction, Jehoiada then proceeded to restore the legitimate king to the throne. He did so through a coronation ceremony in which the new king accepted the *testimonies*:

> So the captains of hundreds did according to all that Jehoiada the priest commanded. And each one of them took his men who were to come in on the sabbath, with those who were to go out on the sabbath, and came to Jehoiada the priest. And the priest gave to the captains of hundreds the spears and shields that had been King David's, which {were} in the house of the LORD. And the guards stood each with his weapons in his hand, from the right side of the house to the left side of the house, by the altar and by the house, around the king. **Then he brought the king's son out and put the crown on him, and {gave him} the testimony;** and they made him king and anointed him, and they clapped their hands and said, "{Long} live the king!"
> (2 Kings 11:9–12)

Finally, Jehoiada saw to the ratification of a covenant between the Lord, the king, and the people of Israel:

*Then **Jehoiada made a covenant between the LORD and the king
and the people**, that they should be the LORD's people, also between the
king and the people.*
(2 Kings 11:17)

The *testimonies* mentioned in connection with the coronation of Joash could perhaps have been the same scroll on
which Samuel wrote "the ordinances of the kingdom" at the
coronation of Saul, the first king of Israel:

*And Samuel said to all the people, "Do you see him whom the LORD has
chosen? Surely there is no one like him among all the people." So all the
people shouted and said, "{Long} live the king!" **Then Samuel told the
people the ordinances of the kingdom, and wrote {them} in the
book and placed {it} before the LORD.** And Samuel sent all the people away, each one to his house.*
(1 Samuel 10:24–25)

Samuel took the scroll on which he had written "the ordinances[30] of the kingdom" and placed it in the sanctuary "before
the Lord." That means this scroll was most likely kept in the
same place as the scroll on which God had written the "ten
words" that were to function as *witnesses* to God's covenant
with the sons of Israel. As Deuteronomy 31:26 indicates, Moses
ordered the Levites to place that scroll in the sanctuary as well.

Since Jehoiada was chief priest, he would have had
access to the scroll on which Moses wrote the **Torah** as well as
the scroll on which Samuel wrote "the ordinances of the kingdom." Therefore, he may have used either scroll in the covenant renewal ceremonies. Nonetheless, the words written on
that scroll must have served as *witnesses* to that covenant just
as "the *testimonies*" written on "the two tablets of the testimonies" served as *witnesses* to the Mosaic Covenant.

---

[30] Although it has been translated as a plural in this case, the Hebrew text
indicates the form is singular—"ordinance" (**mishpat**). The phrase *literally*
says, "the *judgment* of the kingdom" and indicates there was but one condition for which the king was held responsible. See the explanation of the
term "judgment" (**mishpat**) in Chapter 2.

CHAPTER 2:

STATUTES AND *JUDGMENTS*

The biblical text indicates the *testimonies* inside "the ark of the *testimonies*" hidden behind "the veil of the *testimonies*" in "the tent/tabernacle of the *testimonies*" were the Ten Commandments—what the Hebrew text calls "the ten words." Those "ten words" had been etched on the "tablets of the *testimonies*" by the finger of God Himself; and Moses calls the two stone tablets "the two tablets of the *testimonies*" because the purpose of the Ten Commandments God engraved on their surface was to provide *testimony* concerning *Corporate* Israel's adherence to the terms of the Mosaic Covenant.

The evidence adduced so far indicates that it was not just the writing etched on the tablets, but the combination of words written on stone tablets that defined the unique nature of the *testimonies*.[1] However, the writing in particular—that is, the Ten Commandments—is what gave "the tablets of the *testimonies*" their distinctive character as divine *witnesses*. But it

---

[1] The Mosaic Covenant required at least two witnesses to confirm any charge (Deut. 19:15–20). That is an integral part of the *symbolism* inherent in the two stone "tablets of the *testimonies*." One tablet alone would not have provided the minimum number of "witnesses" needed to convict.

would be a mistake to assume that the *testimonies* were nothing more than witnesses to the covenant God made with the sons of Israel.

The "ten words" that God wrote on the two stone tablets while Moses was on the mountain were the totality of the covenant that God made with *Corporate* Israel.[2] They were, in fact, Israel's constitution. Yet just as a constitution does not contain the legal code by which a nation is governed on a daily basis, so too, the Ten Commandments do not contain the legal code by which God expected *Corporate* Israel to be governed.

To function, a government requires laws and regulations that apply to specific situations and carry specific penalties for every infraction. The legal stipulations that filled those needs for *Corporate* Israel were the *statutes* (**chuqqîm/chuqqôt**) and *judgments* (**mishpatîm**). Although these two categories were a logical extension of the *testimonies*, which were the covenant agreement, they were not part of the original agreement. That can be seen from what the Hebrew Scriptures say concerning the covenant renewal ceremony that Joshua orchestrated:[3]

> *"Now, therefore, fear the LORD and serve Him in sincerity and truth; and put away the gods which your fathers served beyond the River and in Egypt, and serve the LORD. And if it is disagreeable in your sight to serve the LORD, choose for yourselves today whom you will serve: whether the gods which your fathers served which were beyond the River, or the gods of the Amorites in whose land you are living; but as for me and my house, we will serve the LORD." And the people answered and said, "Far be it from us that we should forsake the LORD to serve other gods; for the LORD our God is He who brought us and our fathers up out of the land of Egypt, from the house of bondage, and who did these great signs in our sight and*

---

[2] Obedience to all the *commandments, statutes,* and *judgments* of God is inherent in the first two commandments, that is, the concept of worship focused on one god only and the prohibition of idolatry.

[3] In the texts quoted, I have boldfaced and capitalized the English translation of the Hebrew terms **choq/chuqqah** and **mishpat**.

*preserved us through all the way in which we went and among all the peoples through whose midst we passed. And the LORD drove out from before us all the peoples, even the Amorites who lived in the land. We also will serve the LORD, for He is our God." Then Joshua said to the people, "You will not be able to serve the LORD, for He is a holy God. He is a jealous God; He will not forgive your transgression or your sins. If you forsake the LORD and serve foreign gods, then He will turn and do you harm and consume you after He has done good to you." And the people said to Joshua, "No, but we will serve the LORD." And Joshua said to the people, "You are witnesses against yourselves that you have chosen for yourselves the LORD, to serve Him." And they said, "We are witnesses." "Now therefore, put away the foreign gods which are in your midst, and incline your hearts to the LORD, the God of Israel." And the people said to Joshua, "We will serve the LORD our God and we will obey His voice." **So Joshua made a covenant with the people that day, and made for them a STATUTE and an ORDINANCE[4] in Shechem**. And Joshua wrote these words in the book of the law of God; and he took a large stone and set it up there under the oak that was by the sanctuary of the LORD. (Joshua 24:14–26)*

That passage indicates two separate events occurred. First, "Joshua made a covenant with the people." Then, he "made for them a statute and an ordinance." These activities were two entirely separate parts of every covenant ratification process and should not be equated.

The basic distinction that exists between the *testimonies, statutes*, and *judgments* is extremely important to an accurate understanding of the biblical text. The *testimonies* were the terms of the covenant God made with *Corporate* Israel. They outlined the essence of the agreement between the two parties. But in order to implement those covenant terms, more detailed rules and regulations were required. The Scriptures call those detailed laws *statutes* and *judgments*.

The *statutes* and *judgments* mentioned in connection with the Mosaic Covenant were the specific rules and regulations which spelled out how the terms of the covenant were to be

---

[4] The Hebrew term *mishpat* has here been translated "ordinance."

implemented. Therefore, they were a necessary corollary to the covenant agreement, but they were not part of the agreement itself.[5] They merely stipulated how *Corporate* Israel was to keep the terms of the covenant agreement.

Although the *statutes* and *judgments* were not a part of the covenant agreement, they were so necessary to the implementation of that agreement that they could easily be viewed as expressing the essence of it. That is obvious from what Moses says concerning the "whole law" he taught:

> *"See, I have taught you* STATUTES *and* JUDGMENTS *just as the* LORD *my God commanded me, that you should do thus in the land where you are entering to possess it. So keep and do {them}, for that is your wisdom and your understanding in the sight of the peoples who will hear all these statutes and say, 'Surely this great nation is a wise and understanding people.' For what great nation is there that has a god so near to it as is the* LORD *our God whenever we call on Him?* **Or what great nation is there that has** STATUTES **and** JUDGMENTS **as righteous as this whole law which I am setting before you today?"**
> (*Deuteronomy 4:5–8*)

In summary, the Mosaic Covenant (**berith**) consisted in the *testimonies*, which were the specific terms agreed to by the two parties. The establishment of the *testimonies* was a once-for-all-time event.[6] By contrast, the drafting and implementation of *statutes* and *judgments* was an ongoing process. That process began immediately after the sons of Israel ratified the Mosaic

---

[5] The *statute* that governed the observance of the Sabbath is the sole exception. That *statute* was included in the Ten Commandments because of the Sabbath's unique function as the "sign" of the covenant.

[6] Biblical covenants were frequently renewed. In the case of the Mosaic Covenant, Moses ordered the priests to conduct a ceremonial renewal of the covenant every seven years (Deut. 31:9–13). This has led to confusion in the minds of biblical scholars. For example, it appears God ratified at least two covenants with Abraham (Gen. 15 and 17). Were these two covenants one and the same, with the latter account giving a description of a covenant renewal ceremony, or were there two separate covenants?

Covenant, and God expected it to continue as long as *Corporate* Israel existed as a nation.

When God drafted the Mosaic Covenant, He wrote the *testimonies*—that is, the Ten Commandments—on the "tablets of the *testimonies.*" By contrast, Moses wrote the original *statutes* and *judgments* on a scroll.[7]

Since the drafting and implementation of *statutes* and *judgments* would have been the logical next step following a covenant ceremony, it becomes obvious that the biblical text is describing how the sons of Israel had already ratified a covenant with God in the following passage:[8]

---

[7] Exodus 24:4.

[8] The ratification or, to use a better term, the renewal of a covenant is undoubtedly in view in this passage (Ex. 15:22–26). In support of this conclusion is God's statement to Moses that Israel must go three days' journey into the wilderness to offer sacrifice:

> "Go and gather the elders of Israel together, and say to them, 'The LORD, the God of your fathers, the God of Abraham, Isaac and Jacob, has appeared to me, saying, "I am indeed concerned about you and what has been done to you in Egypt. So I said, I will bring you up out of the affliction of Egypt to the land of the Canaanite and the Hittite and the Amorite and the Perizzite and the Hivite and the Jebusite, to a land flowing with milk and honey."' And they will pay heed to what you say; and you with the elders of Israel will come to the king of Egypt, and you will say to him, 'The LORD, the God of the Hebrews, has met with us. So now, please, **let us go a three days' journey into the wilderness, that we may sacrifice to the LORD our God.**'"*
> (Exodus 3:16–18)

This passage refers to the sacrifices that provided the covenant meal the sons of Israel ate when they first ratified the covenant. However, the covenant mentioned in Exodus 15:22–26 was not the first covenant the sons of Israel made with God. That distinction belongs to the covenant they ratified when they ate the Passover meal on the night God delivered them from Egypt. All other covenants God made with *Corporate* Israel were, in one way or another, merely renewals of that first covenant. Moreover, all subsequent covenant renewal ceremonies were for the purpose of emphasizing some symbolic aspect of the *parabolic pantomime* of the Passover Parable. (See "The Passover Parable," *The Voice of Elijah*, July 1991, or *The Passover Parable*, [The Elijah Project: Mesquite, Texas, 2005].)

Then Moses led Israel from the Red Sea, and they went out into the wilderness of Shur; and they went three days in the wilderness and found no water. And when they came to Marah, they could not drink the waters of Marah, for they were bitter; therefore it was named Marah. So the people grumbled at Moses, saying, "What shall we drink?" Then he cried out to the LORD, and the LORD showed him a tree; and he threw {it} into the waters, and the waters became sweet. **There He made for them a STATUTE and REGULATION,**[9] *and there He tested them. And He said, "If you will give earnest heed to the voice of the LORD your God, and do what is right in His sight, and give ear to His commandments, and keep all His statutes, I will put none of the diseases on you which I have put on the Egyptians; for I, the LORD, am your healer."*
(Exodus 15:22–26)

The ratification of a covenant is not specifically mentioned in that passage, but it should be inferred since the text says exactly the same thing as was said in regard to Joshua above: God "made for them a *statute* and a *judgment.*"

The Judgments *of Israel*

Now that you know how the *testimonies* differed from the *statutes* and the *judgments*, it is essential that you also understand the distinction that exists between the *statutes* and the *judgments.* Without insight into the fundamental difference between these two types of legal stipulations, it is impossible to understand the *meaning* and *significance* of specific statements made in the Hebrew Scriptures.

Although the *statutes* and *judgments* are completely different types of laws, they nevertheless complement each other. Therefore, the two are most often mentioned together just as we have seen in the passages quoted above. However, they also occur in conjunction with various other "legal" terms, such as the *commandments* and "*laws*" of God. At times, one or the other of them will also occur in combination with yet a third term, as in the frequently used phrase "justice (*judgment*) and righteous-

---

[9] The Hebrew term **mishpat** has been translated "regulation."

ness."[10] Therefore, it will eventually be necessary to explain their connection to these other terms as well.

The Hebrew term normally translated *"judgment"* is **mishpat**. The individual who handed down a *judgment* (**mishpat**) was, not surprisingly, a "judge" (**shophet**). *Judgments* are exactly what the English word infers—legal decisions that pertain to specific legal circumstances which have been, or must be, adjudicated in a court of law. The nature of the *judgment* becomes clear from the following statement in which the Hebrew term that is normally translated *"judgment"* (**mishpat**) has been translated *ordinance*:

> *"Now these are the ORDINANCES which you are to set before them."*
> *(Exodus 21:1)*

Immediately following that brief introduction is a series of civil/criminal case laws along with the prescribed penalty for each infraction. The following is typical of the *judgments* listed:

> *"If a man steals an ox or a sheep, and slaughters it or sells it, he shall pay five oxen for the ox and four sheep for the sheep. If the thief is caught while breaking in, and is struck so that he dies, there will be no bloodguiltiness on his account. {But} if the sun has risen on him, there will be bloodguiltiness on his account. He shall surely make restitution; if he owns nothing, then he shall be sold for his theft. If what he stole is actually found alive in his possession, whether an ox or a donkey or a sheep, he shall pay double. If a man lets a field or vineyard be grazed {bare} and lets his animal loose so that it grazes in another man's field, he shall make restitution from the best of his own field and the best of his own vineyard. If a fire breaks out and spreads to thorn bushes, so that stacked grain or the standing grain or the field {itself} is consumed, he who started the fire shall surely make restitution. If a man gives his neighbor money or goods to keep {for him}, and it is stolen from the*

---

[10] The two terms "justice" (**mishpat**)—which is sometimes translated "ordinance"—and "righteousness" (**zedeq**) occur together not only in the phrase "justice and righteousness" (cf. Ps. 119:121; Ecc. 5:8) or, inversely, "righteousness and justice" (cf. Ps. 89:14; 97:2; Prov. 1:3; 2:9; Hos. 2:19) but also in tandem, as "righteous judgment" (cf. Deut. 16:18; Ps. 119:7, 62, 106, 160, 164; and Is. 58:2).

*man's house, **if the thief is caught,** he shall pay double. **If the thief is not caught,** then the owner of the house shall appear before the judges, {to} determine whether he laid his hands on his neighbor's property. For every breach of trust, {whether it is} for ox, for donkey, for sheep, for clothing, {or} for any lost thing about which one says, 'This is it,' the case of both parties shall come before the judges; he whom the judges condemn shall pay double to his neighbor."*
(Exodus 22:1–9)

The identifying characteristic of every *judgment* in that list is the conditional particle "if." That particle indicates a "judge" (**shophet**) had to render a "*judgment*/decision/verdict" (**mishpat**) based on whether the facts of the case fell within the limits of the conditions specified in the legal code.[11] It is clear, therefore, that the Hebrew term **mishpat**, which is usually translated "case," "justice," "judgment," or "ordinance," designates what is today called "case law." That is, it is law established by legal precedent or by judicial decision in particular cases. It is judge-made law.[12] That definition accurately reflects the *meaning* and usage of the term **mishpat** in the Hebrew Scriptures.

A *judgment* is any legal or cultic stipulation containing at least one condition that requires the decision of a judge. For example, the stipulations governing the observance of the Passover are called both a *statute*[13] and a "*law*" in Exodus 12,[14] but the term "judgment"—*mishpat*—is never used to refer to stipulations governing the Passover until specific conditions are introduced in Numbers 9:1–14. Then we are twice told that the observance of the Passover is governed by both *stat-*

---

[11] The reader who is interested in viewing the laws of Israel from a purely legal perspective should consult David Daube's *Studies in Biblical Law* (Cambridge: Cambridge University Press, 1947).

[12] *Webster's Third New International Dictionary* (Chicago: G.&C. Merriam Co., 1971).

[13] Exodus 12:14, 17, 24, 43; 13:10.

[14] Exodus 12:49; 13:9.

utes and *judgments*. That is because, although specific conditions are mentioned in connection with the observance of the Passover in Exodus 12,[15] the emphasis in Numbers 9:1–14 is on the conditional aspects of the Passover legislation:

> *Thus the* LORD *spoke to Moses in the wilderness of Sinai, in the first month of the second year after they had come out of the land of Egypt, saying, "Now, let the sons of Israel observe the Passover at its appointed time. On the fourteenth day of this month, at twilight, you shall observe it at its appointed time; you shall observe it according to all its statutes and **according to all its** ORDINANCES."[16] So Moses told the sons of Israel to observe the Passover. And they observed the Passover in the first {month}, on the fourteenth day of the month, at twilight, in the wilderness of Sinai; according to all that the* LORD *had commanded Moses, so the sons of Israel did. But there were {some} men who were unclean because of {the} dead person, so that they could not observe Passover on that day; so they came before Moses and Aaron on that day. And those men said to him, "{Though} we are unclean because of {the} dead person, why are we restrained from presenting the offering of the* LORD *at its appointed time among the sons of Israel?" Moses therefore said to them, "Wait, and I will listen to what the* LORD *will command concerning you." Then the* LORD *spoke to Moses, saying, "Speak to the sons of Israel, saying, 'If any one of you or of your generations becomes unclean because of a {dead} person, or is on a distant journey, he may, however, observe the Passover to the* LORD. *In the second month on the fourteenth day at twilight, they shall observe it; they shall eat it with unleavened bread and bitter herbs. They shall leave none of it until morning, nor break a bone of it; according to all the statute of the Passover they shall observe it. But the man who is clean and is not on a journey, and yet neglects to observe the Passover, that person shall then be cut off from his people, for he did not present the offering of the* LORD *at its appointed time. That man shall bear his sin. And if an alien sojourns among you and observes the Passover to the* LORD, *according to the statute of the Passover and **according to its** ORDINANCE, so he shall do; you shall have one statute, both for the alien and for the native of the land.'"*
> *(Numbers 9:1–14)*

---

[15] Exodus 12:4, 48.

[16] The Hebrew term *mishpat* has again been translated "ordinance."

Likewise, there is no reference to *judgments* in connection with the *symbolic ritual* associated with the burnt offering until the possibility of offering a bird as a burnt offering is mentioned. At that time, the text specifically calls it a *judgment*:

> "But **if he cannot afford a lamb**, then he shall bring to the LORD his guilt offering for that in which he has sinned, two turtledoves or two young pigeons, one for a sin offering and the other for a burnt offering. And he shall bring them to the priest, who shall offer first that which is for the sin offering and shall nip its head at the front of its neck, but he shall not sever {it}. He shall also sprinkle some of the blood of the sin offering on the side of the altar, while the rest of the blood shall be drained out at the base of the altar: it is a sin offering. The second he shall then prepare as a burnt offering **according to the ORDINANCE.**[17] So the priest shall make atonement on his behalf for his sin which he has committed, and it shall be forgiven him."
> (Leviticus 5:7–10)

Later on, the text indicates Aaron offered a burnt offering for the people "according to the *ordinance*," that is, according to the *judgment* (**mishpat**). The use of the term *judgment* makes it clear that Aaron was to make decisions based on specific conditions that relate to the offering of that particular sacrifice:

> Then he presented the people's offering, and took the goat of the sin offering which was for the people, and slaughtered it and offered it for sin, like the first. He also presented the burnt offering, and offered it **according to the ORDINANCE.** Next he presented the grain offering, and filled his hand with some of it and offered {it} up in smoke on the altar, besides the burnt offering of the morning.
> (Leviticus 9:15–17)

By his use of the phrase "according to the ordinance," that is, according to the *judgment* (**mishpat**), Moses is referring to the fact that the priest had to make a decision as to how to proceed with the sacrificial ritual based on what was being sacrificed. That is, the ritual depended on the type of animal or bird offered. That can be seen from the following:

---

[17] The Hebrew term **mishpat** has again been translated "ordinance."

*Then the LORD called to Moses and spoke to him from the tent of meeting, saying, "Speak to the sons of Israel and say to them, 'When any man of you brings an offering to the LORD, you shall bring your offering of animals from the herd or the flock. **If his offering is a burnt offering from the herd**, he shall offer it, a male without defect; he shall offer it at the doorway of the tent of meeting, that he may be accepted before the LORD. And he shall lay his hand on the head of the burnt offering, that it may be accepted for him to make atonement on his behalf. And he shall slay the young bull before the LORD; and Aaron's sons, the priests, shall offer up the blood and sprinkle the blood around on the altar that is at the doorway of the tent of meeting. He shall then skin the burnt offering and cut it into its pieces. And the sons of Aaron the priest shall put fire on the altar and arrange wood on the fire. Then Aaron's sons, the priests, shall arrange the pieces, the head, and the suet over the wood which is on the fire that is on the altar. Its entrails, however, and its legs he shall wash with water. And the priest shall offer up in smoke all of it on the altar for a burnt offering, an offering by fire of a soothing aroma to the LORD. But **if his offering is from the flock, of the sheep or of the goats, for a burnt offering**, he shall offer it a male without defect. And he shall slay it on the side of the altar northward before the LORD, and Aaron's sons, the priests, shall sprinkle its blood around on the altar. He shall then cut it into its pieces with its head and its suet, and the priest shall arrange them on the wood which is on the fire that is on the altar. The entrails, however, and the legs he shall wash with water. And the priest shall offer all of it, and offer it up in smoke on the altar; it is a burnt offering, an offering by fire of a soothing aroma to the LORD. But **if his offering to the LORD is a burnt offering of birds**, then he shall bring his offering from the turtledoves or from young pigeons. And the priest shall bring it to the altar and wring off its head, and offer it up in smoke on the altar; and its blood is to be drained out on the side of the altar. He shall also take away its crop with its feathers, and cast it beside the altar eastward, to the place of the ashes. Then he shall tear it by its wings, {but} shall not sever {it}. And the priest shall offer it up in smoke on the altar on the wood which is on the fire; it is a burnt offering, an offering by fire of a soothing aroma to the LORD.'"*
(Leviticus 1:1–17)

From this passage, it is apparent the priest was required to make specific decisions (***mishpatîm***) based on the various conditions given. That was true of every *judgment*. Consequently, the possibility of perverting the legal/cultic system for one's own benefit was always present. That is why the Hebrew Scriptures time and again insist on the absolute honesty and integrity of the judge, with repeated warnings against distorting or perverting *judgment*:

> *"You shall not pervert the* JUSTICE *{due} to your needy {brother} in his dispute."*
> *(Exodus 23:6)*

> *"You shall do no injustice in* JUDGMENT; *you shall not be partial to the poor nor defer to the great, but you are to* JUDGE *your neighbor fairly."*
> *(Leviticus 19:15)*

> *"You shall appoint for yourself judges and officers in all your towns which the LORD your God is giving you, according to your tribes, and they shall judge the people with righteous* JUDGMENT. *You shall not distort* JUSTICE; *you shall not be partial, and you shall not take a bribe, for a bribe blinds the eyes of the wise and perverts the words of the righteous.* JUSTICE, *{and only}* JUSTICE, *you shall pursue, that you may live and possess the land which the LORD your God is giving you."*
> *(Deuteronomy 16:18–20)*

> *"You shall not pervert the* JUSTICE *due an alien {or} an orphan, nor take a widow's garment in pledge."*
> *(Deuteronomy 24:17)*

> *"'Cursed is he who distorts the* JUSTICE *due an alien, orphan, and widow.' And all the people shall say, 'Amen.'"*
> *(Deuteronomy 27:19)*

In each instance, the Hebrew term *mishpat* has been translated either "judgment" or "justice," depending on the nuance required. But the term's use clearly reveals its direct connection to the activities of the court. The following description of Israel's judicial process further confirms the *meaning* of the root as "that which pertains to judicial decision":

> *Then the daughters of Zelophehad, the son of Hepher, the son of Gilead, the son of Machir, the son of Manasseh, of the families of Manasseh the son of Joseph, came near; and these are the names of his daughters: Mahlah, Noah and Hoglah and Milcah and Tirzah. And they stood*

> *before Moses and before Eleazar the priest and before the leaders and all the congregation, at the doorway of the tent of meeting, saying, "Our father died in the wilderness, yet he was not among the company of those who gathered themselves together against the LORD in the company of Korah; but he died in his own sin, and he had no sons. Why should the name of our father be withdrawn from among his family because he had no son? Give us a possession among our father's brothers." And Moses brought their CASE before the LORD.*
> *(Numbers 27:1–5)*

The "case" mentioned in verse 5 is a translation of the Hebrew term *mishpat*—"*judgment*." Its presence reveals this account deals with the formulation of case law, that is, with a *judgment*. The daughters of Zelophehad were appealing to Moses for a judicial decision concerning the estate of their deceased father. When Moses found he could not arrive at a decision on his own, Moses took the women's case to God for a *judgment* in accordance with the judicial process God had established in Israel. In return, he *received* a "statutory judgment":

> *Then the LORD spoke to Moses, saying, "The daughters of Zelophehad are right in {their} statements. You shall surely give them a hereditary possession among their father's brothers, and you shall transfer the inheritance of their father to them. Further, you shall speak to the sons of Israel, saying, 'If a man dies and has no son, then you shall transfer his inheritance to his daughter. And if he has no daughter, then you shall give his inheritance to his brothers. And if he has no brothers, then you shall give his inheritance to his father's brothers. And if his father has no brothers, then you shall give his inheritance to his nearest relative in his own family, and he shall possess it; and it shall be a STATUTORY ORDINANCE to the sons of Israel, just as the LORD commanded Moses.'"*
> *(Numbers 27:6–11)*

The Hebrew phrase translated "statutory ordinance" in verse 11 *literally* says "*statute of judgment*." The two terms *statute* and *judgment* occurring together as a noun construct confirm that the term *statute* refers to something distinct from, and other than, a *judgment*. If the two terms were interchangeable, they would hardly have been used together to refer to one particular legal rendering.

The Statutes *of Israel*

There are two terms in the Hebrew Scriptures that are normally translated "*statute.*" Both refer to ordinances that "mandate limits" for some fundamental order of existence. These two terms are further restricted in usage to just two types of *statutes,* either those governing the order of nature or those governing the procedure to be followed by the priests in conducting the sacrificial rituals of the tabernacle cult.

The two Hebrew nouns normally translated "*statute*" are the masculine form *choq* and its feminine form *chuqqah*. Both derive from the same root as the verb *chaqaq*, which *means* "to inscribe," "to engrave," or "to mark out." Since the use of the verb *chaqaq* provides a key to understanding the *meaning* of the two nouns, let's take a look at that form first.[18]

First of all, the Hebrew verb *chaqaq* is used in connection with God's creation of the universe:

> "*When He established the heavens, I was there,*
> **When He INSCRIBED** *a circle on the face of the deep,*
> *When He made firm the skies above,*
> *When the springs of the deep became fixed,*
> *When He set for the sea its boundary,*
> *So that the water should not transgress His command,*
> **When He MARKED OUT** *the foundations of the earth.*"
> (*Proverbs 8:27–29*)

The verb *chaqaq* in that passage plainly conveys the sense of etching, or inscribing, marks on something. That is, marking a limit or boundary beyond which something cannot go. That is exactly the sense conveyed by the noun *choq* in this passage:

---

[18] In the following passages, the English translation of *chaqaq, choq,* and *chuqqah* is boldfaced and capitalized.

"Or {who} enclosed the sea with doors,
When, bursting forth, it went out from the womb;
When I made a cloud its garment,
And thick darkness its swaddling band,
And I placed BOUNDARIES *on it,*
And I set a bolt and doors,
And I said, 'Thus far you shall come, but no farther;
And here shall your proud waves stop'?"
(Job 38:8–11)

That passage makes somewhat the same statement as Proverbs 8 above, except the Prophet in this case uses the noun *choq* instead of the verb *chaqaq*. Therefore, we know that both the verbal form *chaqaq* and the nominal form *choq* were used to describe how God instituted the boundaries of created things. That explains why the author of the Book of Job also uses the noun *chuqqah* to tell us there are *statutes* of the heavens that govern the behavior of the Earth. Unfortunately, the term has again been translated "ordinance" instead of *"statute"*:

"Do you know the ORDINANCES *of the heavens,*
Or fix their rule over the earth?"
(Job 38:33)

In the following two passages, Jeremiah reveals that there are also *statutes* (*choq/chuqqah*) of the moon and stars as well as *statutes* of Heaven and Earth:

Thus says the LORD,
Who gives the sun for light by day,
And the FIXED ORDER *of the moon and the stars*
for light by night,
Who stirs up the sea so that its waves roar;
The LORD *of hosts is His name:*
"If this FIXED ORDER *departs*
From before Me," declares the LORD,
"Then the offspring of Israel also shall cease
From being a nation before Me forever."
(Jeremiah 31:35–36)

*"Thus says the LORD, 'If My covenant {for} day and night {stand} not,
{and} the FIXED PATTERNS of heaven and earth I have not established,
then I would reject the descendants of Jacob and David My servant, not
taking from his descendants rulers over the descendants of Abraham,
Isaac, and Jacob. But I will restore their fortunes and will have mercy on
them.'"*
(Jeremiah 33:25–26)

The translator, not understanding the basic nuance of the
noun *choq*, has translated it "fixed order" and "fixed pattern."[19]
That is somewhat inaccurate. Yet you can still see that the basic
meaning of the term has to do with a mandate that sets a limit or
boundary within which something must operate. In the
pasages just quoted, the Prophet uses it to point to the physical
laws of the universe that set limits within which the forces of
nature operate.

From the above, it is obvious that the verb *chaqaq* and the
nouns *choq* and *chuqqah* all convey the sense of an "inscribed
ordinance mandating limits." That *meaning* is confirmed in
several contexts where the noun obviously refers to a different kind of established boundary or limit. In the following
passage it carries the connotation of "what is allowed," "allow-
ance," or "allotment":

*So Joseph bought all the land of Egypt for Pharaoh, for every Egyptian
sold his field, because the famine was severe upon them. Thus the land
became Pharaoh's. And as for the people, he removed them to the cities
from one end of Egypt's border to the other. Only the land of the priests he
did not buy, for the priests had an ALLOTMENT from Pharaoh, and they
lived off the ALLOTMENT which Pharaoh gave them. Therefore, they did
not sell their land. Then Joseph said to the people, "Behold, I have today
bought you and your land for Pharaoh; now, {here} is seed for you, and
you may sow the land. And at the harvest you shall give a fifth to Pharaoh, and four-fifths shall be your own for seed of the field and for your
food and for those of your households and as food for your little ones." So*

---

[19] In Jeremiah 31:35–36, "allotment" might be more in keeping with the
term's use opposite the verb *give*. In Jeremiah 33:25, the term occurs with
covenant and carries the legal nuance *statute*.

*they said, "You have saved our lives! Let us find favor in the sight of my lord, and we will be Pharaoh's slaves." And **Joseph made it a** STATUTE concerning the land of Egypt {valid} to this day, that Pharaoh should have the fifth; only the land of the priests did not become Pharaoh's. (Genesis 47:20–26)*

The words translated "allotment" and "statute" in that passage are all the same noun—*choq*. So the term clearly carries a nuance of "allotment" as well as the general *meaning "statute."* But even in the narrower sense of the term, the "allotment" still depends on an "inscribed ordinance mandating limits." That is, it represents limits established by a *statute*. That is especially *significant* in connection with the *statutes* related to the priestly *allotment*, portion, or due. These *statutes* specified the limit of the portion or *allotment* the priests could take from the sacrifices and offerings.

Statutes *Governing Creation*

The verb ***chaqaq*** and the nouns ***choq/chuqqah*** provide a basic insight into the *meaning* of their root form (***chq***), and the evidence is abundantly clear: God enacted *statutes* to control certain elements of His Creation. In keeping with the basic *meaning* of the consonantal Hebrew root ***chq***, those *statutes* mandate limits beyond which something cannot go. So it is clear that a *statute* is a law which, by setting limits, governs some fundamental order of existence.

To this point, the two nouns ***choq/chuqqah*** have been restricted to just two types of *statutes*: *statutes* that mandate limits for the conduct of nature and *statutes* that govern the conduct of the sacrificial rituals of the tabernacle cult. That restricted use is also apparent in the following survey of passages in which those two noun forms occur:

Limits to Human Life Span

"Man, who is born of woman,
Is short-lived and full of turmoil.

Like a flower he comes forth and withers.
He also flees like a shadow and does not remain.
Thou also dost open Thine eyes on him,
And bring him into judgment with Thyself.
Who can make the clean out of the unclean?
No one!
Since his days are determined,
The number of his months is with Thee,
And his LIMITS Thou hast set so that he cannot pass."
(Job 14:1–5)

Limits to Light and Darkness

"He obscures the face of the full moon,
And spreads His cloud over it.
He has INSCRIBED A CIRCLE on the surface of the waters,
At the boundary of light and darkness."
(Job 26:9–10)

Limits to the Rain

"When He imparted weight to the wind,
And meted out the waters by measure,
When He SET A LIMIT for the rain,
And a course for the thunderbolt,
Then He saw it and declared it;
He established it and also searched it out."
(Job 28:25–27)

Limits to the Sea

"Or {who} enclosed the sea with doors,
When, bursting forth, it went out from the womb;
When I made a cloud its garment,
And thick darkness its swaddling band,
And I PLACED BOUNDARIES on it,
And I set a bolt and doors,
And I said, 'Thus far you shall come, but no farther;
And here shall your proud waves stop'?"
(Job 38:8–11)

"When He established the heavens, I was there,
When He INSCRIBED A CIRCLE on the face of the deep,
When He made firm the skies above,
When the springs of the deep became fixed,
When He set for the sea its BOUNDARY,
So that the water should not transgress His command,
When He MARKED OUT the foundations of the earth."
(Proverbs 8:27–29)

"Do you not fear Me?" declares the LORD.
"Do you not tremble in My presence?
For I have placed the sand as a boundary for the sea,
An ETERNAL DECREE, so it cannot cross over it.
Though the waves toss, yet they cannot prevail;
Though they roar, yet they cannot cross over it."
(Jeremiah 5:22)

"Eternal" Statutes *Governing Cultic Ritual*

In contrast to their use in the passages above, in the Pentateuch the nouns *choq* and *chuqqah* refer only to regulations governing the cultic rituals associated with the tabernacle. Most of those *statutes* are said to be "eternal" (Hebrew: *'olam*[20]), and all of those "eternal statutes" (*choq/chuqqah 'olam*) mandate limits for the conduct of the cultic rituals of the sanctuary. Moreover, the biblical text explicitly states that these eternal limits are absolute. They are not conditional like the *judgments*.

The following passages include all the occurrences of the phrase translated "eternal statute" in the Pentateuch. They reveal that *statutes* governed the observance of the major feast days, the conduct of the priestly ritual, the distribution of the tithes and offerings brought to the sanctuary, and the allocation of *Corporate* Israel's inheritance. In each case, the nouns *choq* and *chuqqah* have been translated as either "statute," "ordi-

---

[20] The English adjective "eternal" is not an accurate translation of the Hebrew noun *'olam*. (See "Questions & Answers," *The Voice of Elijah*, July 2000.) The grammatical construction actually says "*statute* of *'olam*."

nance," "portion," or "due." The word *'olam* is translated as either "permanent," "forever," "perpetual," or "perpetually." Both the word and the phrase are boldfaced and capitalized:

"Eternal" *Statutes* Relating to
the Passover/Feast of Unleavened Bread

> *"'Now this day will be a memorial to you, and you shall celebrate it {as} a feast to the LORD; throughout your generations you are to celebrate it {as} a PERMANENT ORDINANCE. Seven days you shall eat unleavened bread, but on the first day you shall remove leaven from your houses; for whoever eats anything leavened from the first day until the seventh day, that person shall be cut off from Israel. And on the first day you shall have a holy assembly, and {another} holy assembly on the seventh day; no work at all shall be done on them, except what must be eaten by every person, that alone may be prepared by you. You shall also observe the {Feast of} Unleavened Bread, for on this very day I brought your hosts out of the land of Egypt; therefore you shall observe this day throughout your generations as a PERMANENT ORDINANCE. In the first {month}, on the fourteenth day of the month at evening, you shall eat unleavened bread, until the twenty-first day of the month at evening. Seven days there shall be no leaven found in your houses; for whoever eats what is leavened, that person shall be cut off from the congregation of Israel, whether {he is} an alien or a native of the land. You shall not eat anything leavened; in all your dwellings you shall eat unleavened bread.'" Then Moses called for all the elders of Israel, and said to them, "Go and take for yourselves lambs according to your families, and slay the Passover {lamb}. And you shall take a bunch of hyssop and dip it in the blood which is in the basin, and apply some of the blood that is in the basin to the lintel and the two doorposts; and none of you shall go outside the door of his house until morning. For the LORD will pass through to smite the Egyptians; and when He sees the blood on the lintel and on the two doorposts, the LORD will pass over the door and will not allow the destroyer to come in to your houses to smite {you}. And you shall observe this event as an ORDINANCE for you and your children FOREVER."*
> (Exodus 12:14–24)

Thus the LORD spoke to Moses in the wilderness of Sinai, in the first month of the second year after they had come out of the land of Egypt, say-

ing, "Now, let the sons of Israel observe the Passover at its appointed time. On the fourteenth day of this month, at twilight, you shall observe it at its appointed time; you shall observe it **according to all its STATUTES** and according to all its ordinances." So Moses told the sons of Israel to observe the Passover. And they observed the Passover in the first {month}, on the fourteenth day of the month, at twilight, in the wilderness of Sinai; according to all that the LORD had commanded Moses, so the sons of Israel did. But there were {some} men who were unclean because of {the} dead person, so that they could not observe Passover on that day; so they came before Moses and Aaron on that day. And those men said to him, "{Though} we are unclean because of {the} dead person, why are we restrained from presenting the offering of the LORD at its appointed time among the sons of Israel?" Moses therefore said to them, "Wait, and I will listen to what the LORD will command concerning you." Then the LORD spoke to Moses, saying, "Speak to the sons of Israel, saying, 'If any one of you or of your generations becomes unclean because of a {dead} person, or is on a distant journey, he may, however, observe the Passover to the LORD. In the second month on the fourteenth day at twilight, they shall observe it; they shall eat it with unleavened bread and bitter herbs. They shall leave none of it until morning, nor break a bone of it; **according to all the STATUTE of the Passover** they shall observe it. But the man who is clean and is not on a journey, and yet neglects to observe the Passover, that person shall then be cut off from his people, for he did not present the offering of the LORD at its appointed time. That man shall bear his sin. And if an alien sojourns among you and observes the Passover to the LORD, **according to the STATUTE of the Passover** and according to its ordinance, so he shall do; you shall have one STATUTE, both for the alien and for the native of the land.'"
(Numbers 9:1–14)

"Eternal" *Statute* Relating to the Feast of Weeks (Pentecost)

"'You shall also count for yourselves from the day after the sabbath, from the day when you brought in the sheaf of the wave offering; there shall be seven complete sabbaths. You shall count fifty days to the day after the seventh sabbath; then you shall present a new grain offering to the LORD. You shall bring in from your dwelling places two {loaves} of bread for a wave offering, made of two-tenths {of an ephah}; they shall be of a fine flour, baked with leaven as first fruits to the LORD. Along

with the bread, you shall present seven one year old male lambs without defect, and a bull of the herd, and two rams; they are to be a burnt offering to the LORD, with their grain offering and their libations, an offering by fire of a soothing aroma to the LORD. You shall also offer one male goat for a sin offering and two male lambs one year old for a sacrifice of peace offerings. The priest shall then wave them with the bread of the first fruits for a wave offering with two lambs before the LORD; they are to be holy to the LORD for the priest. On this same day you shall make a proclamation as well; you are to have a holy convocation. You shall do no laborious work. It is to be a PERPETUAL STATUTE in all your dwelling places throughout your generations.'"
(Leviticus 23:15–21)

"Eternal" *Statute* Relating to the Day of Atonement

"And {this} shall be a PERMANENT STATUTE for you: in the seventh month, on the tenth day of the month, you shall humble your souls, and not do any work, whether the native, or the alien who sojourns among you; for it is on this day that atonement shall be made for you to cleanse you; you shall be clean from all your sins before the LORD. It is to be a sabbath of solemn rest for you, that you may humble your souls; it is a PERMANENT STATUTE. So the priest who is anointed and ordained to serve as priest in his father's place shall make atonement: he shall thus put on the linen garments, the holy garments, and make atonement for the holy sanctuary; and he shall make atonement for the tent of meeting and for the altar. He shall also make atonement for the priests and for all the people of the assembly. Now you shall have this as a PERMANENT STATUTE, to make atonement for the sons of Israel for all their sins once every year." And just as the LORD had commanded Moses, {so} he did.
(Leviticus 16:29–34)

"Eternal" *Statutes* Relating to Light

"And you shall charge the sons of Israel, that they bring you clear oil of beaten olives for the light, to make a lamp burn continually. In the tent of meeting, outside the veil which is before the testimony, Aaron and his sons shall keep it in order from evening to morning before the LORD; {it shall be} a PERPETUAL STATUTE throughout their generations for the sons of Israel."
(Exodus 27:20–21)

Then the LORD spoke to Moses, saying, "Command the sons of Israel that they bring to you clear oil from beaten olives for the light, to make a lamp burn continually. Outside the veil of testimony in the tent of meeting, Aaron shall keep it in order from evening to morning before the LORD continually; {it shall be} a PERPETUAL STATUTE throughout your generations."
(Leviticus 24:1–3)

"Eternal" *Statute* Relating to Sounding of Trumpets

The LORD spoke further to Moses, saying, "Make yourself two trumpets of silver, of hammered work you shall make them; and you shall use them for summoning the congregation and for having the camps set out. And when both are blown, all the congregation shall gather themselves to you at the doorway of the tent of meeting. Yet if {only} one is blown, then the leaders, the heads of the divisions of Israel, shall assemble before you. But when you blow an alarm, the camps that are pitched on the east side shall set out. And when you blow an alarm the second time, the camps that are pitched on the south side shall set out; an alarm is to be blown for them to set out. When convening the assembly, however, you shall blow without sounding an alarm. The priestly sons of Aaron, moreover, shall blow the trumpets; and this shall be for you a PERPETUAL STATUTE throughout your generations."
(Numbers 10:1–8)

"Eternal" *Statutes* Relating to Consecration/Cleansing

"And for Aaron's sons you shall make tunics; you shall also make sashes for them, and you shall make caps for them, for glory and for beauty. And you shall put them on Aaron your brother and on his sons with him; and you shall anoint them and ordain them and consecrate them, that they may serve Me as priests. And you shall make for them linen breeches to cover {their} bare flesh; they shall reach from the loins even to the thighs. And they shall be on Aaron and on his sons when they enter the tent of meeting, or when they approach the altar to minister in the holy place, so that they do not incur guilt and die. It {shall be} a STATUTE FOREVER to him and to his descendants after him."
(Exodus 28:40–43)

"Then you shall bring Aaron and his sons to the doorway of the tent of meeting, and wash them with water. And you shall take the garments, and put on Aaron the tunic and the robe of the ephod and the ephod and

the breastpiece, and gird him with the skillfully woven band of the ephod; and you shall set the turban on his head, and put the holy crown on the turban. Then you shall take the anointing oil, and pour it on his head and anoint him. And you shall bring his sons and put tunics on them. And you shall gird them with sashes, Aaron and his sons, and bind caps on them, and they shall have the priesthood by **a PERPETUAL STATUTE**. *So you shall ordain Aaron and his sons."*
(Exodus 29:4–9)

"You shall also make a laver of bronze, with its base of bronze, for washing; and you shall put it between the tent of meeting and the altar, and you shall put water in it. And Aaron and his sons shall wash their hands and their feet from it; when they enter the tent of meeting, they shall wash with water, that they may not die; or when they approach the altar to minister, by offering up in smoke a fire {sacrifice} to the LORD. So they shall wash their hands and their feet, that they may not die; and it shall be **a PERPETUAL STATUTE** *for them, for Aaron and his descendants throughout their generations."*
(Exodus 30:18–21)

The LORD then spoke to Aaron, saying, "Do not drink wine or strong drink, neither you nor your sons with you, when you come into the tent of meeting, so that you may not die—it is **a PERPETUAL STATUTE** *throughout your generations—and so as to make a distinction between the holy and the profane, and between the unclean and the clean, and so as to teach the sons of Israel all* **the STATUTES** *which the LORD has spoken to them through Moses."*
(Leviticus 10:8–11)

Then the LORD spoke to Moses and Aaron, saying, "This is the **STATUTE of the LAW** *which the LORD has commanded, saying, 'Speak to the sons of Israel that they bring you an unblemished red heifer in which is no defect, {and} on which a yoke has never been placed. And you shall give it to Eleazar the priest, and it shall be brought outside the camp and be slaughtered in his presence. Next Eleazar the priest shall take some of its blood with his finger, and sprinkle some of its blood toward the front of the tent of meeting seven times. Then the heifer shall be burned in his sight; its hide and its flesh and its blood, with its refuse, shall be burned. And the priest shall take cedar wood and hyssop and scarlet {material}, and cast it into the midst of the burning heifer. The priest shall then wash his clothes and bathe his body in water, and afterward come into the camp, but the*

priest shall be unclean until evening. The one who burns it shall also wash his clothes in water and bathe his body in water, and shall be unclean until evening. Now a man who is clean shall gather up the ashes of the heifer and deposit them outside the camp in a clean place, and the congregation of the sons of Israel shall keep it as water to remove impurity; it is purification from sin. And the one who gathers the ashes of the heifer shall wash his clothes and be unclean until evening; and it shall be *a PERPETUAL STATUTE* to the sons of Israel and to the alien who sojourns among them. The one who touches the corpse of any person shall be unclean for seven days. That one shall purify himself from uncleanness with the water on the third day and on the seventh day, {and then} he shall be clean; but if he does not purify himself on the third day and on the seventh day, he shall not be clean. Anyone who touches a corpse, the body of a man who has died, and does not purify himself, defiles the tabernacle of the LORD; and that person shall be cut off from Israel. Because the water for impurity was not sprinkled on him, he shall be unclean; his uncleanness is still on him. This is the law when a man dies in a tent: everyone who comes into the tent and everyone who is in the tent shall be unclean for seven days. And every open vessel, which has no covering tied down on it, shall be unclean. Also, anyone who in the open field touches one who has been slain with a sword or who has died {naturally}, or a human bone or a grave, shall be unclean for seven days. Then for the unclean {person} they shall take some of the ashes of the burnt purification from sin and flowing water shall be added to them in a vessel. And a clean person shall take hyssop and dip {it} in the water, and sprinkle {it} on the tent and on all the furnishings and on the persons who were there, and on the one who touched the bone or the one slain or the one dying {naturally} or the grave. Then the clean {person} shall sprinkle on the unclean on the third day and on the seventh day; and on the seventh day he shall purify him from uncleanness, and he shall wash his clothes and bathe {himself} in water and shall be clean by evening. But the man who is unclean and does not purify himself from uncleanness, that person shall be cut off from the midst of the assembly, because he has defiled the sanctuary of the LORD; the water for impurity has not been sprinkled on him, he is unclean. So it shall be *a PERPETUAL STATUTE* for them. And he who sprinkles the water for impurity shall wash his clothes, and he who touches the water for impurity shall be unclean until evening.'"
(Numbers 19:1–21)

"Eternal" *Statute* Relating to Israel's Allotment

Then the LORD spoke to Moses, saying, "Speak to the sons of Israel, and say to them, 'When you enter the land which I am going to give to you and reap its harvest, then you shall bring in the sheaf of the first fruits of your harvest to the priest. And he shall wave the sheaf before the LORD for you to be accepted; on the day after the sabbath the priest shall wave it. Now on the day when you wave the sheaf, you shall offer a male lamb one year old without defect for a burnt offering to the LORD. Its grain offering shall then be two-tenths {of an ephah} of fine flour mixed with oil, an offering by fire to the LORD {for} a soothing aroma, with its libation, a fourth of a hin of wine. Until this same day, until you have brought in the offering of your God, you shall eat neither bread nor roasted grain nor new growth. It is to be a PERPETUAL STATUTE throughout your generations in all your dwelling places.'"
(Leviticus 23:9–14)

"Eternal" *Statutes* Relating to the Priestly Allotment[21]

"Then you shall take the breast of Aaron's ram of ordination, and wave it as a wave offering before the LORD; and it shall be your portion. And you shall consecrate the breast of the wave offering and the thigh of the heave offering which was waved and which was offered from the ram of ordination, from the one which was for Aaron and from the one which was for his sons. And it shall be for Aaron and his sons as {their} POR-

---

[21] The *statutes* in the Pentateuch that mandate the "allotment" of the priesthood are also in view in the account of the sin of the sons of Eli:

Now the sons of Eli were worthless men; they did not know the LORD and the custom of the priests with the people. When any man was offering a sacrifice, the priest's servant would come while the meat was boiling, with a three-pronged fork in his hand. Then he would thrust it into the pan, or kettle, or caldron, or pot; all that the fork brought up the priest would take for himself. Thus they did in Shiloh to all the Israelites who came there. Also, before they burned the fat, the priest's servant would come and say to the man who was sacrificing, "Give the priest meat for roasting, as he will not take boiled meat from you, only raw." And if the man said to him, "They must surely burn the fat first, and then take as much as you desire," then he would say, "No, but you shall give {it to me} now; and if not, I will take it by force." Thus the sin of the young men was very great before the LORD, for the men despised the offering of the LORD.
(1 Samuel 2:12–17)

TION FOREVER from the sons of Israel, for it is a heave offering; and it shall be a heave offering from the sons of Israel from the sacrifices of their peace offerings, {even} their heave offering to the LORD."
(Exodus 29:26–28)

"'Now this is the law of the grain offering: the sons of Aaron shall present it before the LORD in front of the altar. Then one {of them} shall lift up from it a handful of the fine flour of the grain offering, with its oil and all the incense that is on the grain offering, and he shall offer {it} up in smoke on the altar, a soothing aroma, as its memorial offering to the LORD. And what is left of it Aaron and his sons are to eat. It shall be eaten as unleavened cakes in a holy place; they are to eat it in the court of the tent of meeting. It shall not be baked with leaven. I have given it as their share from My offerings by fire; it is most holy, like the sin offering and the guilt offering. Every male among the sons of Aaron may eat it; it is a PERMANENT ORDINANCE throughout your generations, from the offerings by fire to the LORD. Whoever touches them shall become consecrated.'"
(Leviticus 6:14–18)

Then the LORD spoke to Moses, saying, "Speak to the sons of Israel, saying, 'He who offers the sacrifice of his peace offerings to the LORD shall bring his offering to the LORD from the sacrifice of his peace offerings. His own hands are to bring offerings by fire to the LORD. He shall bring the fat with the breast, that the breast may be presented as a wave offering before the LORD. And the priest shall offer up the fat in smoke on the altar; but the breast shall belong to Aaron and his sons. And you shall give the right thigh to the priest as a contribution from the sacrifices of your peace offerings. The one among the sons of Aaron who offers the blood of the peace offerings and the fat, the right thigh shall be his as {his} portion. For I have taken the breast of the wave offering and the thigh of the contribution from the sons of Israel from the sacrifices of their peace offerings, and have given them to Aaron the priest and to his sons as {their} DUE FOREVER from the sons of Israel. This is that which is consecrated to Aaron and that which is consecrated to his sons from the offerings by fire to the LORD, in that day when he presented them to serve as priests to the LORD. These the LORD had commanded to be given them from the sons of Israel in the day that He anointed them. It is {their} DUE FOREVER throughout their generations.'"
(Leviticus 7:28–36)

Then Moses spoke to Aaron, and to his surviving sons, Eleazar and Ith-amar, "Take the grain offering that is left over from the LORD's offerings by fire and eat it unleavened beside the altar, for it is most holy. You shall eat it, moreover, in a holy place, because it is your DUE and your sons' DUE out of the LORD's offerings by fire; for thus I have been commanded. The breast of the wave offering, however, and the thigh of the offering you may eat in a clean place, you and your sons and your daughters with you; for they have been given as your DUE and your sons' DUE out of the sacri-fices of the peace offerings of the sons of Israel. The thigh offered by lifting up and the breast offered by waving, they shall bring along with the offer-ings by fire of the portions of fat, to present as a wave offering before the LORD; so it shall be a thing PERPETUALLY DUE you and your sons with you, just as the LORD has commanded."
(Leviticus 10:12–15)

"Then you shall take fine flour and bake twelve cakes with it; two-tenths {of an ephah} shall be {in} each cake. And you shall set them {in} two rows, six {to} a row, on the pure {gold} table before the LORD. And you shall put pure frankincense on each row, that it may be a memorial por-tion for the bread, {even} an offering by fire to the LORD. Every sabbath day he shall set it in order before the LORD continually; it is an everlast-ing covenant for the sons of Israel. And it shall be for Aaron and his sons, and they shall eat it in a holy place; for it is most holy to him from the LORD's offerings by fire, {his} PORTION FOREVER."
(Leviticus 24:5–9)

Then the LORD spoke to Aaron, "Now behold, I Myself have given you charge of My offerings, even all the holy gifts of the sons of Israel, I have given them to you as a PORTION, and to your sons as a PERPETUAL ALLOTMENT. This shall be yours from the most holy {gifts, reserved} from the fire; every offering of theirs, even every grain offering and every sin offering and every guilt offering, which they shall render to Me, shall be most holy for you and for your sons. As the most holy {gifts} you shall eat it; every male shall eat it. It shall be holy to you. This also is yours, the offering of their gift, even all the wave offerings of the sons of Israel; I have given them to you and to your sons and daughters with you, as a PER-PETUAL ALLOTMENT. Everyone of your household who is clean may eat it. All the best of the fresh oil and all the best of the fresh wine and of the grain, the first fruits of those which they give to the LORD, I give them to you. The first ripe fruits of all that is in their land, which they bring to the

LORD, shall be yours; everyone of your household who is clean may eat it. Every devoted thing in Israel shall be yours. Every first issue of the womb of all flesh, whether man or animal, which they offer to the LORD, shall be yours; nevertheless the first-born of man you shall surely redeem, and the first-born of unclean animals you shall redeem. And as to their redemption price, from a month old you shall redeem them, by your valuation, five shekels in silver, according to the shekel of the sanctuary, which is twenty gerahs. But the first-born of an ox or the first-born of a sheep or the first-born of a goat, you shall not redeem; they are holy. You shall sprinkle their blood on the altar and shall offer up their fat in smoke {as} an offering by fire, for a soothing aroma to the LORD. And their meat shall be yours; it shall be yours like the breast of a wave offering and like the right thigh. All the offerings of the holy {gifts,} which the sons of Israel offer to the LORD, I have given to you and your sons and your daughters with you, as *a PERPETUAL ALLOTMENT*. It is an everlasting covenant of salt before the LORD to you and your descendants with you."
(Numbers 18:8–19)

"Eternal" *Statute* Relating to the Levites' Allotment

Then the LORD said to Aaron, "You shall have no inheritance in their land, nor own any portion among them; I am your portion and your inheritance among the sons of Israel. And to the sons of Levi, behold, I have given all the tithe in Israel for an inheritance, in return for their service which they perform, the service of the tent of meeting. And the sons of Israel shall not come near the tent of meeting again, lest they bear sin and die. Only the Levites shall perform the service of the tent of meeting, and they shall bear their iniquity; it shall be *a PERPETUAL STATUTE* throughout your generations, and among the sons of Israel they shall have no inheritance. For the tithe of the sons of Israel, which they offer as an offering to the LORD, I have given to the Levites for an inheritance; therefore I have said concerning them, 'They shall have no inheritance among the sons of Israel.'"
(Numbers 18:20–24)

"Eternal" *Statutes* Relating to the Lord's Allotment

"And from it he shall present his offering as an offering by fire to the LORD, the fat that covers the entrails and all the fat that is on the entrails, and the two kidneys with the fat that is on them, which is on

the loins, and the lobe of the liver, which he shall remove with the kidneys. And the priest shall offer them up in smoke on the altar {as} food, an offering by fire for a soothing aroma; all fat is the LORD's. It is a PERPETUAL STATUTE throughout your generations in all your dwellings: you shall not eat any fat or any blood.'"
(Leviticus 3:14–17)

Then the LORD spoke to Moses, saying, "This is the offering which Aaron and his sons are to present to the LORD on the day when he is anointed; the tenth of an ephah of fine flour as a regular grain offering, half of it in the morning and half of it in the evening. It shall be prepared with oil on a griddle. When it is {well} stirred, you shall bring it. You shall present the grain offering in baked pieces as a soothing aroma to the LORD. And the anointed priest who will be in his place among his sons shall offer it. By a PERMANENT ORDINANCE it shall be entirely offered up in smoke to the LORD. So every grain offering of the priest shall be burned entirely. It shall not be eaten."
(Leviticus 6:19–23)

"'Any man from the house of Israel who slaughters an ox, or a lamb, or a goat in the camp, or who slaughters it outside the camp, and has not brought it to the doorway of the tent of meeting to present {it} as an offering to the LORD before the tabernacle of the LORD, bloodguiltiness is to be reckoned to that man. He has shed blood and that man shall be cut off from among his people. The reason is so that the sons of Israel may bring their sacrifices which they were sacrificing in the open field, that they may bring them in to the LORD, at the doorway of the tent of meeting to the priest, and sacrifice them as sacrifices of peace offerings to the LORD. And the priest shall sprinkle the blood on the altar of the LORD at the doorway of the tent of meeting, and offer up the fat in smoke as a soothing aroma to the LORD. And they shall no longer sacrifice their sacrifices to the goat demons with which they play the harlot. This shall be a PERMANENT STATUTE to them throughout their generations.'"
(Leviticus 17:3–7)

"'Thus it shall be done for each ox, or for each ram, or for each of the male lambs, or of the goats. According to the number that you prepare, so you shall do for everyone according to their number. All who are native shall do these things in this manner, in presenting an offering by fire, as a soothing aroma to the LORD. And if an alien sojourns with you, or one

who may be among you throughout your generations, and he {wishes to} make an offering by fire, as a soothing aroma to the LORD, just as you do, so he shall do. {As for} the assembly, there shall be one statute for you and for the alien who sojourns {with you,} a PERPETUAL STATUTE throughout your generations; as you are, so shall the alien be before the LORD.'" (Numbers 15:11–15)

Statutes *That Are Not "Eternal"*

In addition to the "eternal *statutes*" (*choq/chuqqat 'olam*), there are other *statutes* in the Law of Moses which are not specifically designated as "eternal." Instead, they are called either a *"statute* of *judgment"* (*chuqqat mishpat*) to indicate they contain conditions, or a *"statute* of *Torah"*[22] (Hebrew: *chuqqat hattorah*) to indicate their basic purpose is that of *Torah*.[23]

Statute of *Judgment* Concerning Inheritance of Women

Then the LORD spoke to Moses, saying, "The daughters of Zelophehad are right in {their} statements. You shall surely give them a hereditary possession among their father's brothers, and you shall transfer the inheritance of their father to them. Further, you shall speak to the sons of Israel, saying, 'If a man dies and has no son, then you shall transfer his inheritance to his daughter. And if he has no daughter, then you shall give his inheritance to his brothers. And if he has no brothers, then you shall give his inheritance to his father's brothers. And if his father has no brothers, then you shall give his inheritance to his nearest relative in his own family, and he shall possess it; and it shall be a STATUTORY ORDINANCE to the sons of Israel, just as the LORD commanded Moses.'" (Numbers 27:6–11)

Statute of *Judgment* Concerning Vows of Women

Then Moses spoke to the heads of the tribes of the sons of Israel, saying, "This is the word which the LORD has commanded. If a man makes a vow to the LORD, or takes an oath to bind himself with a binding obligation, he

---

[22] The "eternal" *statute* concerning the red heifer is also called a "*statute* of *Torah*" in Numbers 19:2.

[23] See the explanation of the Hebrew term *torah* in the next chapter.

shall not violate his word; he shall do according to all that proceeds out of his mouth. Also if a woman makes a vow to the LORD, and binds herself by an obligation in her father's house in her youth, and her father hears her vow and her obligation by which she has bound herself, and her father says nothing to her, then all her vows shall stand, and every obligation by which she has bound herself shall stand. But if her father should forbid her on the day he hears {of it,} none of her vows or her obligations by which she has bound herself shall stand; and the LORD will forgive her because her father had forbidden her. However, if she should marry while under her vows or the rash statement of her lips by which she has bound herself, and her husband hears of it and says nothing to her on the day he hears {it,} then her vows shall stand and her obligations by which she has bound herself shall stand. But if on the day her husband hears {of it,} he forbids her, then he shall annul her vow which she is under and the rash statement of her lips by which she has bound herself; and the LORD will forgive her. But the vow of a widow or of a divorced woman, everything by which she has bound herself, shall stand against her. However, if she vowed in her husband's house, or bound herself by an obligation with an oath, and her husband heard {it,} but said nothing to her {and} did not forbid her, then all her vows shall stand, and every obligation by which she bound herself shall stand. But if her husband indeed annuls them on the day he hears {them,} then whatever proceeds out of her lips concerning her vows or concerning the obligation of herself, shall not stand; her husband has annulled them, and the LORD will forgive her. Every vow and every binding oath to humble herself, her husband may confirm it or her husband may annul it. But if her husband indeed says nothing to her from day to day, then he confirms all her vows or all her obligations which are on her; he has confirmed them, because he said nothing to her on the day he heard them. But if he indeed annuls them after he has heard them, then he shall bear her guilt." These are the STATUTES *which the LORD commanded Moses, {as} between a man and his wife, {and as} between a father and his daughter, {while she is} in her youth in her father's house." (Numbers 30:1–16)*

Statute of Judgment Concerning Fleeing to a City of Refuge

Then the LORD spoke to Moses, saying, "Speak to the sons of Israel and say to them, 'When you cross the Jordan into the land of Canaan, then you shall select for yourselves cities to be your cities of refuge, that the manslayer who has killed any person unintentionally may flee there. And the cities shall be to you as a refuge from the avenger, so that the manslayer may not die until he stands before the congregation for trial. And the cities which you are to give shall be your six cities of refuge. You shall give three cities across the Jordan and three cities in the land of Canaan; they are to be cities of refuge. These six cities shall be for refuge for the sons of Israel, and for the alien and for the sojourner among them; that anyone who kills a person unintentionally may flee there. But if he struck him down with an iron object, so that he died, he is a murderer; the murderer shall surely be put to death. And if he struck him down with a stone in the hand, by which he may die, and {as a result} he died, he is a murderer; the murderer shall surely be put to death. Or if he struck him with a wooden object in the hand, by which he may die, and {as a result} he died, he is a murderer; the murderer shall surely be put to death. The blood avenger himself shall put the murderer to death; he shall put him to death when he meets him. And if he pushed him of hatred, or threw something at him lying in wait and {as a result} he died, or if he struck him down with his hand in enmity, and {as a result} he died, the one who struck him shall surely be put to death, he is a murderer; the blood avenger shall put the murderer to death when he meets him. But if he pushed him suddenly without enmity, or threw something at him without lying in wait, or with any deadly object of stone, and without seeing it dropped on him so that he died, while he was not his enemy nor seeking his injury, then the congregation shall judge between the slayer and the blood avenger according to these ordinances. And the congregation shall deliver the manslayer from the hand of the blood avenger, and the congregation shall restore him to his city of refuge to which he fled; and he shall live in it until the death of the high priest who was anointed with the holy oil. But if the manslayer shall at any time go beyond the border of his city of refuge to which he may flee, and the blood avenger finds him outside the border of his city of refuge, and the blood avenger kills the manslayer, he shall not be guilty of blood because he should have remained in his city of refuge until the death of the high priest. But after the death of the high priest the manslayer shall return to the land of his possession. And these things shall be for a STATUTORY ORDINANCE to you throughout your generations in all your dwellings. If anyone kills a person, the murderer shall be put to death at the evidence of witnesses, but no person shall be put to death on the testimony of one witness. Moreover, you shall not take ran-

som for the life of a murderer who is guilty of death, but he shall surely be put to death. And you shall not take ransom for him who has fled to his city of refuge, that he may return to live in the land before the death of the priest. So you shall not pollute the land in which you are; for blood pollutes the land and no expiation can be made for the land for the blood that is shed on it, except by the blood of him who shed it. And you shall not defile the land in which you live, in the midst of which I dwell; for I the LORD am dwelling in the midst of the sons of Israel.'"
(Numbers 35:9–34)

Statute of the *Torah* Concerning Cleansing Spoils of War

Then Eleazar the priest said to the men of war who had gone to battle, "This is the STATUTE of the LAW which the LORD has commanded Moses: only the gold and the silver, the bronze, the iron, the tin and the lead, everything that can stand the fire, you shall pass through the fire, and it shall be clean, but it shall be purified with water for impurity. But whatever cannot stand the fire you shall pass through the water. And you shall wash your clothes on the seventh day and be clean, and afterward you may enter the camp."
(Numbers 31:21–24)

Summary

My purpose in this chapter has been to show you the basic *meaning* of the Hebrew terms normally translated as "*statute*" and "*judgment.*" In Chapter 1, I explained how the biblical evidence indicates the *testimonies* (Hebrew: *'edôt*) were the "ten words"—the Ten Commandments—that God wrote on the two stone tablets Moses *received* on the Mountain of God. Due to a natural tendency to think of the *testimonies* and the two tablets as one, however, the tablets and the writing on them are tacitly identified as "the *testimonies.*" At God's direction, Moses placed "the two tablets of the *testimonies*" in "the ark of the *testimonies*" behind "the veil of the *testimonies*" in "the tabernacle of the *testimonies.*" There they remained as silent *witnesses* to the covenant that God had made with the sons of Israel.

The *testimonies* are never identified in any way as either *statutes* or *judgments.* That is because the *testimonies* were the terms of the covenant agreement, whereas the *statutes* and *judgments* were a logical extension of that agreement. That is, the *statutes* and *judgments* provided the means whereby the *testimonies* were to be implemented.

The Hebrew terms translated *statutes* and *judgments* point to the distinctive characteristics of two entirely different kinds of legal stipulations. That is, they refer to two clearly defined legal categories.

The Hebrew term **mishpat**, which is most frequently translated as *"judgment,"* displays one distinctive feature which sets it apart from every other legal category in the Mosaic legislation. That distinction lies in the fact that the *judgment* specified the condition or conditions a judge had to consider in reaching a *judgment.* Therefore, every *judgment* is associated in some way with a conditional *judgment* that begins with the word *if.*

In contrast to the *judgment,* a *statute* (**choq/chuqqah**) is a legal stipulation that mandates limits to govern some normal cyclical order. Since Israel maintained a favorable relationship with God by carrying out the cultic rituals of the sanctuary, it is not surprising to find that all the *"statutes* of *'olam"* mentioned in the Pentateuch mandate limits within which the priests were to conduct the cultic rituals.

Although they refer to two entirely different types of legal mandates, the *statutes* and *judgments* are not mutually exclusive. In some cases, the two overlap. That is why, on a couple of occasions, a *statute* is said to be a *"statute* of *judgment."* That is, it is a *statute* which contains the conditional *if* of a *judgment.* The first such mention occurs in connection with women inheriting from their father.[24] The second instance describes the legal stipulations relating to the blood avenger

---

[24] Numbers 27:11.

pursuing a manslayer who seeks refuge in the city of refuge.[25] In both instances, however, the conditional *if* occurs as the defining characteristic of the *judgment*. So the conditionality of the *statute* accounts for the term *judgment* in the designation *"statute* of *judgment."* A third *statute* of *judgment* also exists,[26] but it is not specifically called a *statute of judgment*. It clearly is one, however, because it is called a *statute* and contains the characteristic conditional *if* of the *judgment*.

---

[25] Numbers 35:29.
[26] Numbers 30:1–16.

CHAPTER 3:

TORAH AND *MITZVAH*

In the first two chapters, I explained the *meaning* of the three Hebrew terms that are normally translated "*testimonies,*" "*statutes*" and "*judgments.*" In this chapter, I will explain the *meaning* of the two Hebrew terms that are translated "*law*" and "*commandment.*" These two terms are **torah** and **mitzvah**,[1] hence the title.

Any distinction that exists between the terms *law* and *commandment*, insofar as they are used with reference to the Mosaic legislation, is not immediately apparent in the translations. Consequently, it is not possible for an English reader to see how the *commandments* of *The Law of Moses* also include *The Teaching of Moses*. However, if it exists, *The Teaching of Moses* must somehow reside in the *commandments* (**mitzvah**) that God *delivered* to

---

[1] *Mitzvah* is the same Hebrew term one encounters in the Jewish religious ritual, the *Bar Mitzvah*. The phrase *Bar Mitzvah* is a combination of the Aramaic word for "son"— *bar* —and the Hebrew/Aramaic word for "commandment"—*mitzvah*. It translates *literally* as "son of the commandment." The *Bar Mitzvah* is celebrated on the occasion of a Jewish boy's thirteenth birthday. It is the ceremonial admission of the youngster to responsibility for the fulfillment of all the commandments of God. That is, at the age of thirteen he becomes a "son of the commandment."

Moses[2] as the *Torah* to which *Corporate* Israel was to adhere. Therefore, I must first explain the fundamental difference in *meaning* that exists between the Hebrew terms translated "*law*" (*torah*) and "*commandment*" (*mitzvah*) before you can see what Moses hid in the things he wrote.

It should be self-evident that every *commandment* God gave the sons of Israel must also be a *law* of God, just as every *law* of God must be a *commandment*. But it is not as obvious that every one of God's *commandments* must be a *teaching*. To see how that is, one must understand the *meaning* of the two Hebrew terms—*torah* and *mitzvah*—that stand behind what have long been their English translations—"*law*" and "*commandment*." One can easily demonstrate the difference between these two Hebrew terms simply by showing what each one refers to.

In this chapter, I will begin by defining these two Hebrew terms and then explain their essential difference in *meaning*. I will next investigate the Jews' belief that Moses *received* both an *oral Torah* and a *written Torah* at Mt. Sinai. Finally, I will explain how Moses uses the Hebrew term translated "*commandment*" (*mitzvah*) in the Pentateuch. My purpose in that is to show you the term has both a specific referent—which is the *apodictic* "thou shalt" and "thou shalt not" type of *commandments*—as well as a general referent—that is, any of God's requirements that derive from His specific *apodictic commandments*.

The Hebrew noun *mitzvah* comes from the same root as the verb *zavah*, which *means* "to command" or "to order." Therefore, "*commandment*" is a fairly accurate translation of that term. By contrast, the Hebrew word *torah*, which is normally translated "*law*," stems from the same root as the verb *yarah*,

---

[2] In this chapter, I am using the terms *received, delivered,* and *handed down* with the same sense that Jesus, the Apostles, and the scribes and Pharisees used them in the time of Christ—that is, as Greek technical terminology related to the transmission of an *oral tradition*. See "Some People Will Make Light of Anything," *The Voice of Elijah*, April 1994.

which *means* "to point out, teach, instruct." Therefore, although
Moses does use *torah* to refer to legal stipulations,[3] its basic
meaning is not "*law;*" it is "*teaching*" or "*instruction.*" Consequently, the translation "*law*" is totally inaccurate and completely misleading. The following table corrects this error:

HEBREW TERM	USUAL TRANSLATION	ACTUAL MEANING
Mitzvah	**Commandment**	**Commandment**
Torah	**Law**	**Teaching**

The Jews still call the first five books of the Bible "the
Torah."[4] That is precisely what those five books contain: *The
Teaching of Moses*, because Moses hid *The (oral) Teaching* that God
revealed to him in the things he wrote. Knowing that the
Hebrew noun *torah* actually *means* "teaching" instead of
"law" explains why *The Teaching of Moses* could in some way
be identified with the "*commandments*" of God. But why
should anyone be concerned about making such a distinction
between the *meaning* of these two terms? Simply because
Moses himself does in the text of the Hebrew Scriptures. In
the following passage, he plainly states God gave him both a
torah and a *mitzvah*[5] while he was on Mt. Sinai:

> *Now the LORD said to Moses, "Come up to Me on the mountain and
> remain there, and I* ***will give you the stone tablets with the LAW and
> the COMMANDMENT which I have written for their instruction.***"
> *So Moses arose with Joshua his servant, and Moses went up to the
> mountain of God.*
> *(Exodus 24:12–13)*

---

[3] Harper, *Not All Israel Is Israel*, p. 92, fn. 14.

[4] The Jews have called the Pentateuch "the **Torah**" since long before the
time of Christ. That terminology stands behind the New Testament phrase
translated "the *Law* and the Prophets."

[5] "Commandment" is an accurate translation of *mitzvah*, whereas *torah*
has been incorrectly translated "law."

That passage says Moses *received* three things while he was on the Mountain of God:

1. **The Stone Tablets**
2. **The Teaching (*torah*)**
3. **The Commandment (*mitzvah*)**

These three entities are much more clearly distinguished in the Hebrew text than they appear to be in the English translation. The Hebrew text *literally* says, "I will give you the tablets of stone AND[6] the **torah** AND the **mitzvah**." The difficulty in determining what God *meant* by that statement arises in connection with His use of the two words **torah** and **mitzvah**. Unless one arbitrarily assumes that this is a simple case of hendiadys,[7] the text must be implying that the terms **torah** and **mitzvah** represent two entirely different things. That conclusion is bolstered by the fact that the two terms appear in yet another context where both have the possessive pronoun *my* attached:

> Then the LORD said to Moses, "How long do you refuse to keep **My commandments and My instructions**?"
> (*Exodus 16:28*)

Again, the Hebrew word **mitzvah** has been translated "commandment." However, this time the translator translated **torah** as "instruction" because he realized that was the actual

---

[6] The New American Standard Bible translation has taken the simple Hebrew conjunction (ו) to *mean* "with." That is an acceptable translation of the way the Hebrew uses the conjunction. So that translation presents no hurdle to a proper understanding of the Hebrew text. However, that Hebrew conjunction, while often having the *meaning* "and," also conveys a variety of other nuances. Its *meaning* is dependent on the context in which it occurs as well as on whether the word is prefixed to a noun or a verb. For the *meaning* "with," see Ronald J. Williams, *Hebrew Syntax: An Outline* (Toronto: University of Toronto Press, 1967), p. 73.

[7] *Hendiadys* is the use of two nouns joined by a conjunction instead of a noun modified by an adjective. For example, "assault and battery" actually *means* "vicious attack."

meaning of the term. But the use of the two terms together confirms that they must have completely separate and distinct *meaning*. That is, they are not synonyms with absolutely identical *meaning*. So what's the point? Merely that since the Hebrew Scriptures lead us to infer a basic distinction existed between the *meaning* of **torah** and **mitzvah**, anyone who is seeking to understand the Truth should at least try to maintain that same *mental* distinction.[8] That is, a traditional—but inaccurate—translation of **torah** as "law" should not be allowed to distort the Truth: *Torah means "teaching."*

Take a closer look at Exodus 24:12–13, the text quoted above:

> *Now the* LORD *said to Moses, "Come up to Me on the mountain and remain there, and* **I will give you the stone tablets with the** LAW **and the** COMMANDMENT **which I have written for their instruction."** *So Moses arose with Joshua his servant, and Moses went up to the mountain of God.*
> *(Exodus 24:12–13)*

The biblical text says God gave Moses "the stone tablets with the *torah* and the *mitzvah* which I have *written* for their *instruction*." One could assume the author *meant* for his reader to understand that God inscribed only the *"commandment" (mitzvah)* on the stone tablets "for their *instruction*."[9] That

---

[8] The use of **torah** and **mitzvah** together in Exodus 16:28 and 24:12 underlines both their synonymous referent—the legal stipulations associated with the covenant of God—and the difference in their description of the nature of that law, that is, *commandment* vs. *teaching*.

[9] Certainly the stone tablets themselves could not have been *"written* for their instruction" in the same way as the *torah* and the *mitzvah* could be written. So the first conjunction must be taken to mean something other than "and." As stated above (p. 92, fn. 6), the conjunction conveys the sense of "with," just as the translator has understood it. That leaves only the two choices mentioned. Either the *mitzvah* alone was "written for their instruction," or both the *torah* and the *mitzvah* were written. The latter understanding (both written) fits together best with the scriptural account and all the other evidence concerning the *meaning* of the terms **torah** and **mitzvah**.

could be so, but not necessarily. Since the two terms *torah* and the *mitzvah* are conjoined by the Hebrew conjunction "and," the writer could just as easily have *meant* that both "the law *and* the commandment" (that is, both *torah* and *mitzvah*) were "*written* for their *instruction*" on the two stone tablets.

Exodus 24:12 raises a couple of questions which must be answered before anyone can accurately understand the Truth that Moses and the other Prophets of Israel hid in the Hebrew Scriptures. Since the *testimonies* were the only things that God wrote on the two stone tablets,[10] *commandment* (*mitzvah*) must be referring to something in those *testimonies*. But to what does it refer? Likewise, if *The Teaching* (*torah*) was written on the stone tablets "for their instruction," *torah* must also refer to something in the *testimonies*. To what then would it refer?

Given the above, the two terms *torah* and *mitzvah* must have separate and distinct *meaning*. That *means* if both *torah* and *mitzvah* were written on the stone tablets, then *The Teaching* (*torah*) must be something in the *testimonies* which is completely different than the *commandment* (*mitzvah*). But it also *means* that if only the *mitzvah* was written on the tablets, God must have *delivered* the *torah* to Moses *orally*. That is certainly a possible inference one can derive from the text, and is therefore something to be investigated further at this point.

Was There an Oral Torah?

Rabbinic Judaism—the belief system *handed down* to the Jews by the scribes and Pharisees, whom Jesus ridiculed for holding to an *oral tradition* based on ignorance of the Truth—is still today based on the firm conviction that God *delivered* both an *oral Torah* and a *written Torah* to Moses at Mt. Sinai. The Jews also insist that their ancestors, the sons of Israel, were supposed to, and did, *hand down* the *oral Torah* that Moses *received* from one generation to the next—*orally*.

---

[10] See above, pp. 34 ff.

Jewish tradition agrees completely with the incipient Christian belief that Moses recorded *written Torah* in the first five books of the Hebrew Scriptures—the Pentateuch. However, Jewish tradition goes further and claims that Moses *received* not only a *written Torah* at Mt. Sinai, but also an additional *oral Torah*, which he *handed down* to the sons of Israel along with instruction that it continue to be *handed down—orally*. Most Christians are completely unaware of that. The following quotation from *Pirke Avot*—a tractate in a collection of Jewish writings known as the Mishnah—asserts that God *delivered* the *oral Torah* to Moses, who *delivered* it to Joshua, who *delivered* it to the Elders, and so on.[11] But that belief is not founded on fact, as we shall see:

> *Moses received Torah from Sinai and delivered it to Joshua, and Joshua to the Elders, and the Elders to the Prophets, and the Prophets delivered it to the Men of the Great Synagogue. These said three things; Be deliberate in judging, and raise up many disciples, and make a hedge for the Torah.*[12]

One should not ignore, as Christians have for centuries, the Jewish claim that Moses *received* an *oral Torah* at Mt. Sinai. Jewish tradition emphatically states that the *oral Torah* Moses *received* from God and *delivered* to Joshua was finally codified in the Mishnah—from which I took the quote above. This collection of writings—which were compiled sometime around A.D. 200—purportedly records the *oral tradition* that was being *handed down orally* by the Pharisees in Jesus' time. Therefore, the distinctive characteristic of the foundation on which

---

[11] It is tempting to make too much of the English translation *"delivered"* in this passage and see a direct parallel with how the Greek term normally translated *"delivered"* is used in the New Testament. However, *Pirke Avot* was written in Rabbinic Hebrew, whereas the New Testament statements concerning the Pharisees' transmission of their *oral tradition* were written in Greek. Although I am unaware of any direct correspondence between the Greek and Hebrew terms used, one may well exist.

[12] R. Travers Herford, *The Ethics of the Talmud: Sayings of the Fathers* (New York: Schocken Books, 1962), p. 19.

Jewish religious tradition is built—that is, the *oral tradition* enshrined in the Mishnah—is that it is a record of the *oral Torah* the Pharisees claimed had been *handed down* to them from the time of Moses. Most Christians aren't aware of that either. Yet they should be.

No less an authority than Jesus Christ Himself vehemently rejected the *oral tradition* of the Pharisees. That does not bode well for those "Christians" today who turn to Jewish tradition for insight into the Truth, because Judaism is firmly founded on the twin pillars of the Mishnah, which they claim to be the *oral Torah* that Moses *received*, and the Hebrew Scriptures, which they assert contain the *written Torah* he *received*:

> *Precisely what comprised this "Torah" that people were to study? That is the next important question. The answer has two parts. First, the Torah comprised precisely what it had always been: the Hebrew Scriptures ("Old Testament"). But, second, in addition to the Torah—now the Written Torah—certain writings came into being which, in long centuries to come, attained the status of divine revelation, hence of Torah, and so became part of the Torah. The first of these writings, as I shall explain in a moment, was the Mishnah, which was completed in about 200. A generation later, in about 250, a tractate, Avot, the Fathers, joined the Mishnah and explained the authority of the Mishnah in an interesting way. That document began with a list of authorities of the Torah, beginning with Moses at Sinai and ending with names of important authorities cited in the Mishnah itself! The implicit proposition, then, was that what the Mishnah authorities teach forms part of the Torah that Moses received from God at Mount Sinai. In the fifth century, documents such as the Talmud of the land of Israel, ca. A.D. 400 begin to refer to these other writings, including the Mishnah, as "the oral Torah," in the theory that when God revealed the Torah to Moses at Sinai, God gave the Torah in two forms—one in writing, the other orally (that is, in memory)—hence, Torah shebikhtav, Torah in writing, and Torah shebeal peh, Torah in memory, or oral.*[13]

---

[13] Jacob Nuesner, *From Testament to Torah: An Introduction to Judaism in its Formative Age* (Englewood Cliffs, New Jersey: Prentice Hall, 1988), p. 44.

To conservative Jews in our day, the *oral Torah* recorded in the Mishnah and the *written Torah* recorded in the Hebrew Scriptures are both equally authoritative as the revelation of God. That is the legacy they derived from the Pharisees. As one contemporary Jewish scholar has put it:

> *Judaism as we know it—that type of Judaism built upon the doctrine of the dual Torah, oral and written, revealed to Moses by God at Sinai—took shape between the first and the seventh century. It drew heavily on Judaisms of the 500 years before the first century, when the Old Testament was written.*[14]

In the statement "Judaism as we know it ... took shape between the first and the seventh century," the author is referring to Rabbinic Judaism.[15] That form of Judaism evolved out of Pharisaic Judaism, which was the Judaism propounded by the scribes and Pharisees in the time of Christ. A major development in the establishment of Rabbinic Judaism as the normative Judaism of the Jews today was the recording of the *oral Torah*—the *oral tradition* of the Rabbis—in written form sometime around A.D. 200. Before that time, there were various sects in Judaism, the Pharisees being but one.

The Jews today claim that, prior to its being recorded in the Mishnah, the *oral Torah* of the scribes and Pharisees had been *handed down* from generation to generation just as the terminology indicates: *orally*—as an *oral tradition*. That *oral Torah* is the Pharisees' "tradition of the elders" that Mark refers to here:

> *And the Pharisees and some of the scribes gathered together around Him when they had come from Jerusalem, and had seen that some of*

---

[14] Neusner, p. xiii.

[15] The rubric *Rabbinic Judaism* as I have used it here refers to that form of Judaism that came into existence after the destruction of the Temple in Jerusalem in A.D. 70. That event was a crisis to which the majority of the Jews responded with amazing resiliency, adapting to the loss of the Temple as the focal point of their religion by focusing instead on the *oral tradition* of the Pharisees.

*His disciples were eating their bread with impure hands, that is,
unwashed. (For the Pharisees and all the Jews do not eat unless they
carefully wash their hands, {thus} observing **the traditions of the
elders**; and {when they come} from the market place, they do not eat
unless they cleanse themselves; and **there are many other things
which they have received in order to observe**, such as the washing of
cups and pitchers and copper pots.)*
(Mark 7:1–4)

Although Jesus ridiculed the Pharisees for strictly adhering
to the legalistic demands of their *oral tradition*, the adherents of
this Jewish sect firmly believed that *oral tradition* had originated
with Moses. That is what they were referring to when they told
the blind man whom Jesus had healed that they were "disciples
of Moses":

*So a second time they called the man who had been blind, and said to
him, "Give glory to God; we know that this man is a sinner." He therefore answered, "Whether He is a sinner, I do not know; one thing I do
know, that, whereas I was blind, now I see." They said therefore to him,
"What did He do to you? How did He open your eyes?" He answered
them, "I told you already, and you did not listen; why do you want to
hear {it} again? You do not want to become His disciples too, do you?"
And they reviled him, and said, "You are His disciple, but **we are disciples of Moses**. We know that God has spoken to Moses; but as for this
man, we do not know where He is from."*
(John 9:24–29)

The Pharisees were absolutely convinced their *oral tradition*
had been *handed down orally* from Moses, whom they considered to be the first Rabbi in Israel. But the Pharisees were not
the only Jews of their day who believed an *oral **Torah*** had been
delivered to Moses. It is apparent from the Dead Sea Scrolls that
the Jewish sect known as the Essenes must have held a similar
belief[16] as a fundamental tenet in their branch of Judaism. The

---

[16] Future volumes in *The Mystery of Scripture* series will explain the rele-
vance of Essene beliefs.

Apostles and Early Church Fathers also believed they were *handing down The Teaching of Jesus* as an *oral tradition.*[17]

In light of the above, Christians today should not hastily reject the Jewish belief that God *delivered* an *oral Torah* to Moses at Mt. Sinai. That is especially so since Jesus Christ Himself gave credence to their claim when He advised His disciples how to respond to the Pharisees' teaching:

> *Then Jesus spoke to the multitudes and to His disciples, saying, "The scribes and* **the Pharisees have seated themselves in the chair of Moses; therefore all that they tell you, do and observe,** *but do not do according to their deeds; for they say {things}, and do not do {them.} And they tie up heavy loads, and lay them on men's shoulders; but they themselves are unwilling to move them with {so much as} a finger. But they do all their deeds to be noticed by men; for they broaden their phylacteries, and lengthen the tassels {of their garments.} And they love the place of honor at banquets, and the chief seats in the synagogues, and respectful greetings in the market places, and being called by men, Rabbi."* (Matthew 23:1–7)

It is impossible to discount completely the Jews' belief that God *delivered* an *oral Torah* to Moses when Jesus Himself acknowledged that His Own disciples were, in some sense, subject to the authority of the Pharisees because they had "seated themselves in the chair of Moses."[18] Jesus knew full well the Pharisees claimed their *oral tradition* was an *oral Torah* that had been *handed down* to them from the time of Moses.

---

[17] Matthew 28:19–20; Luke 24:27; and 1 Corinthians 11:2. See also "Where Are Jesus' Disciples?" *The Voice of Elijah*, April 1991 and "Some People Will Make Light of Anything," *The Voice of Elijah*, April 1994. Later volumes in this series will provide additional evidence in support of that view.

[18] Jesus is not validating the Pharisees' claim that the Pharisees were legitimately "seated" "in the chair of Moses." Although He does confirm that such a "chair" existed, He rejects the Pharisees' beliefs by saying they had "seated themselves" in that "chair." *The Mystery of Scripture* series will show that the Pharisees were usurpers. They had "seated themselves in the chair of Moses" more than a century earlier, after deposing the legitimate occupants of that "chair"—the priests who descended from Zadok.

The "chair of Moses" to which He refers was the position Moses held as the first Rabbi (teacher) in Israel:

> *The central conception distinguishing Rabbinic Judaism from all other conceptions of Judaism, past and present, is the belief in the myth of Moses as "our rabbi," and the conception that when God—also conceived in the model of the rabbi—revealed the Torah to Moses, he gave the Torah in two parts, one in writing, the other as tradition handed on orally. The tradition handed on orally is now contained in the Mishnah and its cognate literature, Tosefta, Babylonian and Palestinian Talmuds, the various Midrashim, and the like. Accordingly, at the center of Rabbinic Judaism are the concept of the dual Torah and the fundamental conviction that the written Torah is not the whole record of revelation. Indeed one may say that just as the New Testament is represented by Christianity as the completion and fulfillment of the Old Testament, so the Mishnah is understood by Rabbinic Judaism as the other half of the Tanakh.[19]*

As I stated above, the Jews today consider the Mishnah to be a written record of the *oral Torah* that their ancestors *handed down* from the time of Moses. They also consider that *oral Torah* to be divine revelation with an authority equal to the Hebrew Scriptures. However, a central item of scholarly debate even among Jews themselves is whether or not the written record of the Rabbis' *oral Torah* provides all that much information about Judaism as it existed before the time the Mishnah was written (ca. A.D. 200).

Some Jewish scholars seriously doubt the *oral tradition* recorded in the Mishnah and its cognate literature is a reliable source of information about any Jewish beliefs earlier than the time in which it was recorded. Few would dare suggest that the Mishnah contains an accurate recording of the *oral Torah* that God *delivered* to Moses some 1700 years before, if indeed they would even admit that Moses *received* any such *oral Torah*.

The skepticism of scholars is understandable. Until the discovery of the Dead Sea Scrolls in 1947, not much was

---

[19] Jacob Nuesner, *Early Rabbinic Judaism* (Leiden: E.J. Brill, 1975), p. 3. The *Tanakh* is what the Jews call the Hebrew Scriptures.

known about the origins of the Pharisaic Judaism from which
Rabbinic Judaism evolved. Even less was known about the
various other sects of Judaism as they existed before the time
of Jesus Christ.

Still today, more than fifty years after the Dead Sea Scrolls
were discovered, important questions still remain unan-
swered, questions as to the origin of the various Jewish sects
that existed in the time of Christ—the Sadducees, Essenes,
Zealots, Pharisees, and Christians. The Dead Sea Scrolls provided important insight into that era, beginning with the time
of Antiochus Epiphanes and the Maccabean revolt (ca. 165
B.C.). Yet whatever form Judaism had before it splintered into
these various sects, one should not casually reject the distinct
possibility that it included a firm belief that Moses, the first
Rabbi in Israel, *received* both a *written* **Torah** and an *oral* **Torah**
at Mt. Sinai.

The Jewish belief in regard to a dual **Torah**—both *oral* and
written—raises an interesting question in light of Exodus
24:12. If their belief that God *delivered* an *oral* **Torah** to Moses
has any basis in fact, could the statement "the stone tablets
with the **torah** and the **mitzvah** which I have *written* for their
instruction" be meant to tell us God *delivered* the **Torah** (*The
Teaching*) to Moses *orally* and the **mitzvah** (the commandment)
in written form? If that be the case, and God *delivered* the
Torah to Moses *orally* rather than in writing, why then do the
Jews say there was both an *oral* **Torah** and a *written* **Torah**? We
will examine those and other issues a bit later. They have
more than a little *significance* as far as *The Mystery of Scripture* is
concerned. However, we must first define the characteristics
of a *commandment*.

The **Commandments** *of God*

We already know that God told Moses many things that
were not written on the two stone tablets. Moses made that

abundantly clear by what he said to the sons of Israel on the plains of Moab shortly before his death:

> *"These words the* LORD *spoke to all your assembly at the mountain from the midst of the fire, {of} the cloud and {of} the thick gloom, with a great voice, and He added no more. And He wrote them on two tablets of stone and gave them to me.* And it came about, when you heard the voice from the midst of the darkness, while the mountain was burning with fire, that you came near to me, all the heads of your tribes and your elders. And you said, 'Behold, the LORD our God has shown us His glory and His greatness, and we have heard His voice from the midst of the fire; we have seen today that God speaks with man, yet he lives. Now then why should we die? For this great fire will consume us; if we hear the voice of the LORD our God any longer, then we shall die. For who is there of all flesh, who has heard the voice of the living God speaking from the midst of the fire, as we {have}, and lived? Go near and hear all that the LORD our God says; then speak to us all that the LORD our God will speak to you, and we will hear and do {it.}' And the LORD heard the voice of your words when you spoke to me, and the LORD said to me, 'I have heard the voice of the words of this people which they have spoken to you. They have done well in all that they have spoken. Oh that they had such a heart in them, that they would fear Me, and keep all My commandments always, that it may be well with them and with their sons forever! Go, say to them, "Return to your tents." But **as for you, stand here by Me, that I may speak to you all the commandments and the statutes and the judgments which you shall teach them, that they may observe {them} in the land which I give them to possess.'"**
> (Deuteronomy 5:22–31)

That passage unambiguously describes circumstances under which God appears to have *delivered* an *oral* **Torah** (*Teaching*) to Moses. After reiterating how God had spoken the Ten Commandments—the *testimonies*—from the top of Mt. Sinai, Moses says, "He wrote them on two tablets of stone and gave them to me." Thus he confirms that the *testimonies*—the Ten Commandments—were all that God wrote on the two stone tablets. But he just as clearly indicates that God told him other things on that occasion—"the commandments, and the statutes and the judgments"—which were not *written* on the stone tablets. Moses says God *delivered* those things to him *orally* and expected him to teach them to the people.

The details in that passage fit together perfectly with the Jewish belief that Moses *received* an *oral **Torah*** at Mt. Sinai.[20] However, if one admits, for the sake of argument, that God *delivered* both an *oral **Torah*** and a *written **Torah*** to Moses, the mention of an *oral **Torah*** in this passage would argue in favor of the conclusion that the ***Torah*** mentioned in Exodus 24:12 was the *written **Torah*** that Moses *received*. Keeping that in mind, let's carefully define the *meaning* of the term ***mitzvah*** and see if there is any other evidence that would indicate the same thing.

---

[20] An interesting side question is, Did everything God revealed to Moses *orally* find *written* expression in the Hebrew Scriptures, thus becoming a part of what the Jews consider to be the *written **Torah*** Moses *received,* or did God expect some of the things Moses *received* as *oral **Torah*** to be *handed down* from generation to generation *orally* as the Jews themselves claim? That question should not be casually dismissed on the basis of some traditional Christian belief concerning the nature and purpose of the Hebrew Scriptures. Certainly one cannot flatly deny—without some inquiry as to whether it might be true—the fundamental tenet on which Judasim has been based for at least 2000 years, that is, the belief that an *oral **Torah*** accompanied and supplemented the Hebrew Scriptures that the Jews hold to be *written **Torah***.

If Jesus *delivered* a *Teaching* to the Apostles through revelation and expected Christian leaders to *hand down* that *Teaching orally* from generation to generation as I have argued elsewhere (see "Where Are Jesus' Disciples?" *The Voice of Elijah*, April 1991; "The Protestant Confession: The Church Lost The Teaching," *The Voice of Elijah*, January 1992; "Did You Mean That Literally?" *The Voice of Elijah*, January 1993; and "Some People Will Make Light of Anything," *The Voice of Elijah*, April 1994), the same could well have been true of ancient Israel.

Judaism may retain a faint echo of the same Truth concerning an even more distant past. As *The Mystery of Scripture* series will show, God did indeed *deliver* an *oral **Torah*** to Moses, and He expected Israel to *hand* it *down* from generation to generation *orally*. Contrary to what the Jews claim, however, the ancient Israelites failed to do as God expected. That is how *The Teaching* became *The Mystery* hidden in the Hebrew Scriptures.

The text of Deuteronomy 5:22–31 (quoted above) expressly states that God communicated both *statutes* and *judgments* to Moses *orally*. It also makes it abundantly clear that the *statutes* and *judgments* that Moses was supposed to *teach* all Israel were not a part of the covenant stipulations— the *testimonies*—that God wrote on the stone tablets. That agrees with my earlier explanation regarding the two terms *statutes* and *judgments*.[21] The *statutes* and *judgments* were instituted as part of the covenant relationship; but they were not included in the covenant text itself. They were instead an extension of the covenant terms, a dynamic implementation of those terms as part of the continuing covenant relationship.

What about the *commandments* (**mitzvah**) mentioned in Deuteronomy 5:31? That verse plainly indicates God gave the *commandments* to Moses *orally*, while Exodus 24:12 just as clearly states, and cannot be interpreted otherwise, that the *commandment* was "*written* for their instruction." Since the *commandment* mentioned in Exodus 24:12 can hardly refer to anything other than something in the *testimonies* which were inscribed on the two stone tablets, how can the use of the term in these two passages be explained?

The only way to reconcile the two accounts is to understand the *commandments* of God as a broader category in which not only *statutes* and *judgments,* but also some part of the *testimonies,* can fit. That *means* the Hebrew terms normally translated "*commandments*" and "*testimonies*" must not have identical *meaning*. *Commandments* must refer to something that is contained in or is somehow a part of the *testimonies*. Likewise, if God did indeed write the **Torah** on the stone tablets, that **Torah** must also be a part of the *testimonies*.

It is clear not only from the foregoing but also from the root *meaning* of the verb **zavah**, which means "to order or command," that a **mitzvah** is just that. It is an order—that is, a

---

[21] See above, pp. 53 ff.

commandment—from God. Therefore, you can easily see why the Hebrew Scriptures support an understanding of *mitzvah* as a broad category which encompasses other, more narrowly defined, categories. That is, they indicate God gave *Corporate* Israel various kinds of *commandments* through Moses.

In Psalm 119, for example, where the psalmist delights in using various legal terms in a paean to *The Teaching of Moses*, the author uses the term *commandment* as a synonym for several other terms. There are *testimonies, precepts, statutes,* and *judgments,* not to mention God's Word and His *Torah.*[22] In fact, all of the terms mentioned in Psalm 119 are in some sense synonyms for the term *mitzvah—commandment*. However, that is so only because they are all smaller, more specific, categories of the larger category. *Mitzvah*, when used as a general term, designates any of the *commandments* of God, which is how Moses uses the term in the following passages:

> *"But when you unwittingly fail and do not observe* **all these commandments***, which the* LORD *has spoken to Moses, {even} all that the* LORD *has commanded you through Moses, from the day when the* LORD *gave commandment and onward throughout your generations, then it shall be, if it is done unintentionally, without the knowledge of the congregation, that all the congregation shall offer one bull for a burnt offering, as a soothing aroma to the* LORD*, with its grain offering, and its libation, according to the ordinance, and one male goat for a sin offering."*
> *(Numbers 15:22–24)*

> *"And now, O Israel, listen to the statutes and the judgments which I am teaching you to perform, in order that you may live and go in and take possession of the land which the* LORD*, the God of your fathers, is giving you. You shall not add to the word which I am commanding you, nor take away from it, that you may keep* **the commandments** *of the* LORD *your God which I command you."*
> *(Deuteronomy 4:1–2)*

---

[22] It is not my purpose here to explain Psalm 119. Suffice it to say the Psalm is a hymn lauding the wisdom God has hidden in *The Teaching of Moses* and *The Teaching of the Prophets.*

The Hebrew term *mitzvah*—"*commandment*"—also has a much more narrowly defined and specific use. It has that restricted *meaning* in Exodus 24:12 and in these passages:

> *"Speak to the sons of Israel, saying, 'If a person sins unintentionally in* **any of the things which the LORD has commanded not to be done**, *and commits any of them …'"*
> *(Leviticus 4:2)*

> *"Now if the whole congregation of Israel commits error, and the matter escapes the notice of the assembly, and they commit* **any of the things which the LORD has commanded not to be done**, *and they become guilty …"*
> *(Leviticus 4:13)*

> *"When a leader sins and unintentionally does* **any one of all the things which the LORD God has commanded not to be done**, *and he becomes guilty …"*
> *(Leviticus 4:22)*

> *"Now if anyone of the common people sins unintentionally in doing* **any of the things which the LORD has commanded not to be done**, *and becomes guilty …"*
> *(Leviticus 4:27)*

> *"Now if a person sins and does* **any of the things which the LORD has commanded not to be done**, *though he was unaware, still he is guilty, and shall bear his punishment."*
> *(Leviticus 5:17)*

The translator of those verses should be commended for his consistent translation of five (almost) identical Hebrew phrases. As you saw in the last chapter from the various ways the Hebrew words for *statutes* and *judgments* were translated, not all translators are as reliable in their treatment of the biblical text. However, in spite of this translator's consistency, the five verses above still conceal the presence of the Hebrew term *mitzvah*. That is so because the translator has translated the Hebrew noun *mitzvah* ("*commandment*") into English as a verb—"commanded."

The use of the Hebrew term *mitzvah* in the passages above provides all the information you need to gain insight into its specific *meaning*. But you first need a more *literal* translation of the biblical text. The Hebrew *literally* says, "the *commandments* of the LORD that are not to be done." Even this translation is somewhat enigmatic until one realizes the noun *mitzvah* in this case refers to a specific type of legal stipulation. That is, it designates a *"commandment"* that contains a prohibition against doing things "that are not to be done."

Only one type of legal stipulation in the Hebrew Scriptures contains a prohibition. That is the category known as *apodictic* law—the "thou shalt" and "thou shalt not" type of law. Now you can see why Exodus 24:12 says, "the *commandment* which I have *written* for their instruction." The Ten Commandments—the *testimonies*—written on the two stone tablets are, in large part, *apodictic* law. That is, they are "thou shalt" and "thou shalt not" laws.

You should now be able to see that, although *apodictic* law has a form completely different from the conditional *judgments* and the *statutes* that mandate limits, it provides the basis for both. That is, there is no reason for an "if someone does" without a prior "thou shalt not," just as there is no reason for a "these are the limits" without a prior "thou shalt."

Apodictic law differs markedly from the *judgment* and the *statute*, yet it provides the basis for the issuance of both. That explains why the strictly defined categories of legal stipulations known as *statutes* and *judgments* can easily be considered *commandments* even according to the narrower definition of *mitzvah* as *apodictic* law. They are merely further defining the implementation of the *apodictic commandments* on which they are based.

The Ten Commandments are not the only *apodictic* laws in *The Law of Moses*. Various other such laws are scattered throughout Deuteronomy. The following is but a sample:

"None of the daughters of Israel shall be a cult prostitute, nor shall any of the sons of Israel be a cult prostitute. You shall not bring the hire of a harlot or the wages of a dog into the house of the LORD your God for any votive offering, for both of these are an abomination to the LORD your God. You shall not charge interest to your countrymen: interest on money, food, {or} anything that may be loaned at interest. You may charge interest to a foreigner, but to your countryman you shall not charge interest, so that the LORD your God may bless you in all that you undertake in the land which you are about to enter to possess."
(Deuteronomy 23:17–20)

There are also *apodictic* laws in the later chapters of the Book of Leviticus:

"You shall not eat {anything} with the blood, nor practice divination or soothsaying. You shall not round off the side-growth of your heads, nor harm the edges of your beard. You shall not make any cuts in your body for the dead, nor make any tattoo marks on yourselves: I am the LORD. Do not profane your daughter by making her a harlot, so that the land may not fall to harlotry, and the land become full of lewdness. You shall keep My sabbaths and revere My sanctuary; I am the LORD. Do not turn to mediums or spiritists; do not seek them out to be defiled by them. I am the LORD your God. You shall rise up before the gray-headed, and honor the aged, and you shall revere your God; I am the LORD. When a stranger resides with you in your land, you shall not do him wrong. The stranger who resides with you shall be to you as the native among you, and you shall love him as yourself; for you were aliens in the land of Egypt: I am the LORD your God. You shall do no wrong in judgment, in measurement of weight, or capacity. You shall have just balances, just weights, a just ephah, and a just hin: I am the LORD your God, who brought you out from the land of Egypt. You shall thus observe all My statutes, and all My ordinances, and do them: I am the LORD."
(Leviticus 19:26–37)

Chapters 28 and 29 of the Book of Numbers contain a series of *apodictic* laws as well. They are introduced as follows:

Then the LORD spoke to Moses, saying, "Command the sons of Israel and say to them, 'You shall be careful to present My offering, My food for My offerings by fire, of a soothing aroma to Me, at their appointed

*time.' And **you shall** say to them, 'This is the offering by fire which **you
shall** offer to the LORD; two male lambs one year old without defect
{as} a continual burnt offering every day. **You shall** offer the one lamb
in the morning, and the other lamb **you shall** offer at twilight.'"*
(Numbers 28:1–4)

The text following that brief introduction goes on to list
various legal stipulations. All are *commandments* that fall
within the narrower definition of *"commandment"* as *apodictic*
law. Yet if you note the topics covered by the *commandments* in
those two chapters, you will find that all have been covered
elsewhere by legal stipulations designated as either a *statute*
or a ***Torah***, and in some cases, as both. Therefore, it is clear that
the *mitzvah*, although having a specific *apodictic* form, still
provided the basis for the *statute*. By logical extension, it was
used as a general term to denote any *commandment*, that is,
any legal stipulation, that God issued.

Since *apodictic* law is the simplest form of *commandment*, it
is also the most easily recognized. Yet any legal stipulation
that originated with God could be called a ***mitzvah*** of God—
that is, a divine *commandment*. That is precisely how the term
mitzvah is used in many cases. For example, in the passage
quoted above, God said to Moses:

*"But as for you, stand here by Me, that I may speak to you **all the commandments and the statutes and the judgments which you shall
teach them**, that they may observe {them} in the land which I give
them to possess."*
(Deuteronomy 5:31)

The phrase translated "all the commandments AND the
statutes and the judgments which you shall teach them"
should be translated "all the commandments, EVEN[23] the statutes and the judgments, which you shall teach them." The
difference in translation would only serve to indicate that the

---

[23] The use of the conjunction in this instance and in the instances mentioned below should be taken as *explicative*. See R. J. Williams, *Hebrew Syntax: An Outline*, p. 72.

phrase "*EVEN* the statutes and the judgments" stands in apposition to "the commandments," telling the reader that "the statutes and the judgments" are component parts of "the commandments." That understanding of the verse is similar to the *meaning* conveyed by the grammatical construction encountered just three verses later, where there can be little doubt as to the *meaning* intended:

> "Now **this is the commandment, the statutes and the judgments** which the LORD your God has commanded {me} to teach you, that you might do {them} in the land where you are going over to possess it, so that you and your son and your grandson might fear the LORD your God, to keep all His statutes and His commandments, which I command you, all the days of your life, and that your days may be prolonged."
> (Deuteronomy 6:1–2)

Later in the chapter, the same grammatical construction occurs again:

> "You should diligently keep **the commandments** of the LORD your God, **and His testimonies and His statutes** which He has commanded you."
> (Deuteronomy 6:17)

As was the case in Deuteronomy 5:31, the phrase "and His testimonies and His statutes" should be translated "*EVEN* His testimonies and His statutes" to indicate that the phrase is again explaining what *commandments* are in view. Three verses later, a similar construction occurs. However, this time the phrase "the commandments" has been replaced with "the testimonies":

> "When your son asks you in time to come, saying, 'What {do} **the testimonies and the statutes and the judgments** {mean} which the LORD our God commanded you?'"
> (Deuteronomy 6:20)

Keeping in mind that the *statutes* and *judgments* mentioned in that verse are an extension of the *testimonies* that God wrote on the stone tablets, it is obvious that the first conjunction should be translated "and." And, since the *testimonies* refer specifically to the Ten Commandments, these three terms together must be *meant* to encompass the total spectrum of legal stipulations in *The Law of Moses*.[24] That is confirmed a bit later in the text where, in a father's response to a question posed by his son, "all these statutes" is summarized as "all this commandment":

> *"So the* LORD *commanded us to observe* **all these statutes***, to fear the* LORD *our God for our good always and for our survival, as {it is} today. And it will be righteousness for us if we are careful to observe* **all this commandment** *before the* LORD *our God, just as He commanded us."*
> *(Deuteronomy 6:24–25)*

With either the general *meaning* "mandated limits," or with the specific *meaning* "mandated cultic limits," the use of the term *statute* in this context fits the question asked and the answer given. The *statutes* of the Mosaic legislation mandated the most visible observances—the *symbolic rituals*—of the sacrificial cult, and thus governed the things most likely to raise questions in the mind of a child.

The singular "all this commandment" in Deuteronomy 6:25, as well as "the commandment" in Deuteronomy 6:1 above, refers to the totality of the Mosaic legislation. That only serves to reinforce what has already been explained: The term translated "commandment" (*mitzvah*) is often used as a general term to encompass all the directives God gave *Corporate* Israel

---

[24] The New Testament Book of James emphasizes the strict unity of the Mosaic legislation in what he says concerning the Ten Commandments:

> *But if you show partiality, you are committing sin {and} are convicted by the law as transgressors.* **For whoever keeps the whole law and yet stumbles in one {point,} he has become guilty of all.** *For He who said, "*DO NOT COMMIT ADULTERY," *also said, "*DO NOT COMMIT MURDER." *Now if you do not commit adultery, but do commit murder, you have become a transgressor of the law. So speak and so act, as those who are to be judged by {the} law of liberty.*
> *(James 2:9–12)*

through Moses. In this case, the singular form emphasizes the
unity of the Mosaic legislation: The *statutes* and the *judgments*
are nothing more than extensions of the *apodictic commandments*
found in the *testimonies*. You have seen the term used that way
before:

> Now the LORD said to Moses, "Come up to Me on the mountain and
> remain there, and **I will give you the stone tablets with the law and
> the commandment which I have written for their instruction."** So
> Moses arose with Joshua his servant, and Moses went up to the moun-
> tain of God.
> (Exodus 24:12–13)

The *commandment* (**mitzvah**) mentioned in this text refers
to the *apodictic* laws found in the "ten words"—the Ten Commandments—that were written on the two stone tablets. But
what about the "law," that is, the **Torah**? What does that term
refer to? Is there something more to the Ten Commandments
than just *apodictic* law—the "thou shalt" and "thou shalt not"
commandments? Is there something in those "ten words"
that should not be lumped together with the *statutes* and *judgments* as just another type of legal stipulation that seeks to
implement an *apodictic commandment*? Indeed there is, and it
must be kept completely separate, as you will see in the next
chapter.

Summary

In this chapter, I began by defining the two Hebrew terms
torah and **mitzvah**. I told you the Hebrew noun **mitzvah** comes
from the same root as the verb **zavah**, which *means* "to command or order." Therefore, *"commandment"* is a fairly accurate
translation of that term. But the Hebrew word **torah**, which is
normally translated *"law,"* is from the same root as the verb
yarah, which *means* "to point out, teach, instruct." Therefore, I
told you that although Moses does use the term to refer to legal

stipulations, its basic *meaning* is not "*law;*" it is "*teaching*" or "*instruction.*"

I next briefly investigated the Jews' belief that Moses *received* both an *oral Torah* and a *written Torah* at Mt. Sinai. I showed you where Moses clearly states God explained *commandments, statutes,* and *judgments* to him *orally.*

Finally, I explained how Moses used the Hebrew term translated "*commandment*" (**mitzvah**) in the Pentateuch and showed you the term has both a specific referent—which is the *apodictic* "thou shalt" and "thou shalt not" type of *commandments*—as well as a general referent—that is, any of God's requirements that derive from His specific *apodictic commandments.*

Chapter 4:

Torah as Teaching

In the first three chapters, I explained the *meaning* of the five Hebrew terms that are sometimes translated "*testimonies,*" "*statutes,*" "*judgments,*" "*commandments,*" and "*laws.*" But I have, to this point, only explained how the first four of those five terms are used. Therefore, in this chapter I will explain the usage of the fifth Hebrew term, *torah,* which is normally translated "*law*" but actually *means "teaching."*

I will show how, in Exodus, Leviticus, and Numbers, the term **torah** refers almost exclusively to *The (oral) Teaching of Moses* that explained the *meaning* of the *symbolic rituals* mandated by the *statutes.* That reveals why the biblical text appears to refer to those *statutes* as **Torah.** The sole exception to that usage of the term is its reference to the single *written* **Torah** in the *testimonies.* That **Torah** explains the *meaning* of the *symbolic ritual* of the Sabbath. Moses *received* that **Torah** as *written* **Torah** when God wrote it on the stone tablets He gave to him. That is not to say, however, that Moses did not also receive additional *oral* **Torah** that explained the *meaning* and *significance* of the *symbolic ritual* of the Sabbath. Indeed he did.[1]

---

[1] See Exodus 16:23–29; 31:14–16; 35:2–3; Leviticus 23:3–32; *et. al.*

It will eventually become clear that God did, in fact, *deliver* both an *oral Torah* (*The Teaching*) and a *written Torah* to Moses just as the Jews say He did. Although Judaism mistakenly contends the Pentateuch is the *written Torah* that Moses *received* at Mt. Sinai, the Hebrew Scriptures contradict that belief. They indicate the *written Torah* that Moses *received* can only be found in the *testimonies*, that is, in the Ten Commandments, which God *wrote* on the two stone "tablets of the testimonies." That *written Torah* is the *written* explanation of the *meaning* and *significance* of the *statute* that mandates the *symbolic ritual* of observing every seventh day as a Sabbath.[2]

In addition to the *written* account of Moses *receiving* the *written Torah* (*The Teaching*) regarding the Sabbath on Mt. Sinai, there are various other *written* accounts scattered throughout the Pentateuch that describe him *receiving oral Torah*—that is, *The Teaching of Moses*. But those *written* accounts do not become *written Torah* just because they were written down. The designation "*written Torah*" can apply only to the *written* explanation of the *meaning* and *significance* of the *statute* that governed the *symbolic ritual* of observing the Sabbath because that is the only *Torah written* by the finger of God Himself.

As I indicated above, Exodus, Leviticus, and Numbers show Moses *orally delivering* to the sons of Israel the *oral Torah* (*The Teaching of Moses*) that explains the *meaning* and *significance* of the *symbolic rituals* mandated by the *statutes*. By contrast, in the Book of Deuteronomy Moses relates how he *orally delivered* to them the complete *oral Torah* (*The Teaching of Moses*)*, which explains not only the *meaning* and *significance* of the *statutes* but also the *meaning* and *significance* of all the *apodictic commandments* and *judgments*. That is, in Deuteronomy Moses describes how he *handed down* to the sons of Israel *The (oral) Teaching* that explains the *meaning* and *significance* of

---

[2] Exodus 20:8–11; Deuteronomy 5:12–15.

every *apodictic commandment,* every *statute*, and every *judgment* mentioned in the Pentateuch.

The Rabbis erroneously assert that the entire Pentateuch
is the *written* **Torah** that God *delivered* to Moses because Moses
intentionally expanded the scope of the term ***torah*** in the
Book of Deuteronomy. In that book alone, Moses uses the
term to refer not only to God's explanation of the *meaning* and
significance of the *symbolic rituals* mandated by the *statutes* but
also to His explanation of the *meaning* and *significance* of the
symbolic rituals associated with the *apodictic commandments* and
conditional *judgments.* He did that at that time because, as I
will explain in Chapters 7 and 8, he also expanded the scope
of the priesthood to include the entire tribe of Levi and gave
the Levites responsibility for judging the sons of Israel.

The Rabbis erred because they lost sight of the fact that
the only *written* **Torah** that Moses *received* at Mt. Sinai was the
single *written* **Torah** in the *testimonies* that explains the *meaning*
of the *symbolic ritual* of the Sabbath. God wrote that **Torah** on
"the two tablets of the *testimonies*" he gave Moses. Since
Moses later expanded the scope of the term ***torah*** to include
all of the legal stipulations found in the Pentateuch, the Rabbis erroneously assumed the *written* **Torah** was the *written* text
of the Pentateuch. That assumption is not true. The Pentateuch is nothing more than a *written* account that explains
why God *delivered* an *oral* **Torah** to Moses and told him to *hand*
it *down* to the sons of Israel with instructions that they *hand* it
down to future generations. It is not the *written* **Torah** Moses
received at Mt. Sinai.

In *Not All Israel Is Israel,* I explain that the ancient Semites
considered their priests to be the keepers of *the divine myster-
ies.*[3] I also explain how, in accordance with that belief, a primary function of the ancient Semitic priestly "family" was to
provide a conduit through which the gods conveyed their

---

[3] Harper, *Not All Israel Is Israel,* pp. 90 ff.

secrets to mankind. Consequently, whether the discernment of divine knowledge was by divine oracle or by priestly divination, the responsibility for making that esoteric body of knowledge known to humanity lay with the priesthood.

God appropriated the ancient belief that the priesthood alone had been granted divine insight and used that concept as part of the *parabolic imagery* of *The Teaching of Moses* in which *Corporate* Israel ("all Israel") is the Firstborn Son and High Priest of God.[4] In keeping with that *parabolic image*, God's intent for *Corporate* Israel has always been that His Firstborn Son would be "a kingdom of priests,"[5] that is, a priestly family, in which every member would be well-versed in *The Teaching* that explains *The Mystery*.

According to the plan outlined in the Old Testament, God expected *Corporate* Israel to be the mediator through which He would convey *The (oral) Teaching* to all the other peoples of the Earth. That was supposed to be a primary part of the ministry of the sons of Israel as His priestly family. By God's design, it was the responsibility of Moses, the first Prophet of Israel, to equip the priestly Teachers of Israel for their ministry to the sons of Israel by making sure they were taught—*orally*—*The Teaching* that God *delivered* to him. Each new generation of Teachers was then expected to *hand down The Teaching* to the next generation *orally*, just as they had *received* it.

In this volume of *The Mystery of Scripture*, I will show you how Moses accomplished his appointed task as the first Prophet of Israel before he died. But the priestly Teachers of Israel who followed him made a miserable mess of things. In the remaining volumes of this series, I will explain how, after God *delivered* to Moses *The Teaching* that explained *The Mystery*, and Moses *handed* it *down* to the priestly Teachers of Israel—*orally*—as *The Teaching of Moses*, *Corporate* Israel failed to live up

---

[4] Exodus 4:22–23.

[5] Exodus 19:6.

to its role as the priestly family of all the Earth. I will also show you how, because the priestly Teachers of Israel failed, *The Teaching of Moses* once again became *The Mystery* of God, wanting only a High Priest fully qualified to explain it once more—*orally*—to those with ears to hear. It finally found that High Priest in the Person of Jesus Christ, Who explained *The Mystery of Scripture* to His disciples and told them to *hand* it *down* to the next generation by teaching it—*orally*—to their disciples.[6]

---

[6] The author of the Book of Hebrews begins his treatise on the high-priestly work of Christ as the divinely appointed Teacher of Israel saying:

*God, after He spoke long ago to the fathers in the prophets in many portions and in many ways, **in these last days has spoken to us in {His} Son**, whom He appointed heir of all things, through whom also He made the world.*
(Hebrews 1:1–2)

Matthew describes how after His resurrection, Jesus Christ transferred the authority He had for teaching Israel to His disciples:

*And Jesus came up and spoke to them, saying, "All authority has been given to Me in heaven and on earth. Go therefore and **make disciples** of all the nations, baptizing them in the name of the Father and the Son and the Holy Spirit, **teaching them** to observe all that I commanded you; and lo, I am with you always, even to the end of the age."*
(Matthew 28:18–20)

The Apostle Peter emphasizes that the priestly role of Christian Believers is one in which they are to make known the Truth of *The Apostolic Teaching*:

*But you are A CHOSEN RACE, A royal PRIESTHOOD, A HOLY NATION, A PEOPLE FOR {God's} OWN POSSESSION, that you may **proclaim** the excellencies of Him who has called you out of darkness into His marvelous light.*
(1 Peter 2:9)

I have explained elsewhere how the Church lost *The Apostolic Teaching*. (See "The Protestant Confession: The Church Lost The Teaching," ***The Voice of Elijah***, January 1992 and the two articles "Did You Mean That Literally?" and "The Origen of Folly," *The Voice of Elijah*, January 1993.) The sad epitaph regarding the Church's failure to carry out the Great Commission has already been succinctly put:

Professing to be wise, they became fools, and exchanged the glory of the incorruptible God for an image in the form of corruptible man and of birds and four-footed animals and crawling creatures.
(Romans 1:22–23)

Torah *in Exodus, Leviticus, and Numbers*

Although the Hebrew word **torah** is normally translated "*law*," I have already shown you why that traditional understanding of the term is totally inaccurate and completely misleading. The term actually *means "teaching."*[7] It has been taken to *mean "law"* only because Moses sometimes *seems* to use it as a synonym for the term **mitzvah**—"*commandment.*" The Truth is, *teaching* does not describe a TYPE of *commandment.* It is sometimes used to describe a CHARACTERISTIC (*teaching*) of a *commandment* in the same way that the term *commandment* is sometimes used to describe a fundamental CHARACTERISTIC (*command*) of the *statutes* and the *judgments.* That is so because any "*commandment*" (**mitzvah**) can also have a specific purpose in keeping with the basic *meaning* of the term **torah.** That is, it can be used to *teach.*

By now, you should be able to see the incredible difficulty that one faces in trying to ferret out (and restore) *The (oral) Teaching of Moses* from all the places where Moses might have concealed it in the Pentateuch. Some of it is obviously hidden in those parts of the Mosaic legislation that are clearly labeled **Torah** ("teaching"). However, Moses may well have hidden crucial bits of information in other places in the Pentateuch as well. But one can only begin to understand how *The Law of*

---

[7] That statement is not precisely true. Although "teaching" does reflect a strong nuance of the term **torah**, it does not accurately capture its precise *meaning.* The English language has no equivalent term. **Torah** can best be understood by looking to the verbal root from which it is derived—*yarah*. The verb *yarah* means "to point out, to direct, lead" as in "to show *the way*" (cf. Gen. 46:28; Ex. 15:25). It therefore carries the *meaning* "to teach by demonstration" or "to show someone *the way*" to do something rather than simply "to teach by speaking." That *meaning* is apparent from the way the verb is used elsewhere. For example, teaching by demonstration was the way Bezalel (Ex. 35:34) and the priests (Lev. 10:11; 14:57; Deut. 17:10, 11; 24:8) "taught" the sons of Israel. Hence, **torah** must carry a *meaning* something on the order of "teaching by demonstration as to *the way* to do something."

Moses is also *The Teaching of Moses* by carefully investigating those covenant stipulations that are designated as "*Torah.*"

When we look closely at those parts of the Mosaic legislation that Moses calls "*Torah,*" we will discover that much of *The (oral) Teaching of Moses* can actually be recovered quite easily by just carefully reading what Moses says about all the *symbolic rituals* described in the Pentateuch. That is because the Truth of the *oral Torah* (*The Teaching*) that Moses *received* in the wilderness explains the *meaning* and *significance* of those *symbolic rituals.*[8]

In the first three books of the Bible that contain the legal stipulations of the covenant that the sons of Israel ratified at Mt. Sinai (Exodus, Leviticus, and Numbers),[9] the Hebrew term *torah* always refers to divine stipulations that have but

---

[8] The notion of teaching via *symbolic ritual* fits in perfectly with the basic *meaning* of the term *torah* as "teaching by demonstration as to *the way* to do something." In the Scriptures, God has keyed on the specific nuance of *torah* as "pointing out *The Way*" of the Lord. The purpose of God's *torah* is "to point out *The Way* in which Israel is to *walk.*" This chapter will touch briefly on the idiom "walk in *The Way.*" However, a complete discussion of the matter must be postponed until it can be addressed directly in the next volume in this series.

[9] The only occurrence of the word *torah* in the Book of Genesis is found in God's *promise* to Isaac:

And the LORD appeared to him and said, "Do not go down to Egypt; stay in the land of which I shall tell you. Sojourn in this land and I will be with you and bless you, for to you and to your descendants I will give all these lands, and I will establish the oath which I swore to your father Abraham. And I will multiply your descendants as the stars of heaven, and will give your descendants all these lands; and by your descendants all the nations of the earth shall be blessed; because Abraham obeyed Me and kept My charge, My commandments, My statutes and My laws."
(Genesis 26:2–5)

Although it is not obvious that *torah* refers to *symbolic ritual* in this passage, it probably does since it occurs with the terms *commandments* and *statutes*. Unless one assumes there is no distinction between these terms, *torah* surely refers to the *symbolic ritual* of circumcision (at least in part).

one thing in common—*symbolic ritual.*[10] That becomes evident from the following passages, which contain all of the occurrences of the term ***torah*** in those three books. In those cases where a *symbolic ritual* is not obviously in view, the *meaning* of the term ***torah*** as "teaching" or "instruction" clearly is. In a few instances, both are equally evident. As you read, keep in mind that the Hebrew term ***torah*** (the boldfaced and capitalized word) has most often been inaccurately translated "law." In spite of the translators' lack of insight into the *meaning* of the term, however, you should notice that it has in some instances still been translated "instruction."

1. The Passover Ritual:

"The same LAW shall apply to the native as to the stranger who sojourns among you." Then all the sons of Israel did {so;} they did just as the LORD had commanded Moses and Aaron. And it came about on that same day the LORD brought the sons of Israel out of the land of Egypt by their hosts.
(Exodus 12:49–51)

2. The Ritual for the Feast of Unleavened Bread:

"And it shall serve as a sign to you on your hand, and as a reminder on your forehead, that the LAW of the LORD may be in your mouth; for with a powerful hand the LORD brought you out of Egypt. Therefore, you shall keep this ordinance at its appointed time from year to year."
(Exodus 13:9–10)

3. The Ritual for Gathering Manna:

Then the LORD said to Moses, "Behold, I will rain bread from heaven for you; and the people shall go out and gather a day's portion every day, that I may test them, whether or not they will walk in My INSTRUCTION."
(Exodus 16:4)

---

[10] Exodus 12:49; 13:9; 16:4, 28; 18:16, 20; 24:12; Leviticus 6:9, 14, 25; 7:1, 7, 11, 37; 11:46; 12:7; 13:59; 14:2, 32, 54, 57; 15:32; 26:46; Numbers 5:29, 30; 6:13, 21(2 times); 15:16, 29; 19:2, 14; 31:21. See also the forthcoming book, *The Inheritance of the Believer,* by the current author.

4. The Sabbath Ritual:

Then the LORD said to Moses, "How long do you refuse to keep My commandments and My INSTRUCTIONS? *See, the LORD has given you the sabbath; therefore He gives you bread for two days on the sixth day. Remain every man in his place; let no man go out of his place on the seventh day." So the people rested on the seventh day.*
(Exodus 16:28–30)

5. The Teaching of Moses:

"When they have a dispute, it comes to me, and I judge between a man and his neighbor, and make known the statutes of God and His LAWS." *And Moses' father-in-law said to him, "The thing that you are doing is not good. You will surely wear out, both yourself and these people who are with you, for the task is too heavy for you; you cannot do it alone. Now listen to me: I shall give you counsel, and God be with you. You be the people's representative before God, and you bring the disputes to God, then **teach them** the statutes and the* LAWS, *and make known to them the way in which they are to walk, and the work they are to do."*
(Exodus 18:16–20)

6. The Writing on the Two Stone Tablets:

Now the LORD said to Moses, "Come up to Me on the mountain and remain there, and I will give you the stone tablets with the LAW *and the commandment which I have written for their instruction."*
(Exodus 24:12)

7. The Ritual for the Burnt Offering:

"Command Aaron and his sons, saying, 'This is the LAW *for the burnt offering: the burnt offering itself {shall remain} on the hearth on the altar all night until the morning, and the fire on the altar is to be kept burning on it.'"*
(Leviticus 6:9)

8. The Ritual for the Grain Offering:

"Now this is the LAW *of the grain offering: the sons of Aaron shall present it before the LORD in front of the altar."*
(Leviticus 6:14)

9. The Ritual for the Sin Offering:

"Speak to Aaron and to his sons, saying, 'This is the LAW of the sin offering: in the place where the burnt offering is slain the sin offering shall be slain before the LORD; it is most holy.'"
(Leviticus 6:25)

10. The Ritual for the Guilt Offering:

"Now this is the LAW of the guilt offering; it is most holy."
(Leviticus 7:1)

11. The Ritual for the Sin Offering:

"The guilt offering is like the sin offering, there is one LAW for them; the priest who makes atonement with it shall have it."
(Leviticus 7:7)

12. The Ritual for the Peace Offering:

"Now this is the LAW of the sacrifice of peace offerings which shall be presented to the LORD."
(Leviticus 7:11)

13. The Ritual for All the Sacrificial Offerings:

This is the LAW of the burnt offering, the grain offering and the sin offering and the guilt offering and the ordination offering and the sacrifice of peace offerings.
(Leviticus 7:37)

14. The Ritual Identification of Edible Creatures:

This is the LAW regarding the animal, and the bird, and every living thing that moves in the waters, and everything that swarms on the earth, to make a distinction between the unclean and the clean, and between the edible creature and the creature which is not to be eaten.
(Leviticus 11:46–47)

15. The Ritual for Cleansing After Childbirth:

"Then he shall offer it before the LORD and make atonement for her; and she shall be cleansed from the flow of her blood. This is the LAW for her who bears {a child, whether} a male or a female."
(Leviticus 12:7)

16. The Ritual for Cleansing Garments:

This is the LAW for the mark of leprosy in a garment of wool or linen, whether in the warp or in the woof, or in any article of leather, for pronouncing it clean or unclean.
(Leviticus 13:59)

17. The Ritual for Cleansing Lepers:

"This shall be the LAW of the leper in the day of his cleansing. Now he shall be brought to the priest, …"
(Leviticus 14:2)

"This is the LAW {for him} in whom there is an infection of leprosy, whose means are limited for his cleansing."
(Leviticus 14:32)

This is the LAW for any mark of leprosy—even for a scale, and for the leprous garment or house, and for a swelling, and for a scab, and for a bright spot—to teach when they are unclean, and when they are clean. This is the LAW of leprosy.
(Leviticus 14:54–57)

18. The Ritual for Cleansing From Unclean Discharge:

This is the LAW for the one with a discharge, and for the man who has a seminal emission so that he is unclean by it, and for the woman who is ill because of menstrual impurity, and for the one who has a discharge, whether a male or a female, or a man who lies with an unclean woman.
(Leviticus 15:32–33)

19. All the Rituals God Established:

These are the statutes and ordinances and LAWS which the LORD established between Himself and the sons of Israel through Moses at Mount Sinai.
(Leviticus 26:46)

20. The Ritual for Suspected Adultery:

"This is the LAW of jealousy: when a wife, {being} under {the authority of} her husband, goes astray and defiles herself, or when a spirit of jealousy comes over a man and he is jealous of his wife, he shall then make the woman stand before the LORD, and the priest shall apply all this LAW to her."
(Numbers 5:29–30)

21. The Ritual for the Nazirite:

"Now this is the LAW *of the Nazirite when the days of his separation are fulfilled, he shall bring the offering to the doorway of the tent of meeting."*
(Numbers 6:13)

"This is the LAW *of the Nazirite who vows his offering to the* LORD *according to his separation, in addition to what {else} he can afford; according to his vow which he takes, so he shall do according to the* LAW *of his separation."*
(Numbers 6:21)

22. The Ritual for Libations Accompanying Offerings:

"There is to be one LAW *and one ordinance for you and for the alien who sojourns with you."*
(Numbers 15:16)

23. The Ritual for Congregational Atonement:

"You shall have one LAW *for him who does {anything} unintentionally, for him who is native among the sons of Israel and for the alien who sojourns among them."*
(Numbers 15:29)

24. The Ritual of the Red Heifer:

"This is the statute of the LAW *which the* LORD *has commanded, saying, 'Speak to the sons of Israel that they bring you an unblemished red heifer in which is no defect, {and} on which a yoke has never been placed.'"*
(Numbers 19:2)

25. The Ritual for Cleansing From a Corpse:

"This is the LAW *when a man dies in a tent: everyone who comes into the tent and everyone who is in the tent shall be unclean for seven days."*
(Numbers 19:14)

26. The Ritual for Cleansing Spoils of War:

Then Eleazar the priest said to the men of war who had gone to battle, "This is the statute of the LAW *which the* LORD *has commanded Moses: only the gold and the silver, the bronze, the iron, the tin and the lead, everything that can stand the fire, you shall pass through the fire, and it*

shall be clean, but it shall be purified with water for impurity. But whatever cannot stand the fire you shall pass through the water. And you shall wash your clothes on the seventh day and be clean, and afterward you may enter the camp."
(Numbers 31:21–24)

Torah *as an Explanation of Symbolic Ritual*

The passages above disclose that, in Exodus, Leviticus, and Numbers at least, Moses never uses the Hebrew term ***torah*** to refer to any of the *apodictic commandments* such as the following, which relate to civil/criminal cases:

*"Now in case a countryman of yours becomes poor and his means with regard to you falter, then **you are** to sustain him, like a stranger or a sojourner, that he may live with you. **Do not** take usurious interest from him, but revere your God, that your countryman may live with you. **You shall not** give him your silver at interest, nor your food for gain. I am the LORD your God, who brought you out of the land of Egypt to give you the land of Canaan {and} to be your God."*
(Leviticus 25:35–38)

Neither does Moses ever use the term ***torah*** in Exodus, Leviticus, and Numbers to refer to any of the conditional civil/criminal *judgments* like these:

*"**If a man steals** an ox or a sheep, and slaughters it or sells it, he shall pay five oxen for the ox and four sheep for the sheep. **If the thief is caught** while breaking in, and is struck so that he dies, there will be no bloodguiltiness on his account. {But} **if the sun has risen** on him, there will be bloodguiltiness on his account. He shall surely make restitution; **if he owns nothing**, then he shall be sold for his theft. **If what he stole is actually found alive** in his possession, whether an ox or a donkey or a sheep, he shall pay double. **If a man lets a field or vineyard be grazed** {bare} and lets his animal loose so that it grazes in another man's field, he shall make restitution from the best of his own field and the best of his own vineyard. **If a fire breaks out and spreads** to thorn bushes, so that stacked grain or the standing grain or the field {itself} is consumed, he who started the fire shall surely make restitution. **If a man gives** his neighbor money or goods to keep {for him,} and it is stolen from the*

*man's house, **if the thief is caught**, he shall pay double. **If the thief is not caught**, then the owner of the house shall appear before the judges, {to} determine whether he laid his hands on his neighbor's property. For every breach of trust, {whether it is} for ox, for donkey, for sheep, for clothing, {or} for any lost thing about which one says, 'This is it,' the case of both parties shall come before the judges; he whom the judges condemn shall pay double to his neighbor."*
(Exodus 22:1–9)

If the term ***torah*** never refers to *apodictic commandments* or to conditional *judgments*, logic dictates Moses must be intentionally using it to refer only to the *statutes* that regulated the *symbolic rituals*. As you will see shortly, that is precisely the case; and, with the sole exception of the Sabbath ***Torah** written* on the stone tablets, he always uses the Hebrew term ***torah*** to refer to *oral* instructions that God gave him concerning the conduct of the *symbolic rituals* of the sacrificial cult. That is because, with the possible exception of the ***Torah*** associated with the *symbolic ritual* of gathering manna, the Aaronic priesthood had complete responsibility for seeing to it that *Corporate* Israel adhered to the *statutes* that governed the conduct of those *symbolic rituals.*[11]

Since the legal stipulations called *"statutes"* are primarily concerned with the *symbolic rituals* of the sacrificial cult, it is easy to understand why, in Exodus, Leviticus, and Numbers at least, Moses only uses the term ***torah*** to refer to an explanation of the *meaning* and *significance* of those *statutes*. That is because the primary purpose of the *statutes* governing the *symbolic rituals* of the tabernacle was to *teach* some concept *nonverbally* through *symbolic ritual* rather than to govern the moral conduct of the individual members of *Corporate* Israel. The biblical text plainly states that was the purpose of the ***Torah*** (translated "law") concerning leprosy:

---

[11] The Aaronic priesthood of the wilderness wandering was restricted to the sons of Aaron, unlike the *Levitical* priesthood described in the Book of Deuteronomy, which included the entire tribe of Levi. Chapter 8 explains the *significance* of that change.

"to teach when they are unclean, and when they are clean. This is the LAW of leprosy."
(Leviticus 14:57)

To better understand how God used *symbolic ritual* to *teach* the sons of Israel, one can look first at the *symbolic ritual* of gathering manna on six days out of seven. The *oral Torah* concerning that *symbolic ritual* is an excellent example of the *oral Torah* that explained the *meaning* of the *symbolic rituals* that God required the sons of Israel to observe. Moreover, the biblical text tells us God had a specific purpose in mind when He instituted the *symbolic ritual* of gathering manna:

> Then the LORD said to Moses, *"Behold, I will rain bread from heaven for you; and the people shall go out and gather a day's portion every day,* **that I may test them, whether or not they will walk in My instruction."**
> *(Exodus 16:4)*

As Moses clearly states, God used the *symbolic ritual* of gathering manna to *test* the sons of Israel, to see "whether or not they will *walk in My Teaching (Torah)*."[12] God is obviously referring to *oral Torah* He had given Moses earlier. That *oral Torah* would have included an explanation of the *meaning* and *significance* of gathering manna in the proper manner. However, Moses indicates God's purpose in testing the people was in addition to the basic *teaching* purpose of that *Torah*. Moses reminded the sons of Israel of the dual purpose of this *symbolic ritual* in his remarks to them shortly before he died:

> *"All the commandments that I am commanding you today you shall be careful to do, that you may live and multiply, and go in and possess the land which the LORD swore {to give} to your forefathers. And you shall remember all the way which the LORD your God has led you in the wilderness these forty years, that He might humble you,* **testing you, to know what was in your heart, whether you would keep His com-**

---

[12] Note this idiomatic expression well. I have explained the *meaning* and *significance* of the Hebrew idiom "walk in The Way" in *The Way, The Truth, The Life*. For now it is enough to note that *means* He expected the sons of Israel to "walk in His *Torah* (teaching)" *mentally*.

mandments or not. And He humbled you and let you be hungry, and fed you with manna which you did not know, nor did your fathers know, **that He might make you understand that man does not live by bread alone,** *but man lives by everything that proceeds out of the mouth of the LORD."*
(Deuteronomy 8:1–3)

Moses is reminding us again why God instituted the *symbolic ritual* of gathering manna. It was to *test* Israel. But he also confirms that the basic purpose of that *symbolic ritual* was to *teach* the people ("make you understand") what God would have them understand:

"… man does not live by bread alone, but man lives by everything that proceeds out of the mouth of the LORD."
(Deuteronomy 8:3b)

As I have already explained,[13] God established the *symbolic ritual* of gathering manna to *teach* the sons of Israel that an understanding of the Truth of *The (oral) Teaching* that He revealed to Moses is more necessary to life than physical food.[14] But notice what God said to Moses after the people tried to gather manna on the Sabbath, thereby proving they were not willing to "walk in" God's *torah (Teaching)*:

Then the LORD said to Moses, **"How long do you refuse to keep My commandments and My instructions?** *See, the LORD has given you the sabbath; therefore He gives you bread for two days on the sixth day. Remain every man in his place; let no man go out of his place on the seventh day." So the people rested on the seventh day.*
(Exodus 16:28–30)

The word translated "instructions" in Exodus 16:4 (quoted above) and 16:28 (quoted here) is *torah*. In both cases, the term

---

[13] Harper, *Not All Israel Is Israel*, pp. 178 ff.

[14] The Truth that Moses taught the sons of Israel is intimately related to their understanding of, and belief in, Corporate Israel's *parabolic pantomime* of the death, burial, and resurrection of the Egyptian Pharaoh—*The Passover Parable*. (See "The Passover Parable," **The Voice of Elijah**, July 1991, or *The Passover Parable*.)

refers to the *oral* explanation God gave Moses concerning the
meaning and *significance* of the *symbolic ritual* of gathering
manna. That is because *teaching* was the primary purpose of the
statute related to the people gathering manna on six days out of
seven. However, *teaching* was also the purpose of all the other
symbolic rituals mandated by Moses—that is, every *statute* that
God instituted. That becomes clear from what Moses says
regarding the *symbolic ritual* of the Feast of Unleavened Bread:

> *And Moses said to the people, "Remember this day in which you went out
> from Egypt, from the house of slavery; for by a powerful hand the LORD
> brought you out from this place. And nothing leavened shall be eaten. On
> this day in the month of Abib, you are about to go forth. And it shall be
> when the LORD brings you to the land of the Canaanite, the Hittite, the
> Amorite, the Hivite and the Jebusite, which He swore to your fathers to
> give you, a land flowing with milk and honey, that you shall observe this
> rite in this month. For seven days you shall eat unleavened bread, and on
> the seventh day there shall be a feast to the LORD. Unleavened bread shall
> be eaten throughout the seven days; and nothing leavened shall be seen
> among you, nor shall any leaven be seen among you in all your borders.
> And **you shall tell your son on that day, saying, 'It is because of
> what the LORD did for me when I came out of Egypt.' And it shall
> serve as a sign to you on your hand, and as a reminder on your fore-
> head, that the law of the LORD may be in your mouth;** for with a pow-
> erful hand the LORD brought you out of Egypt. Therefore, you shall keep
> **this ordinance** at its appointed time from year to year."*
> *(Exodus 13:3–10)*

Moses calls the stipulations governing the observance of
the Feast of Unleavened Bread "this *statute*," which has here
been translated "this ordinance." He also says the purpose of
the *statute* was to provide a "sign" the people could use to *teach*
their children. His point becomes much clearer if one understands that the term **torah**—which has been translated "law" in
verse 9—actually *means* "teaching." The *statute* itself was not
"*The Teaching* of the Lord." The **Torah** (*Teaching*) was instead a
detailed *oral* explanation of what the *symbolic ritual* mandated
by the *statute* actually *meant*. That is, the *symbolic ritual* man-

dated by the *statute* was supposed to provide a visual aid the sons of Israel could use when they *taught* their children *orally*— "that *The Teaching* of the Lord may be in your mouth."

The underlying purpose of the *statute* governing the *symbolic ritual* of observing the Feast of Unleavened Bread for seven days, like the *statute* establishing the *symbolic ritual* of gathering manna on six days out of seven, was to establish a *parabolic pantomime* that illustrated some Truth God wanted the sons of Israel to understand. That is why Moses said the *statute* related to the *symbolic ritual* of the Feast of Unleavened Bread was to provide a "sign" to remind them of *The (oral) Teaching* related to the *symbolic ritual* so that "the **Torah** (*Teaching*) of the Lord may be in your mouth."

The Sabbath Torah

Now that you know the basic *meaning* of the term **torah**, take another look at the *testimonies* God wrote on the two stone tablets. See if you can find any **Torah** written there:

> Then God spoke all these words, saying, "I am the LORD your God, who brought you out of the land of Egypt, out of the house of slavery.
>
> **You shall have no** other gods before Me.
>
> **You shall not** make for yourself an idol, or any likeness of what is in heaven above or on the earth beneath or in the water under the earth.
>
> **You shall not** worship them or serve them; for I, the LORD your God, am a jealous God, visiting the iniquity of the fathers on the children, on the third and the fourth generations of those who hate Me, but showing lovingkindness to thousands, to those who love Me and keep My commandments.
>
> **You shall not** take the name of the LORD your God in vain, for the LORD will not leave him unpunished who takes His name in vain.
>
> **Remember** the sabbath day, to keep it holy.
>
> Six days you shall labor and do all your work, but the seventh day is a sabbath of the LORD your God; {in it} you shall not do any work, you or your son or your daughter, your male or your female servant or your cattle or your sojourner who stays with you. For in six days the LORD

made the heavens and the earth, the sea and all that is in them, and rested on the seventh day; therefore the LORD *blessed the sabbath day and made it holy.*

Honor *your father and your mother, that your days may be prolonged in the land which the* LORD *your God gives you.*

You shall not *murder.*

You shall not *commit adultery.*

You shall not *steal.*

You shall not *bear false witness against your neighbor.*

You shall not *covet your neighbor's house; you shall not covet your neighbor's wife or his male servant or his female servant or his ox or his donkey or anything that belongs to your neighbor."*
(Exodus 20:1–17)

The explanation as to *why* the sons of Israel were to conduct the *symbolic ritual* of observing the Sabbath day as one day of rest out of every seven stands out in stark relief among all the *apodictic commandments* in the Ten Commandments. It is the only one of the *testimonies* which not only is not an *apodictic commandment* but also has a supplementary explanation (**Torah**) as to *why* God instituted its observance. That distinguishing characteristic makes it easy to see that the explanatory **Torah** is not the *statute*, which is "Remember the sabbath day, to keep it holy," but is instead the explanation as to *why Corporate* Israel was to conduct that *symbolic ritual—as parabolic pantomime.*

Additionally, the *statute* concerning the Sabbath is the only one of the *testimonies* not directly concerned with protecting the health or well-being of either God or man. That is, the person who breaks any other *commandment* has done something to the detriment of God or his fellow man. By contrast, the observance of the Sabbath every seventh day is strictly a *symbolic ritual* whose observance God instituted for the purpose of illustrating *The (oral) Teaching* Moses had taught the sons of Israel concerning the seventh day of Creation.

From the foregoing, we can be fairly certain that *Corporate* Israel's observance of the Sabbath was a *symbolic ritual* the sons of Israel were supposed to use to *teach* their children the Truth concerning the seventh day of Creation.[15] However, the *written* explanation of the *meaning* and *significance* of *Corporate* Israel's observance of the *symbolic ritual* of the Sabbath is nowhere explicitly called "*Torah*." Nonetheless, that is obviously what it is. But only by understanding that *The Teaching of Moses* (*Torah*) is the *oral* explanation of the *meaning* and *significance* of the *symbolic rituals* mandated by the *statutes*—and by paying close attention to what Exodus 24:12 says concerning the presence of *Torah* in the *testimonies*—do we know for certain that is the case.

The foregoing is not the only evidence in the Hebrew Scriptures that the explantion of the *meaning* and *significance* of the *symbolic ritual* of observing the Sabbath is *Torah*. There are other indications as well. For example, what God says to Moses concerning the Sabbath as a "sign" is an important clue:

> *And the LORD spoke to Moses, saying, "But as for you, speak to the sons of Israel, saying, 'You shall surely observe My sabbaths; for {**this**} **is a sign**[16] **between Me and you** throughout your generations, that you may know that I am the LORD who sanctifies you. Therefore you are to observe the sabbath, for it is holy to you. Everyone who profanes it shall surely be put to death; for whoever does any work on it, that person shall be cut off from among his people. For six days work may be done, but on the seventh*

---

[15] See "Questions & Answers," *The Voice of Elijah*, January 1998, and "Transformed Into the Image and Likeness of God," *The Voice of Elijah*, April 2003.

[16] Because of its use in connection with the miracles of Moses (Ex. 4:8, 9, 17, 28, 30; 7:3; 10:1, 2), there is a tendency to attach more *meaning* to the Hebrew word for "sign" (*'ot*) than what it actually carries. The term does not have the nuance of "convincing sign/wonder." It conveys only the notion of "visible reminder." That is clear from its use to denote:

1. The rainbow as the sign of God's covenant with Noah (Gen. 9:12, 13, 17).

2. Circumcision as the sign of God's covenant with Abraham (Gen. 17:11).

3. The blood on the doorposts and lintel as a sign that God would observe and pass over the house (Ex. 12:13).

4. The standards of the twelve tribes of Israel (Num. 2:2).

5. The bronze censers of Korah and his company that were made into plating for the altar (Num. 16:38).

day there is a sabbath of complete rest, holy to the LORD; whoever does any work on the sabbath day shall surely be put to death. So the sons of Israel shall observe the sabbath, to celebrate the sabbath throughout their generations as a perpetual covenant.' **It is a sign between Me and the sons of Israel forever;** *for in six days the LORD made heaven and earth, but on the seventh day He ceased {from labor,} and was refreshed."* *(Exodus 31:12–17)*

In Exodus 13:9–17 above, we saw that God established the *symbolic ritual* of the Feast of Unleavened Bread to provide a "sign" the people could use to teach their children.[17] In this passage, Moses confirms that their observance of the *symbolic ritual* of the Sabbath was for that same purpose—to provide a "sign." Logic alone suggests that both signs had *teaching* as their common purpose. So we can be fairly certain that Moses' *oral* explanation of the *meaning* and *significance* of *Corporate* Israel's observance of the *symbolic ritual* of the Sabbath was *Torah*. Yet there is still more scriptural evidence that argues this was the case.

Exodus 16:4 plainly states that God intended the *symbolic ritual* of gathering manna to be a *test* that would reveal whether the sons of Israel would "walk in the *Torah*"[18] Moses had already explained to them:

Then the LORD said to Moses, "Behold, I will rain bread from heaven for you; and the people shall go out and gather a day's portion every day, ***that I may test them, whether or not they will walk in My instruction."*** *(Exodus 16:4)*

Since the *statute* governing the daily gathering of manna conflicted with another *statute*—the Sabbath *Torah*—the strict observance of both of these *symbolic rituals* was not possible. That is, one could not gather manna every day of the week and still rest (not do any such work) on the seventh day of the week. Therefore, the Lord resolved the conflict by indicating

---

[17] Exodus 13:9, 16.

[18] Keep in mind that ***torah*** has been translated "instruction" in this verse.

the people should observe the *symbolic ritual* of gathering manna by gathering enough for two days on the sixth day. That would make it possible for them to observe the *symbolic ritual* of resting on the seventh day, which was the Sabbath:

> *So it came about at evening that the quails came up and covered the camp, and in the morning there was a layer of dew around the camp. When the layer of dew evaporated, behold, on the surface of the wilderness there was a fine flake-like thing, fine as the frost on the ground. When the sons of Israel saw {it}, they said to one another, "What is it?" For they did not know what it was. And Moses said to them, "It is the bread which the LORD has given you to eat. This is what the LORD has commanded, 'Gather of it every man as much as he should eat; you shall take an omer apiece according to the number of persons each of you has in his tent.'" And the sons of Israel did so, and {some} gathered much and {some} little. When they measured it with an omer, he who had gathered much had no excess, and he who had gathered little had no lack; every man gathered as much as he should eat. And Moses said to them, "Let no man leave any of it until morning." But they did not listen to Moses, and some left part of it until morning, and it bred worms and became foul; and Moses was angry with them. And they gathered it morning by morning, every man as much as he should eat; but when the sun grew hot, it would melt. Now it came about on the sixth day they gathered twice as much bread, two omers for each one. When all the leaders of the congregation came and told Moses, then he said to them, "This is what the LORD meant: Tomorrow is a sabbath observance, a holy sabbath to the LORD. Bake what you will bake and boil what you will boil, and all that is left over put aside to be kept until morning." So they put it aside until morning, as Moses had ordered, and it did not become foul, nor was there any worm in it. And Moses said, "Eat it today, for today is a sabbath to the LORD; today you will not find it in the field. Six days you shall gather it, but on the seventh day, {the} sabbath, there will be none." And it came about on the seventh day that some of the people went out to gather, but they found none. Then the LORD said to Moses, "How long do you refuse to keep **My commandments and My instructions**? See, the LORD has given you the sabbath; therefore He gives you bread for two days on the sixth day. Remain every man in his place; let no man go out of his place on the seventh day." So the people rested on the seventh day.*
>
> *(Exodus 16:13–30)*

The combination of the *symbolic ritual* for gathering manna with the *symbolic ritual* for observing the Sabbath day of rest every seventh day *meant* there was not just one *statute*—one *symbolic ritual*—to be observed on the Sabbath; there were two. That explains why the Hebrew words **torah** (*Teaching*) and **mitzvah** (*commandment*) are both plural in God's question to Moses: "How long do you refuse to keep My *commandments* and My *instructions*?" That also explains why He immediately follows His question with an explanation of how He intended the two *symbolic rituals* to be combined:

> *"See, the LORD has given you the sabbath; therefore He gives you bread for two days on the sixth day. Remain every man in his place; let no man go out of his place on the seventh day." So the people rested on the seventh day.*
> *(Exodus 16:29–30)*

In contrast to every other *statute*—*symbolic ritual*—in the Mosaic legislation, God included only the *statute* mandating the Sabbath in the *testimonies* He wrote on "the two tablets of the *testimonies*." The reason for that lies squarely in the function for which He ordained the seventh day as a day of rest. The observance of the Sabbath by the sons of Israel was *meant* to be the sign of His eternal covenant with them just as the rainbow is the sign of His covenant with Noah[19] and circumcision was the sign of His covenant with Abraham:[20]

> *"So the sons of Israel shall observe the sabbath, to celebrate the sabbath throughout their generations as a perpetual covenant. It is a sign between Me and the sons of Israel forever; for in six days the LORD made heaven and earth, but on the seventh day He ceased {from labor,} and was refreshed."*
> *(Exodus 31:16–17)*

The *symbolic ritual* of the sons of Israel observing the Sabbath as a sign of their covenant with God was intended to

---

[19] Genesis 9:12, 13, 17.

[20] Genesis 17:11.

serve as a visual illustration that explained the essence of the
oral Torah (*Teaching*) they were to *hand down*. That is why the
Prophet Ezekiel assailed *Corporate* Israel not only generally for
breaking God's *statutes* and *judgments* but also specifically for
failing to maintain a proper observance of the Sabbath:

> *"And I said to their children in the wilderness, 'Do not walk in the statutes
> of your fathers, or keep their ordinances, or defile yourselves with their
> idols. I am the* LORD *your God;* **walk in My statutes, and keep My
> ordinances, and observe them. And sanctify My sabbaths; and they
> shall be a sign between Me and you, that you may know that I am
> the* LORD *your God.' But the children rebelled against Me; they did not
> walk in My statutes, nor were they careful to observe My ordi-
> nances,** by which, {if} a man observes them, he will live;* **they profaned
> My sabbaths.** *So I resolved to pour out My wrath on them, to accom-
> plish My anger against them in the wilderness. But I withdrew My hand
> and acted for the sake of My name, that it should not be profaned in the
> sight of the nations in whose sight I had brought them out. Also I swore to
> them in the wilderness that I would scatter them among the nations and
> disperse them among the lands, because* **they had not observed My
> ordinances, but had rejected My statutes, and had profaned My
> sabbaths,** *and their eyes were on the idols of their fathers."*
> (*Ezekiel 20:18–24*)

Torah *in Deuteronomy*

The evidence in Exodus, Leviticus, and Numbers indicates
God gave Moses a *written Torah* at Mt. Sinai, just as the Jews
have claimed for thousands of years. That *written Torah* was the
Torah (*Teaching*) that explained the *meaning* and *significance* of
the *statute* mandating the observance of the Sabbath. That was
the only **Torah** (*Teaching*) that God wrote on "the two tablets of
the *testimonies*." However, He also *delivered* an *oral Torah* to
Moses in the wilderness of Sinai. That *oral Torah* included an
explanation of the *meaning* and *significance* of all the other *statutes* that governed the *symbolic rituals* of the sacrificial cult.[21]

---

[21] Deuteronomy 5:31.

Insight into this bit of Truth presents yet another issue to be resolved. In spite of the fact that the *written Torah* Moses *received* is obviously the *Torah* that God inscribed on the stone tablets, the Jews still claim the entire Pentateuch is the *written Torah* that God gave to Moses. So how did the Rabbis come to believe the *written Torah* was the Pentateuch instead of just the Sabbath *Torah* God wrote on the two stone tablets? They did so because of statements Moses made to the sons of Israel shortly before his death.

As I explained above, Exodus, Leviticus, and Numbers contain a *written* record of Moses *receiving* both a *written Torah* (*Teaching*) and an *oral Torah* (*The Teaching of Moses*) from God in the wilderness of the Sinai peninsula. In that account, the term *torah* refers to an explanation (both *written* and *oral*) of the *meaning* and *significance* of the *symbolic rituals* mandated by the *statutes* of God. That is because teaching is the basic purpose of every *statute* in those three books of the Scriptures. That is, all of the *symbolic rituals* of the sacrificial cult were *meant* to teach *The Teaching of Moses nonverbally* through *parabolic pantomime*.

One cannot deny, however, that every legal dictate that God *delivered* to *Corporate* Israel through Moses (not just the *statutes* governing the *symbolic rituals* of the sacrificial cult) must have been intended, in one way or another, to teach the people something about God. Therefore, the *meaning* and *significance* of all of the *commandments* of God—the *apodictic commandments* and the *judgments,* as well as the *statutes*—must have been explained by the *oral Torah* that Moses *received* from God. That is made abundantly clear by Moses' use of the term *torah* in the Book of Deuteronomy.

In his final words, Moses refers to the contents of the Book of Deuteronomy as the embodiment of all the stipulations of the covenant God made with *Corporate* Israel. At that time, he repeatedly called all the covenant stipulations "this *Torah*"[22] and

---

[22] Harper, *Not All Israel Is Israel*, pp. 58 ff.

"this commandment," clearly seeking to identify the entire corpus of covenant stipulations—*judgments* as well as *statutes*—as *Torah* in a way that had not been the case during the wilderness wandering of Israel. In so doing, he intentionally expanded the scope of the term *torah*, including within it much more than just the few *statutes* governing the *symbolic rituals* of the tabernacle cult that God had required the people to observe in the wilderness.

Why would Moses make such a drastic change in his use of terminology?[23] In seeking the answer to that question, the logical place to begin is by looking at all the occurrences of the term *torah* in the Book of Deuteronomy.

1. "All the Words" of Deuteronomy are *Torah*:

Across the Jordan in the land of Moab, **Moses undertook to expound this** LAW, *saying,* "The LORD *our God spoke to us at Horeb, saying, 'You have stayed long enough at this mountain. Turn and set your journey, and go to the hill country of the Amorites, and to all their neighbors in the Arabah, in the hill country and in the lowland and in the Negev and by the seacoast, the land of the Canaanites, and Lebanon, as far as the great river, the river Euphrates. See, I have placed the land before you; go in and possess the land which the* LORD *swore to give to your fathers, to Abraham, to Isaac, and to Jacob, to them and their descendants after them.'"* (Deuteronomy 1:5–8)

"And it shall be with him, and he shall read it all the days of his life, that he may learn to fear the LORD *his God,* **by carefully observing all the words of this** LAW **and these statutes***, that his heart may not be lifted up above his countrymen and that he may not turn aside from the com-*

---

[23] In making this statement, I am obviously viewing the Pentateuch from the perspective of one who believes Moses wrote it. I realize most scholars prefer to cling to their recently contrived *tradition* which holds the Pentateuch to be nothing more than the redacted product of an anonymous editor who drew from several earlier sources. That theory hardly merits recognition except to state that had its author understood what the author of the Pentateuch *meant* by what he said, he might have been less likely to resort to such fantasy.

mandment, to the right or the left; in order that he and his sons may continue long in his kingdom in the midst of Israel."
(Deuteronomy 17:19–20)

"So it shall be on the day when you shall cross the Jordan to the land which the LORD your God gives you, that you shall set up for yourself large stones, and coat them with lime and **write on them all the words of this** LAW, when you cross over, in order that you may enter the land which the LORD your God gives you, a land flowing with milk and honey, as the LORD, the God of your fathers, promised you."
(Deuteronomy 27:2–3)

"And you shall write on the stones **all the words of this** LAW very distinctly."
(Deuteronomy 27:8)

"Cursed is he who does not confirm **the words of this** LAW by doing them." And all the people shall say, "Amen."
(Deuteronomy 27:26)

"If you are not careful to observe **all the words of this** LAW which are written in this book, to fear this honored and awesome name, the LORD your God, then the LORD will bring extraordinary plagues on you and your descendants, even severe and lasting plagues, and miserable and chronic sicknesses. And He will bring back on you all the diseases of Egypt of which you were afraid, and they shall cling to you. Also every sickness and every plague which, not **written in the book of this** LAW, the LORD will bring on you until you are destroyed."
(Deuteronomy 28:58–61)

"The LORD shall never be willing to forgive him, but rather the anger of the LORD and His jealousy will burn against that man, and every curse which is written in this book will rest on him, and the LORD will blot out his name from under heaven. Then the LORD will single him out for adversity from all the tribes of Israel, according to all the curses of the covenant which are **written in this book of the** LAW."
(Deuteronomy 29:20–21)

"The secret things belong to the LORD our God, but the things revealed belong to us and to our sons forever, that we may observe **all the words of this** LAW."
(Deuteronomy 29:29)

*"Then the LORD your God will prosper you abundantly in all the work of your hand, in the offspring of your body and in the offspring of your cattle and in the produce of your ground, for the LORD will again rejoice over you for good, just as He rejoiced over your fathers; if you obey the LORD your God to keep His commandments and His statutes which are **written in this book of the** LAW, if you turn to the LORD your God with all your heart and soul."*
(Deuteronomy 30:9–10)

*So **Moses wrote this** LAW **and gave it to the priests**, the sons of Levi who carried the ark of the covenant of the LORD, and to all the elders of Israel. Then Moses commanded them, saying, "At the end of {every} seven years, at the time of the year of remission of debts, at the Feast of Booths, when all Israel comes to appear before the LORD your God at the place which He will choose, you shall read **this** LAW in front of all Israel in their hearing. Assemble the people, the men and the women and children and the alien who is in your town, in order that they may hear and learn and fear the LORD your God, and be careful to observe **all the words of this** LAW. And their children, who have not known, will hear and learn to fear the LORD your God, as long as you live on the land which you are about to cross the Jordan to possess."*
(Deuteronomy 31:9–13)

*And it came about, when **Moses finished writing the words of this** LAW **in a book until they were complete**, that Moses commanded the Levites who carried the ark of the covenant of the LORD, saying, "Take **this book of the** LAW and place it beside the ark of the covenant of the LORD your God, that it may remain there as a witness against you."*
(Deuteronomy 31:24–26)

*When Moses had finished speaking all these words to all Israel, he said to them, "Take to your heart all the words with which I am warning you today, which you shall command your sons to observe carefully, {even} **all the words of this** LAW. For it is not an idle word for you; indeed it is your life. And by this word you shall prolong your days in the land, which you are about to cross the Jordan to possess."*
(Deuteronomy 32:45–47)

"Moses charged us with a LAW,
A possession for the assembly of Jacob."
(Deuteronomy 33:4)

And of Levi he said,
"{Let} Thy Thummim and Thy Urim {belong} to Thy godly man,
Whom Thou didst prove at Massah,
With whom Thou didst contend at the waters of Meribah;
Who said of his father and his mother,
'I did not consider them;'
And he did not acknowledge his brothers,
Nor did he regard his own sons,
For they observed Thy word,
And kept Thy covenant.
They shall teach *Thine ordinances to Jacob,*
And **Thy LAW** *to Israel.*
They shall put incense before Thee,
And whole burnt offerings on Thine altar.
O LORD, bless his substance,
And accept the work of his hands;
Shatter the loins of those who rise up against him,
And those who hate him, so they may not rise {again}."
(Deuteronomy 33:8–11)

2. Testimonies, Statutes, and Judgments are Torah:

"Or **what great nation is there that has statutes and judgments as** **righteous as this whole LAW which I am setting before you** **today?"**
(Deuteronomy 4:8)

Now **this is the LAW** *which Moses set before the sons of Israel;* **these** **are the testimonies and the statutes and the ordinances which** **Moses spoke** *to the sons of Israel, when they came out from Egypt,* *across the Jordan, in the valley opposite Beth-peor, in the land of Sihon* *king of the Amorites who lived at Heshbon, whom Moses and the sons* *of Israel defeated when they came out from Egypt.*
(Deuteronomy 4:44–46)

"If any case is too difficult for you to decide, between one kind of homi- *cide or another, between one kind of lawsuit or another, and between one* *kind of assault or another, being cases of dispute in your courts, then* *you shall arise and go up to the place which the LORD your God chooses.* *So you shall come to the Levitical priest or the judge who is {in office}* *in those days, and you shall inquire {of them,} and they will declare to*

you the verdict in the case. And you shall do according to the terms of
the verdict which they declare to you from that place which the LORD
chooses; and you shall be careful to observe according to all that they
teach you. ***According to the terms of the LAW which they teach you,***
and according to the verdict which they tell you, you shall do; you
shall not turn aside from the word which they declare to you, to
the right or the left."
(Deuteronomy 17:8–11)

A quick reading of Moses' final words to the sons of Israel
in the passages above clearly indicates he intended the term
torah to include much more than just an explanation of the
meaning and *significance* of the *statutes* that governed the *sym-*
bolic rituals of the sacrificial cult. Therefore, the evidence in
Exodus, Leviticus, and Numbers stands in sharp contrast to
Moses' statements in Deuteronomy, where he obviously
includes *judgments* as a part of "this whole ***Torah***." That can
only *mean* he intended his reader to understand that the *judg-*
ments also governed *symbolic rituals* which were *meant* to *teach*.
He says as much in the following passage:

"See, ***I have taught you statutes and judgments just as the LORD***
my God commanded me*, that you should do thus in the land where*
you are entering to possess it. So keep and do {them}, for that is your
wisdom and your understanding in the sight of the peoples who will
hear all these statutes and say, 'Surely this great nation is a wise and
understanding people.' For what great nation is there that has a god so
near to it as is the LORD our God whenever we call on Him? Or ***what***
great nation is there that has statutes and judgments as righteous
as this whole law which I am setting before you today?"
(Deuteronomy 4:5–8)

Nowhere in his account of Israel's wilderness wandering
(Exodus, Leviticus, and Numbers) does Moses ever refer to
the civil/criminal *judgments* as ***Torah***. Therefore, by specifically
subsuming an explanation of the conditional *judgments* under
the rubric "this whole ***Torah***," he has clearly elevated the *sym-*
bolic rituals of all of the *commandments* to the status of ***Torah***. In
the next chapter, I will begin to explain the circumstances

under which Moses made that radical change. For now, it is enough to note that the evidence from Deuteronomy makes it quite clear that God must have intended *Corporate* Israel's observance of the entire legal code of the Mosaic Covenant to be an integrated set of *symbolic rituals* the sons of Israel could use to teach His Truth to subsequent generations.

Deuteronomy states that Moses wrote this "expanded" *Torah* on a scroll and gave it to the priests. The priests, in turn, were expected to use that scroll to teach the people the things they needed to know about the covenant stipulations:

> So **Moses wrote this** LAW **and gave it to the priests**, *the sons of Levi who carried the ark of the covenant of the LORD, and to all the elders of Israel. Then Moses commanded them, saying, "At the end of {every} seven years, at the time of the year of remission of debts, at the Feast of Booths, when all Israel comes to appear before the LORD your God at the place which He will choose, you shall read* **this** LAW *in front of all Israel in their hearing. Assemble the people, the men and the women and children and the alien who is in your town, in order that they may hear and learn and fear the LORD your God, and be careful to observe* **all the words of this** LAW. *And their children, who have not known, will hear and learn to fear the LORD your God, as long as you live on the land which you are about to cross the Jordan to possess."*
> (Deuteronomy 31:9–13)

From the foregoing, it becomes apparent that the Book of Deuteronomy is the source of the Jewish belief that the *written Torah* is the Pentateuch. Throughout Deuteronomy, Moses repeatedly says the legal stipulations he wrote on the scroll he gave the priests were "this *Torah*."[24] That would seem to settle the issue. We are, after all, talking about the first edition of the Scriptures—the edition penned by Moses himself. However, there is much more to the story than readily meets the eye. Moses calls the *written* text of the Pentateuch "this *Torah*" only because *he hid the Truth of the oral Torah in that written text.*

---

[24] Deuteronomy 1:5; 4:8; 17:18, 19; 27:3, 8, 26; 28:58, 61; 29:21, 29; 30:10; 31:9, 11, 12, 24, 26; 32:46.

The Rabbis erred because they were unaware of what Moses was referring to by "this *Torah*." Their ignorance in that regard was due to the fact that the sons of Israel had long since given up *The (oral) Teaching of Moses* and had fallen for Satan's "big lie." So the Rabbis incorrectly made Moses' use of the term *torah* in Deuteronomy apply retroactively to the time of the wilderness wandering—the time when he *received* both *written Torah* and *oral Torah*. Thus the entire Pentateuch became identified as the *written Torah* that God *delivered* to Moses. In one sense, that is a legitimate designation, since teaching is the purpose of everything Moses recorded in the Pentateuch. Yet that half-truth should not be allowed to conceal the fact that the Pentateuch is not the original *written Torah*.

The *written Torah* that God *delivered* to Moses can only be found in the *testimonies* that were written by the finger of God on "the two tablets of the *testimonies*." Moses *received* that *Torah* while he was on the Mountain of God. Therefore, any other *Torah* he *received* from God must have been *oral Torah*, in spite of its having subsequently been recorded in *written* form in the Pentateuch.

Where should one look to gain insight into the *content* of the *oral Torah* that Moses *received* from God in the wilderness of Sinai? The most logical place to begin would be where Moses concealed the most important parts of it—in the first five books of the Hebrew Scriptures. Yet even if one understands all that Moses recorded there, the possibility still exists that the Jews are correct in asserting that God *orally delivered* much more *Teaching* to Moses than he recorded in the first five books of the Old Testament. The Prophets indicate the Jews are undoubtedly correct in that assertion, since they provide much more detail concerning God's purpose in the life, death, and resurrection of Jesus Christ. The remaining volumes in this series will explain the evidence that supports that conclusion.

Summary

It is important that you, the reader, understand the *meaning* and *significance* of the five terms I have explained thus far, since I am going to build on the basic distinction I have shown you exists between the *testimonies, statutes, judgments, commandments,* and *torah.* Therefore, let's review briefly.

As I explained in the first three chapters, the *testimonies* are the Ten Commandments that God wrote on the two stone tablets; the *judgments* are the legal stipulations containing condition(s) which make the *judgment* of a *judge* necessary; and the *statutes* are those dictates which mandate limits of one sort or another.

In contrast to these three terms, the Hebrew term translated "*commandment*" has both a specific and a general referent. Specifically, it refers to the *apodictic* "thou shalt" and "thou shalt not" commands. But Moses also uses it at times to refer generally to any of the *commandments*—the *statutes* and *judgments*—that derive from those *apodictic commandments.*

In this chapter, I explained that the Hebrew term **torah** refers specifically to an explanation of the legal stipulations that governed the *symbolic rituals* for which teaching was the primary purpose. Consequently, Moses indicates that the only *Torah* he taught the sons of Israel during the wilderness wandering was an *oral* explanation of the *meaning* of the *symbolic rituals* governed by the *statutes.* But shortly before his death, Moses expanded the scope of *Torah* to include an *oral* explanation of all of the *commandments* he *received* from God. He specifically included the conditional *judgments* as part of the *Torah* because he gave the priests responsibility for supervising the judges of Israel at that time.

It is clear from the foregoing that God gave Moses both an *oral Torah* and a *written Torah* at Mt. Sinai. The *written Torah* was an explanation of the solitary *statute* in the Ten Commandments that mandated the *symbolic ritual* of observing the

Sabbath. By contrast, there are accounts of Moses *receiving oral Torah* throughout the Pentateuch. However, the Jews are undoubtedly correct in their understanding that Moses *received* more *oral Torah* than he recorded in the Pentateuch. The Pentateuch contains only part of *The (oral) Teaching* that Moses *received* at Mt. Sinai. The Prophets supply sufficient insight to understand the rest. But if one ever hopes to master the *oral Torah* the sons of Israel were supposed to *hand down—orally*—from one generation to the next, one must begin by paying close attention to what Moses wrote.

All of the above information is absolutely essential to an accurate understanding of *The Mystery* that Moses and the other Prophets of Israel hid in the Hebrew Scriptures. However, one also needs insight into the key role played by Moses, the first Prophet of Israel, to see exactly how God intended the sons of Israel to *hand down* His *oral Torah* (*The Teaching of Moses*) from one generation to the next. We will investigate that next.

CHAPTER 5:

MOSES, PROPHET OF GOD

In light of the true *meaning* of the Hebrew word **torah** and the way Moses used it in the Pentateuch, it is obvious the scriptural record should provide at least some insight into *The (oral) Teaching* that God *delivered* to Moses to *hand down* to the sons of Israel as an *oral tradition*. It is just as clear that *The Teaching of Moses* must reside in the *meaning* and *significance* of the *symbolic rituals* of the sacrificial cult and the other legal prescriptions that God required the sons of Israel to observe. That much, at least, is easy enough to comprehend. Achieving a complete understanding of *The (oral) Teaching of Moses* is a bit more difficult.

The major difficulty related to the quest for insight into *The Teaching of Moses* lies in determining where Moses hid an explanation of the *meaning* and *significance* of the *symbolic rituals* in the *written* text of the Scriptures and how to coax those things out of hiding. That is the ultimate objective of The Resurrection Theology Series.[1] My only purpose in this current

---

[1] A forthcoming volume in The Resurrection Theology Series—*The Inheritance of the Believer*—will provide a basic explanation of how the rituals and laws of the Pentateuch convey *The Teaching of Moses*.

series[2] is to show you how, from Genesis through Revelation, the Scriptures are an account of what happened to *The (oral) Teaching of Moses.* They do that cryptically by referring to it as *"The Way."*[3] Before I can show you that, however, I must first show you exactly when Moses first *received oral* **Torah**. Contrary to what one might expect, it was not on the Mountain of God. Not at all. Moses *received* an understanding of *The Teaching* quite some time before that, and his instruction in the *parabolic imagery* of *The Mystery*[4] continued long after he came down from the mountain.

According to the biblical text, God spoke the *testimonies,* which were for the most part a series of *apodictic commandments,* from a cloud that rested atop Mt. Sinai. As we have seen, the *testimonies* contained the only *written* **Torah** that Moses *received* at Mt. Sinai. God inscribed that **Torah**—the **Torah** that explained the *meaning* and *significance* of the *symbolic ritual* of observing a Sabbath day of rest every seventh day—on "the two tablets of the *testimonies*" He gave Moses while Moses was on the mountain. The biblical text specifically states that **Torah** was *written* on those stone tablets along with "the commandment"—"for their instruction":

> Now the LORD *said to Moses, "Come up to Me on the mountain and remain there, and **I will give you the stone tablets with the law and the commandment which I have written for their instruction.***" (Exodus 24:12)

God most definitely gave Moses *written* **Torah** while he was on the mountain. But keep in mind, Moses *received* that *written* **Torah** *after* he went up the mountain.

---

[2] *The Mystery of Scripture* series will ultimately fill at least three volumes.

[3] See L. Harper, *The Way, The Truth, The Life.* The Jewish literature from the Intertestamental Period and the writings of the Early Church Fathers use the same terminology to refer to *The Teaching.*

[4] In these pages, *The Mystery* is used interchangeably with *The Teaching.* As explained in the introduction, *The Mystery* becomes *The Teaching* when it is known and reverts back to *The Mystery* when it is lost.

Logic alone dictates a much more extensive *oral **Torah*** must have accompanied the briefly worded *written **Torah*** that God inscribed on the tablets. However, Exodus 25:1–31:18 is the only record we have of what God said to Moses while he was on Mt. Sinai. And that account only details various instructions that God gave Moses concerning how to construct the tabernacle and how to conduct its *symbolic rituals*. Those instructions appear to be nothing more than straightforward statements concerning how to do this and how to do that. So that tells us Moses must have *received* an even more comprehensive *oral* explanation of the *meaning* and *significance* of those things—as *oral **Torah***—some other time.[5] The question is: When?

Moses tells us he understood much of *The (oral) Teaching* (***Torah***) even before he went up the mountain to *receive* "the two tablets of the *testimonies*." Moreover, he carefully (and cryptically) explains how he came into possession of that information. For one thing, he says God had already given him *oral **Torah*** at the foot of the mountain. That *oral **Torah*** explained "all the commandments, EVEN the statutes and the judgments"[6] that he was supposed to teach the people:

> *"These words the LORD spoke to all your assembly at the mountain from the midst of the fire, {of} the cloud and {of} the thick gloom, with a great voice, and He added no more. And He wrote them on two tablets of stone and gave them to me. And it came about, when you heard the voice from the midst of the darkness, while the mountain was burning with fire, that you came near to me, all the heads of your tribes and your elders. And you said, 'Behold, the LORD our God has shown us His glory and His greatness, and we have heard His voice from the midst of the fire; we have seen today that God speaks with man, yet he lives. Now then why should we die? For this great fire*

---

[5] The sole purpose of the tabernacle and its sacrificial cult was to provide **torah** through *symbolic ritual*. That is, the *symbolic rituals* of the tabernacle cult were intended "*to point out The Way in which Israel was to walk.*" That being the case, God must have told Moses exactly what those rituals *meant*.

[6] Deuteronomy 5:31.

*will consume us; if we hear the voice of the LORD our God any longer, then we shall die. For who is there of all flesh, who has heard the voice of the living God speaking from the midst of the fire, as we {have}, and lived? Go near and hear all that the LORD our God says; then speak to us all that the LORD our God will speak to you, and we will hear and do {it}.' And the LORD heard the voice of your words when you spoke to me, and the LORD said to me, 'I have heard the voice of the words of this people which they have spoken to you. They have done well in all that they have spoken. Oh that they had such a heart in them, that they would fear Me, and keep all My commandments always, that it may be well with them and with their sons forever! Go, say to them, "Return to your tents." **But as for you, stand here by Me, that I may speak to you all the commandments and the statutes and the judgments which you shall teach them, that they may observe {them} in the land which I give them to possess.'"***
(Deuteronomy 5:22–31)

That passage makes it abundantly clear that Moses *received oral* **Torah** immediately *after* God spoke the *testimonies* from the cloud and *before* he went up the Mountain of God to *receive* the two stone tablets on which the *testimonies* were *written*. It agrees precisely with the parallel account in Exodus 20, where it says the people were afraid to approach the cloud after it descended on the mountain and God spoke "the *testimonies*" from the top of the mountain. So they asked Moses to be their intermediary and tell them what God said. He did as they requested, thereby functioning as God's first Prophet:

*And all the people perceived the thunder and the lightning flashes and the sound of the trumpet and the mountain smoking; and when the people saw {it,} they trembled and stood at a distance. **Then they said to Moses, "Speak to us yourself and we will listen; but let not God speak to us, lest we die."** And Moses said to the people, "Do not be afraid; for God has come in order to test you, and in order that the fear of Him may remain with you, so that you may not sin." **So the people stood at a distance, while Moses approached the thick cloud where God {was.}***
(Exodus 20:18–21)

Immediately following that account, the biblical text lists some of the legal stipulations that God *delivered* to Moses *orally* at the foot of Mt. Sinai.[7] From a survey of those stipulations, it is clear that the *oral Torah* that Moses *received* included an explanation of the *meaning* and *significance* of *apodictic commandments* as well as conditional *judgments*. However, the stipulations governing the Feast of Unleavened Bread, the Feast of Harvest, and the Feast of Ingathering[8] are also mentioned in the things that Moses *received orally* at the foot of the mountain. Since those are all called "eternal statutes" elsewhere,[9] Moses must have *received* an explanation of the *meaning* and *significance* of those *statutes* as well. That confirms Deuteronomy 5:31, which says God *delivered* "all this commandment, EVEN the statutes and judgments" (my translation) to Moses *orally* after He spoke the Ten Commandments from the cloud.

The biblical text makes it abundantly clear that Moses *received* an *oral Torah* (*Teaching*) from God at the foot of Mt. Sinai. That *oral Torah* explained various things related to the *meaning* and *significance* of the *statutes* and *judgments* as well as the *apodictic commandments*. However, when Moses tells us what God said to him, he mentions only *judgments* (here translated "ordinances") and "the words of the Lord":

> *Then He said to Moses, "Come up to the LORD, you and Aaron, Nadab and Abihu and seventy of the elders of Israel, and you shall worship at a distance. Moses alone, however, shall come near to the LORD, but they shall not come near, nor shall the people come up with him." Then* **Moses came and recounted to the people all the words of the LORD and all the ordinances;** *and all the people answered with one voice, and said, "All the words which the LORD has spoken we will do!" (Exodus 24:1–3)*

In spite of that general statement in which Moses describes what God said to him *before* he went up the mountain to *receive*

---

[7] Exodus 21:1–23:33.
[8] Exodus 23:14–19.
[9] Leviticus 23:21, 31, 41.

the two stone tablets on which God had inscribed the *written Torah*,[10] Deuteronomy 5:31 clearly says Moses *received* an *oral Torah* (*Teaching*) related to specific *commandments, statutes,* and *judgments* at that time. But what about prior to that time? Is there any evidence that Moses *received oral Torah* (*Teaching*) before Israel arrived at Mt. Sinai? Certainly, and one need only apply a small bit of deductive reasoning to determine where that evidence is hidden.

Exodus 24:15 says Moses ascended the Mountain of God immediately *after Corporate* Israel ratified the Mosaic Covenant. Before he went up the mountain, however, he first made a *written* record of the things God told him to teach the people. The biblical text says he wrote those things in "the Book of the Covenant"[11] and then used that *written* record as the basis for Israel's *reaffirmation* of its covenant with God:[12]

> *And **Moses wrote down all the words of the** Lord. Then he arose early in the morning, and built an altar at the foot of the mountain with twelve pillars for the twelve tribes of Israel. And he sent young men of the sons of Israel, and they offered burnt offerings and sacrificed young bulls as peace offerings to the* Lord. *And Moses took half of the blood and put {it} in basins, and the {other} half of the blood he sprinkled on the altar. **Then he took the book of the covenant and read {it} in the***

---

[10] Deuteronomy 5:31.

[11] The purpose of the "Book of the Covenant" was most likely the same as the "Book of *the Teaching*" that Moses wrote and gave to the Levitical priests (Deut. 31:9–11, 24–29). It was intended to supplement the "witness" of "the *testimonies*" while providing a written basis for teaching the sons of Israel the *meaning* of the *symbolic rituals.*

[12] As has already been pointed out above (see p. 56, fn. 6), the sons of Israel entered into a covenant relationship with God at the time of the first Passover. They renewed that covenant after a three-day journey into the wilderness (Ex. 15:25). One could hardly expect them to accept such an obligation without some explanation as to why God demanded that they adhere to His *statutes* and *judgments.* That alone would indicate Moses must have taught the sons of Israel what the covenant stipulations *meant* prior to arriving at Mt. Sinai. If that be so, God would have given Moses an *oral Torah* at some earlier time.

hearing of the people; and they said, "All that the LORD has spoken we will do, and we will be obedient!" So Moses took the blood and sprinkled {it} on the people, and said, "Behold the blood of the covenant, which the LORD has made with you in accordance with all these words." Then Moses went up with Aaron, Nadab and Abihu, and seventy of the elders of Israel, and they saw the God of Israel; and under His feet there appeared to be a pavement of sapphire, as clear as the sky itself. Yet He did not stretch out His hand against the nobles of the sons of Israel; and they beheld God, and they ate and drank.
(Exodus 24:4–11)

Moses clearly indicates the sons of Israel willingly entered into a covenant relationship with God at the foot of Mt. Sinai. The specific characteristics of a covenant ceremony are all present—the reading and recording of covenant terms, the sacrifice of an animal, and the eating of a covenant meal. Therefore, *Corporate* Israel quite obviously stood in a covenant relationship with God *before* Moses ascended the mountain to *receive* the *written* **Torah** that God inscribed on "the two tablets of the testimonies." Again, simple logic dictates Moses must have taught the people something concerning the *meaning* and *significance* of the *symbolic rituals* of that covenant *before* they ratified it. His explanation of those covenant terms would have been part of the *oral* **Torah** he *received* from God at the foot of the mountain.

However, God's statement concerning *Corporate* Israel's sin while Moses was still on the mountain provides overwhelming evidence that Moses already understood a comprehensive *oral* **Torah** *(The Teaching)* long *before* the sons of Israel arrived at Mt. Sinai. It also confirms that Moses had also taught the sons of Israel the basics of that *oral* **Torah** *(Teaching) before* he ascended the mountain:

Now when the people saw that Moses delayed to come down from the mountain, the people assembled about Aaron, and said to him, "Come, make us a god who will go before us; as for this Moses, the man who brought us up from the land of Egypt, we do not know what has become of him." And Aaron said to them, "Tear off the gold rings which are in

the ears of your wives, your sons, and your daughters, and bring {them} to me." Then all the people tore off the gold rings which were in their ears, and brought {them} to Aaron. And he took {this} from their hand, and fashioned it with a graving tool, and made it into a molten calf; and they said, "This is your god, O Israel, who brought you up from the land of Egypt." Now when Aaron saw {this,} he built an altar before it; and Aaron made a proclamation and said, "Tomorrow {shall be} a feast to the LORD." So the next day they rose early and offered burnt offerings, and brought peace offerings; and the people sat down to eat and to drink, and rose up to play. Then the LORD spoke to Moses, "Go down at once, for your people, whom you brought up from the land of Egypt, have corrupted {themselves.} **They have quickly turned aside from the way which I commanded them**. *They have made for themselves a molten calf, and have worshiped it, and have sacrificed to it, and said, 'This is your god, O Israel, who brought you up from the land of Egypt!'" And the LORD said to Moses, "I have seen this people, and behold, they are an obstinate people. Now then let Me alone, that My anger may burn against them, and that I may destroy them; and I will make of you a great nation."*
(Exodus 32:1–10)

God's simple declaration that the sons of Israel had "quickly *turned aside from The Way* which I commanded them" is decisive. That is no vague statement with uncertain *meaning*. The Hebrew idiom "turn aside from *The Way*" carries specific *meaning* with potent implications in this context. *The Way* is a *parabolic image* the Prophets use to *parabolically* depict *The Teaching* (the *oral Torah*) that Moses *received* at Mt. Sinai and *handed down* to the sons of Israel in the wilderness.[13] Jesus Christ and the Apostles use it as well.[14] The Hebrew idiom "walk in *The Way*" *means* "believe *The Teaching*," and the idiom "turn aside from *The Way*" *means* "to disbelieve *The Teaching*." Since only a fool would contend someone can disbelieve something he has not heard explained, logic again demands Moses must have

---

[13] See L. Harper, *The Way, The Truth, The Life.*
[14] Matthew 5:25, 7:13–14, 21:32; John 14:1–6; Acts 9:2, 18:25–26, 19:9, 23, 24:14, 22; Hebrews 9:8; 2 Peter 2:2, 15, 21.

explained *The Way* (*The Teaching*) to the sons of Israel *before* he ascended Mt. Sinai.

Only by understanding the *meaning* and *significance* of the idiom "turn aside from *The Way*" and other idioms related to it does one have any hope at all of ever gaining complete insight into the *content* of the *oral Torah* Moses taught. Therefore, the second volume in this series will show how the Prophets used the Hebrew idioms "walk in *The Way*" and "turn aside from *The Way*" to conceal the *meaning* of what they wrote about the loss of *The Teaching of Moses*. For now, it is enough to show when and how Moses first *received oral Torah*.

The idiom "turn aside from *The Way*" reveals Moses must have taught the sons of Israel *The Teaching* (*The Way*) before he ascended the Mountain of God. How would they have been able to "turn aside from *The Way*," that is, "disbelieve *The (oral) Teaching of Moses*," if it were otherwise? That idiomatic statement would make no sense if the sons of Israel did not already know what God expected of them. But one does not have to rely solely on insight into the *meaning* of that one idiom alone. In several passages, the Scriptures explicitly state that Moses taught the sons of Israel *The (oral) Teaching* he *received* from God long *before* they arrived at Mt. Sinai. The following is but one:

> And it came about the next day that Moses sat to judge the people, and the people stood about Moses from the morning until the evening. Now when Moses' father-in-law saw all that he was doing for the people, he said, "What is this thing that you are doing for the people? Why do you alone sit {as judge} and all the people stand about you from morning until evening?" And Moses said to his father-in-law, "Because **the people come to me to inquire of God. When they have a dispute, it comes to me, and I judge between a man and his neighbor, and make known**[15] **the statutes of God and His laws.**"
> (Exodus 18:13–16)

---

[15] Moses uses a verb here which has the general *meaning* "make known" (*hôdîʿa*) rather than one with a more specific *meaning*. The importance of the author's use of such terminology becomes evident later on.

Since the word translated "laws" in that passage is the plural form of the Hebrew word *torah*, the text of Exodus 18:13–16 confirms that Moses understood the *meaning* and *significance* of more than one of the *symbolic rituals*. Therefore, God must have given him insight into those things at some earlier time.

Moses told his father-in-law that the people were coming to him to "inquire of God." Given what Moses said immediately after that, one could assume that *meant* they were coming to him only for the purpose of having a dispute settled. But that is not necessarily the case with everyone who came "to inquire of God." Some of them may have come just to hear Moses "make known" the *meaning* and *significance* of the *statutes* of God and His *Torah*.

In saying Moses would "make known" the *statutes* of God and His *Torah*, the Hebrew text clearly indicates Moses was teaching the people an *oral Torah*—that is, *The (oral) Teaching of Moses*—that he already understood. That *oral Torah* would have almost certainly explained the *meaning* and *significance* of the *statutes*—the *symbolic rituals*—that God had previously commanded the sons of Israel to observe. That indicates Moses was settling disputes according to his understanding of God's *statutes, judgments,* and *commandments*—that is, according to the *oral Torah (The Teaching)* he had already *received*.

One need not rely only on Moses' statements in this one passage alone. Jethro's assessment of Moses' activities also confirms that Moses had already *received*, and was teaching, an *oral Torah before* the sons of Israel arrived at the Mountain of God. On finding that Moses was overly burdened with the dual tasks of judging and teaching the sons of Israel, Jethro gave his son-in-law some sage advice. It was blunt and to the point. He advised him to separate the two tasks, letting others judge Israel so that he could devote himself to teaching:

And Moses' father-in-law said to him, "The thing that you are doing is not good. You will surely wear out, both yourself and these people who

are with you, for the task is too heavy for you; you cannot do it alone.
Now listen to me: I shall give you counsel, and God be with you. You be
the people's representative before God, and you bring the disputes to
*God, then **teach them the statutes and the laws, and make known***
***to them the way in which they are to walk**, and the work they are to*
do. Furthermore, you shall select out of all the people able men who fear
God, men of truth, those who hate dishonest gain; and you shall place
{these} over them, {as} leaders of thousands, of hundreds, of fifties and
of tens. And let them judge the people at all times; and let it be that
every major dispute they will bring to you, but every minor dispute
they themselves will judge. So it will be easier for you, and they will
bear {the burden} with you."
(Exodus 18:17–22)

Now there is no doubt. In talking about Moses' responsibility as a Teacher, Jethro recommended that Moses "enlighten" the sons of Israel in regard to the *statutes* and the **Torah** and "make known to them *The Way* in which they are to walk."[16] That is exactly the same "way" God said the people had "turned aside from" while Moses was on the Mountain of God *receiving* the stone tablets.[17] That is, Jethro is speaking in terms of the *meaning* of the Hebrew idiom "walk in *The Way*," which is the opposite of the idiom "turn aside from *The Way*." It *means* "to believe *The Teaching*."

The two Hebrew idioms—"walk in *The Way*" and "turn aside from *The Way*"—do not occur in just the two passages

---

[16] This passage is *significant* for several reasons. First, it tells us Moses, on the advice of Jethro, delegated the day-to-day responsibility for judging Israel to others but retained for himself the responsibility for teaching Israel. More importantly, it alerts us to the fact that the author is being extremely careful in his use of terminology related to Moses teaching Israel. He does not tell us Jethro used either of the two Hebrew verbs most commonly associated with the teaching task—*limmed* ("to teach, cause to learn") or *yarah* ("to point out, show"). Rather, he says Jethro used a verb that is seldom used outside the Prophets—*hizhir* ("to give light, enlighten")—and the verb Moses used earlier—*hôdî'a* ("to make known"). We will discuss the *significance* of this terminology later.

[17] Exodus 32:8.

you have seen so far. They can be found scattered throughout the Hebrew Scriptures, and their frequent occurrence will allow us to define their *meaning* with a great deal of precision later on. Their *meaning* will, in turn, solidly confirm that Moses was indeed teaching the sons of Israel an *oral Torah* (*The Teaching*) on this occasion. For now, we must content ourselves with ascertaining when God began to give Moses *oral Torah* (*The Teaching*).

Moses and God's Torah

Exodus 18:13–20 clearly indicates that Moses was teaching the sons of Israel an *oral Torah* (*The Teaching*) before they arrived at Mt. Sinai. But what was the content of that *Torah*? When did he learn it? How was he taught? In trying to answer these questions, we will find that Moses—the author of the Pentateuch—has intentionally hidden, or at least partially veiled from sight, the unique role that his brother Aaron played in God's delivery of the sons of Israel from Pharaoh's bondage.

Moses plainly states the sons of Israel had observed the following four *symbolic rituals* before they arrived at Mt. Sinai. Therefore, an explanation of their *meaning* and *significance* must have been part of the *oral Torah* (*The Teaching*) that Moses was teaching the people when Jethro offered his advice. Keep in mind that the Hebrew word *torah* has been translated either "law" or "instruction" in the following passages:

1. The Passover Ritual:

> *"The same LAW shall apply to the native as to the stranger who sojourns among you." Then all the sons of Israel did {so;} they did just as the LORD had commanded Moses and Aaron. And it came about on that same day that the LORD brought the sons of Israel out of the land of Egypt by their hosts.*
> *(Exodus 12:49–51)*

2. The Ritual for the Feast of Unleavened Bread:

"And it shall serve as a sign to you on your hand, and as a reminder on your forehead, that the LAW of the LORD may be in your mouth; for with a powerful hand the LORD brought you out of Egypt. Therefore, you shall keep this ordinance at its appointed time from year to year."
(Exodus 13:9–10)

3. The Ritual for Gathering Manna:

Then the LORD said to Moses, "Behold, I will rain bread from heaven for you; and the people shall go out and gather a day's portion every day, that I may test them, whether or not they will walk in My INSTRUCTION."
(Exodus 16:4)

4. The Sabbath Ritual:

Then the LORD said to Moses, "How long do you refuse to keep My commandments and My INSTRUCTIONS? See, the LORD has given you the sabbath; therefore He gives you bread for two days on the sixth day. Remain every man in his place; let no man go out of his place on the seventh day." So the people rested on the seventh day.
(Exodus 16:28–30)

When Moses accepted Jethro's advice, he must have already understood the *oral **Torah*** related to those *symbolic rituals*, which were mandated by four of the *statutes* listed in Chapter 2. Therefore, *The (oral) Teaching of Moses* mentioned in Exodus 18:17–20 included, at the very least, an explanation of their *meaning* and *significance*. That *means* God must have given Moses insight into that *oral **Torah*** at some earlier time. If so, Moses should give some indication as to when, where, and how that happened. Indeed he does. He begins in the account of his calling, where he describes his first encounter with God:

Now Moses was pasturing the flock of Jethro his father-in-law, the priest of Midian; and he led the flock to the west side of the wilderness, and came to Horeb, the mountain of God. And the angel of the LORD appeared to him in a blazing fire from the midst of a bush; and he looked,

and behold, the bush was burning with fire, yet the bush was not consumed. So Moses said, "I must turn aside now, and see this marvelous sight, why the bush is not burned up." When the LORD saw that he turned aside to look, God called to him from the midst of the bush, and said, "Moses, Moses!" And he said, "Here I am." Then He said, "Do not come near here; remove your sandals from your feet, for the place on which you are standing is holy ground." He said also, "I am the God of your father, the God of Abraham, the God of Isaac, and the God of Jacob." Then Moses hid his face, for he was afraid to look at God.
(Exodus 3:1–6)

Having gotten Moses' attention, God then explained what He wanted Moses to do. The text not only reveals God intended to deliver the sons of Israel from Egypt, it also says He had chosen Moses as their deliverer:

*And the LORD said, "I have surely seen the affliction of My people who are in Egypt, and have given heed to their cry because of their taskmasters, for I am aware of their sufferings. So **I have come down to deliver them from the power of the Egyptians, and to bring them up from that land to a good and spacious land,** to a land flowing with milk and honey, to the place of the Canaanite and the Hittite and the Amorite and the Perizzite and the Hivite and the Jebusite. And now, behold, the cry of the sons of Israel has come to Me; furthermore, I have seen the oppression with which the Egyptians are oppressing them. **Therefore, come now, and I will send you to Pharaoh, so that you may bring My people, the sons of Israel, out of Egypt.**"*
(Exodus 3:7–10)

After hearing what God had in mind, Moses questioned his own qualifications. God responded by giving him a "sign" whereby Moses would know God had chosen him. He told Moses that he would bring the sons of Israel back to worship Him at the mountain where he had encountered the burning bush. That "sign" would confirm that God had sent him:

*But Moses said to God, "Who am I, that I should go to Pharaoh, and that I should bring the sons of Israel out of Egypt?" And He said, "Certainly I will be with you, and this shall be the sign to you that it is I who have sent you: **when you have brought the people out of Egypt, you***

shall worship God at this mountain."
(Exodus 3:11–12)

At that point, Moses turns to a more enigmatic concern. In a question that seems somewhat odd—if not completely irrelevant—to the modern mind-set, Moses asks God to reveal His "name":[18]

Then Moses said to God, "Behold, I am going to the sons of Israel, and I shall say to them, 'The God of your fathers has sent me to you.' Now they may say to me, 'What is His name?' What shall I say to them?" And God said to Moses, "I AM WHO I AM"; and He said, "Thus you shall say to the sons of Israel, 'I AM has sent me to you.'"[19] And God, furthermore, said to Moses, "Thus you shall say to the sons of Israel, 'The LORD, the God of your fathers, the God of Abraham, the God of Isaac, and the God of Jacob, has sent me to you.' This is My name forever, and this is My memorial-name to all generations."
(Exodus 3:13–15)

---

[18] The names of divine beings were of special interest to the ancients. Not only Moses but also Jacob inquired concerning the divine name (Gen. 32:29; cf. Jdg. 13:17–18). The ancient mind-set is puzzling to the modern mind. Yet in the mythologies of the peoples of the Fertile Crescent, one finds evidence that the ancients believed a person or thing could not exist without a name because the name was, in some sense, the embodiment of the individual. Therefore, it was not something that was chosen and bestowed without due consideration (Gen. 25:24–26; 30:6–24).

Moreover, a name could be changed as the circumstances of the person changed (Gen. 17:5, 15; 32:28). The ancient Semites were particularly concerned that a man have a son who could "cause his name to be remembered" after he died (2 Sam. 18:18). The next chapter will explain some things regarding the importance the ancients attached to having a male offspring who could continue to "carry" one's "name." Future volumes in The Resurrection Theology Series will continue the explanation regarding *The Name* that is begun in this work.

[19] The *meaning* and *significance* of God's revelation of His name has perplexed biblical scholars for centuries. Yet God apparently explained as much as He felt was required, and one must assume that what He said was intelligible to Moses. For an explanation of the text, see "They Got God at a Fire Sale Price (and a Whole Lot More Than They Bargained For)—Part I," *The Voice of Elijah*, April 1999.

Having answered Moses' inquiry concerning His name, God then told him to return to Egypt and begin the mission for which he had been called. God specifically told him to ask Pharaoh to allow the sons of Israel to go three days into the wilderness to offer sacrifices to God:[20]

> *"Go and gather the elders of Israel together, and say to them, 'The LORD, the God of your fathers, the God of Abraham, Isaac and Jacob, has appeared to me, saying, "I am indeed concerned about you and what has been done to you in Egypt. So I said, I will bring you up out of the affliction of Egypt to the land of the Canaanite and the Hittite and the Amorite and the Perizzite and the Hivite and the Jebusite, to a land flowing with milk and honey."' And they will pay heed to what you say; and **you with the elders of Israel will come to the king of Egypt, and you will say to him, 'The LORD, the God of the Hebrews, has met with us. So now, please, let us go a three days' journey into the wilderness, that we may sacrifice to the LORD our God.'"***
> *(Exodus 3:16–18)*

Although God began by telling Moses what to ask of Pharaoh, He went on to remind him that His ultimate goal was to attain much more than just permission for the sons of Israel to offer sacrifices in the wilderness. From the outset, God expected them to plunder the Egyptians and escape completely from bondage:

> *"But I know that the king of Egypt will not permit you to go, except under compulsion. **So I will stretch out My hand, and strike Egypt with all My miracles which I shall do in the midst of it; and after that he will let you go.** And I will grant this people favor in the sight of the Egyptians; and it shall be that when you go, you will not go empty-handed. But every woman shall ask of her neighbor and the woman who lives in her house, articles of silver and articles of gold, and*

---

[20] The three-day journey into the wilderness to offer sacrifices to God is mentioned again in Exodus 8:27. Then, in Exodus 15:22–26, it says the sons of Israel went three days into the wilderness, where God "made for them a statute and a regulation." As stated above (see p. 56, fn. 6), that indicates they ratified a covenant at that time. The sacrifices mentioned were part of the covenant ratification ceremony.

*clothing; and you will put them on your sons and daughters. **Thus you will plunder the Egyptians**."*
(Exodus 3:19–22)

On hearing what God wanted him to do, Moses had doubts that the sons of Israel would believe him. When he raised that issue, God responded by providing a series of three "signs" that Moses could show the sons of Israel. These signs involved his staff, his hand, and water from the Nile River:

> *Then Moses answered and said, "What if they will not believe me, or listen to what I say? For they may say, 'The LORD has not appeared to you.'" And the LORD said to him, "What is that in your hand?" And he said, "A staff." Then He said, "Throw it on the ground." So he threw it on the ground, and it became a serpent; and Moses fled from it. But the LORD said to Moses, "Stretch out your hand and grasp {it} by its tail"—so he stretched out his hand and caught it, and it became a staff in his hand—"that they may believe that the LORD, the God of their fathers, the God of Abraham, the God of Isaac, and the God of Jacob, has appeared to you." And the LORD furthermore said to him, "Now put your hand into your bosom." So he put his hand into his bosom, and when he took it out, behold, his hand was leprous like snow. Then He said, "Put your hand into your bosom again." So he put his hand into his bosom again; and when he took it out of his bosom, behold, it was restored like {the rest of} his flesh. And it shall come about that if they will not believe you or heed the witness of the first sign, they may believe the witness of the last sign. But it shall be that if they will not believe even these two signs or heed what you say, then you shall take some water from the Nile and pour it on the dry ground; and the water which you take from the Nile will become blood on the dry ground."*
> *(Exodus 4:1–9)*

In bringing up the issue of the unbelief of the sons of Israel, Moses appears to be seeking a valid reason why he cannot do what God wants him to do. That supposition is further strengthened by the fact that, after God settled that issue by providing a way for Moses to give the people three different supernatural demonstrations of divine power, Moses fixed on a final issue he felt posed a problem. He pointed out that he was not eloquent:

> *Then Moses said to the LORD, "Please, Lord, I have never been eloquent, neither recently nor in time past, nor since Thou hast spoken to Thy servant; for I am slow of speech and slow of tongue." And the LORD said to him, "Who has made man's mouth? Or who makes {him} dumb or deaf, or seeing or blind? Is it not I, the LORD? Now then go, and I, even I, will be with your mouth, and teach you what you are to say."*
> *(Exodus 4:10–12)*

This passage reveals precisely how Moses *received* instruction from God. The text says God promised He would "point out"[21] ("teach") what Moses was to say while Moses was speaking and then direct his mouth to say what God wanted him to say. Given those circumstances, the education of Moses must have been an ongoing process. Whenever Moses taught the sons of Israel, God was simultaneously "pointing out" what he was to say and making it possible for him to say it. Therefore, when Moses tells us "the Lord said

---

[21] The Hebrew verb used in Exodus 4:12 and 15 is *yarah*, the verbal root of *torah*. Its *significance* in this context should not be overlooked. The text indicates Moses *received* instruction from God *mentally*, with God "pointing out" the things he needed to say. God used this verb instead of one with a *meaning* like "to reveal" or "to make known" because Moses already understood the things he taught Israel. God had only to "point out" the Truth in what Moses already believed. (See "The Passover Parable," *The Voice of Elijah*, July 1991, or *The Passover Parable*.)

This view of the ministry of Moses contradicts conventional wisdom, according to which Moses was the purveyor of an entirely new set of religious concepts. Conventional wisdom is only partly correct. Moses was the purveyor of an entirely new *understanding* of an *already existing* set of religious concepts. *The Teaching of Moses* is all about the death and resurrection of *The Name* of God—the One known to us as Jesus Christ. Moses and the Prophets knew Him as *The Man*, that is, the coming Messiah of Israel. By contrast, the Egyptians believed essentially the same things about the god they knew as Osiris, just as the Canaanites did about their god Baal. That is why the Prophets took *mythological imagery* from these religions and turned it into *parabolic imagery* that speaks concerning Jesus Christ.

unto Moses," it can only *mean* his education was proceeding just as God promised.

In the following passage, God not only specifically states that Moses was a Prophet, He also confirms that He was indeed "pointing out" to Moses what Moses needed to know when he needed to know it. Furthermore, He indicates He worked with all the Prophets the same way He worked with Moses. He put His words in their mouth and told them what to say when they were to say it:

> "For those nations, which you shall dispossess, listen to those who practice witchcraft and to diviners, but as for you, the LORD your God has not allowed you {to do} so. The LORD your God will raise up for you a prophet like me from among you, from your countrymen, you shall listen to him. This is according to all that you asked of the LORD your God in Horeb on the day of the assembly, saying, 'Let me not hear again the voice of the LORD my God, let me not see this great fire anymore, lest I die.' And the LORD said to me, 'They have spoken well. **I will raise up a prophet from among their countrymen like you, and I will put My words in his mouth, and he shall speak to them all that I command him.** And it shall come about that whoever will not listen to My words which he shall speak in My name, I Myself will require {it} of him.'"
> (Deuteronomy 18:14–19)

In a postscript to the Book of Deuteronomy, an anonymous Prophet (most likely Jeremiah) makes the following statement concerning Moses, God's first Prophet—that is, the man who functioned as the first "mouth" of God:

> Now Joshua the son of Nun was filled with the spirit of wisdom, for Moses had laid his hands on him; and the sons of Israel listened to him and did as the LORD had commanded Moses. **Since then no prophet has risen in Israel like Moses, whom the LORD knew face to face**, for all the signs and wonders which the LORD sent him to perform in the land of Egypt against Pharaoh, all his servants, and all his land, and for all the mighty power and for all the great terror which Moses performed in the sight of all Israel.
> (Deuteronomy 34:9–12)

Summary

In this chapter, I explained that even before the sons of Israel arrived at Mt. Sinai, God had already explained to Moses the *meaning* and *significance* of the Passover ritual, the ritual of the Feast of Unleavened Bread, the ritual of gathering manna, and the ritual of observing the Sabbath. Moses taught these things to the sons of Israel as "*The Way* of the Lord."

I also explained how God *delivered The Teaching* to Moses. Prior to the erection of the Tabernacle, in which He began speaking to Moses "face to face," God "pointed out" the things Moses needed to know by "speaking" to him *mentally.*

CHAPTER 6:

AARON, PROPHET OF MOSES

In telling Moses that He would "point out" what he needed to know while he was speaking and also enable him to say it, God had finally given Moses a response he could not counter. Yet even after God had effectively paried all of his objections, Moses was still not completely willing to do what God wanted. He resigned himself to the task nonetheless:

But he said, "Please, Lord, now send {the message} by whomever Thou wilt."
(Exodus 4:13)

As the text indicates, Moses only grudgingly consented to do what God required—provided God couldn't find anyone else to do it. Because Moses' attitude was a whole lot less than what He desired, God immediately responded in anger. Thus it was, as a direct result of Moses not trusting Him, that God made Aaron a "mouth" for Moses in the same way that He had made Moses His Own "mouth":

*Then the anger of the LORD burned against Moses, and He said, **"Is there not your brother Aaron the Levite? I know that he speaks fluently.** And moreover, behold, he is coming out to meet you; when he sees you, he will be glad in his heart. **And you are to speak to him and put the***

words in his mouth; and I, even I, will be with your mouth and his
mouth, and I will teach you what you are to do. Moreover, he shall
speak for you to the people; and it shall come about that he shall be
as a mouth for you, and you shall be as God to him. And you shall
take in your hand this staff, with which you shall perform the signs."
(Exodus 4:14–17)

In this passage, Moses tells us God made Aaron his "prophet" at the same time that He made Moses His Own Prophet. God specifically defines Aaron's role when He tells Moses, "he shall speak for you to the people." At the same time, He reaffirms His promise that He would "point out" ("teach") what Moses needed to know while Moses was speaking. Just as importantly, however, the passage discloses that God expected Moses to use a very definite method of communicating the things he gained by divine revelation.

Moses, the Prophet of God, was supposed to tell Aaron, the "prophet" of Moses, what God had given him to understand. Aaron would then tell the people. Under that arrangement, whenever God "pointed out" something He wanted Moses to teach the people, Moses functioned as the Prophet of God and Aaron functioned as God's Teacher. Take note of that Prophet/Teacher relationship; it will become important to your understanding of the ongoing relationship that God established between the Prophets and Priests (Teachers) of Israel.

A bit later, Moses tells us he and Aaron did just as God commanded them. God "spoke" (*mentally*) to Moses; Moses spoke (*audibly*) to Aaron; and Aaron spoke (*audibly*) to the people, while performing the signs God had given Moses:

Now the LORD said to Aaron, "Go to meet Moses in the wilderness." So
he went and met him at the mountain of God, and he kissed him. And
Moses told Aaron all the words of the LORD with which He had sent him,
and all the signs that He had commanded him {to do.} **Then Moses and**
Aaron went and assembled all the elders of the sons of Israel; and
Aaron spoke all the words which the LORD had spoken to Moses. He

then performed the signs in the sight of the people. So the people believed; and when they heard that the LORD was concerned about the sons of Israel and that He had seen their affliction, then they bowed low and worshiped.
(Exodus 4:27–31)

From that passage, it is readily apparent that Aaron had already assumed his role as Moses' "prophet." In Exodus 4:16 (quoted above), God tells Moses that Aaron is supposed to *"speak for you to the people."* The passage just quoted confirms that is exactly what Aaron did. Although the biblical text does not say God expected Aaron to function in that same role when Moses spoke to the Pharaoh, it does say that both men spoke to the king of Egypt. That indicates they must have used the same method of communication:

*And **afterward Moses and Aaron came and said to Pharaoh**, "Thus says the LORD, the God of Israel, 'Let My people go that they may celebrate a feast to Me in the wilderness.'" But Pharaoh said, "Who is the LORD that I should obey His voice to let Israel go? I do not know the LORD, and besides, I will not let Israel go." **Then they said**, "The God of the Hebrews has met with us. Please, let us go a three days' journey into the wilderness that we may sacrifice to the LORD our God, lest He fall upon us with pestilence or with the sword."*
(Exodus 5:1–3)

The unique relationship that God established between Moses and Aaron explains why the text says *"Moses and Aaron came and said* to Pharaoh" in verse one, and *"they said"* in verse three. Moses spoke to Aaron, and Aaron in turn spoke to the Pharaoh because the two men were continuing to function in the extraordinary *parabolic* roles God had assigned them.

Apparently, Moses thought the relationship he had with his brother Aaron on these two occasions was only temporary. That is revealed by what happened next. Not long after the two spoke to Pharaoh, God "spoke" (*mentally*) to Moses again, telling him things He wanted him to say to the sons of Israel. This time, however, Moses spoke to the people himself.

In contrast to the time before when the people heeded Aaron, they now refused to listen to Moses:

> **God spoke further to Moses and said to him,** *"I am the LORD; and I appeared to Abraham, Isaac, and Jacob, as God Almighty, but {by} My name, LORD, I did not make Myself known to them. And I also established My covenant with them, to give them the land of Canaan, the land in which they sojourned. And furthermore I have heard the groaning of the sons of Israel, because the Egyptians are holding them in bondage; and I have remembered My covenant.* **Say, therefore, to the sons of Israel,** *'I am the LORD, and I will bring you out from under the burdens of the Egyptians, and I will deliver you from their bondage. I will also redeem you with an outstretched arm and with great judgments. Then I will take you for My people, and I will be your God; and you shall know that I am the LORD your God, who brought you out from under the burdens of the Egyptians. And I will bring you to the land which I swore to give to Abraham, Isaac, and Jacob, and I will give it to you {for} a possession; I am the LORD.'"* **So Moses spoke thus to the sons of Israel, but they did not listen to Moses on account of {their} despondency and cruel bondage.**
> *(Exodus 6:2–9)*

The biblical text says the sons of Israel "did not *listen to Moses* on account of {their} despondency and cruel bondage" (emphasis mine). Therefore, we know their lack of response had nothing whatsoever to do with the way Moses talked. However, when God told Moses to speak to Pharaoh again, Moses hesitated. He thought the people had not listened to him because of his inability to speak fluently:

> *Now the LORD spoke to Moses, saying, "Go, tell Pharaoh king of Egypt to let the sons of Israel go out of his land." But Moses spoke before the LORD, saying,* **"Behold, the sons of Israel have not listened to me; how then will Pharaoh listen to me, for I am unskilled in speech?"**
> *(Exodus 6:10–12)*

Since Moses mentions his lack of eloquence again, it is fairly obvious he must have spoken to the people himself rather than speaking through Aaron. That explains why, this time, God accepted his concern as legitimate rather than as just an excuse. In deference to his concerns, God reestablished the same Prophet/Teacher relationship Moses had with Aaron before:

> *Then the LORD spoke to Moses and to Aaron, and gave them a charge to the sons of Israel and to Pharaoh king of Egypt,* to bring the sons of Israel out of the land of Egypt.
> (*Exodus 6:13*)

In that passage, God again commissions Aaron as Moses' "mouth" because Moses was still preoccupied with his lack of fluency. The text says God gave both men together "*a charge* to the sons of Israel and to Pharaoh king of Egypt." Their Prophet/Teacher relationship is obviously in view here because later in the chapter, when the text specifically mentions Moses' concern over his lack of eloquence, it also describes Aaron's reconfirmation as the "prophet" of Moses:

> *It was {the same} Aaron and Moses to whom the LORD said, "Bring out the sons of Israel from the land of Egypt according to their hosts." They were the ones who spoke to Pharaoh king of Egypt about bringing out the sons of Israel from Egypt; it was {the same} Moses and Aaron. Now it came about on the day when the LORD spoke to Moses in the land of Egypt,[1] that the LORD spoke to Moses, saying, "I am the LORD; speak to Pharaoh king of Egypt all that I speak to you." But Moses said before the LORD, "Behold, I am unskilled in speech; how then will Pharaoh listen to me?"* **Then the LORD said to Moses, "See, I make you {as} God to Pharaoh, and your brother Aaron shall be your prophet. You shall speak all that I command you, and your brother Aaron shall speak to Pharaoh that he let the sons of Israel go out of his land."**
> (*Exodus 6:26–7:2*)

This passage mentions the Prophet/Teacher relationship of Moses and Aaron only in the context of their speaking to the

---

[1] The phrase "in the land of Egypt" in this context is intended to point the reader back to the events described in Exodus 6:10–13 rather than to those mentioned in Exodus 4:10–17. The first time Moses raised the issue of his lack of fluency was at "Horeb, the mountain of God" (Ex. 3:1) "in Midian" (Ex. 4:19) rather than "in the land of Egypt."

Pharaoh. The biblical account also confirms that the two did exactly what God commissioned them to do in that regard:

> *So Moses and Aaron did {it;} as the Lord commanded them, thus they did. And Moses was eighty years old and Aaron eighty-three, when they spoke to Pharaoh.*
> *(Exodus 7:6–7)*

In this passage, Moses is concerned only with recounting that he and Aaron spoke to Pharaoh. In Exodus 6:13, however, he specifically said God *"gave them a charge* to the sons of Israel and to Pharaoh king of Egypt, *to bring the sons of Israel out of the land of Egypt."* That means God must have intended the same Prophet/Teacher relationship to govern their ministry to the sons of Israel throughout the entirety of the Exodus from Egypt, which it did.

Moses, Aaron, and Pharaoh

Moses' account of how he and Aaron delivered the sons of Israel from Egypt is replete with evidence that illustrates how the Prophet/Teacher relationship worked in practice. For example, when the two brothers first approached Pharaoh, the king refused to accede to their requests in spite of Aaron's awesome demonstration of the power of Moses' staff.[2] So God spoke to Moses again, telling him what he and Aaron should do the next time they spoke to Pharaoh. Notice how Moses describes their relationship:

> **Then the Lord said to Moses,** *"Pharaoh's heart is stubborn; he refuses to let the people go. Go to Pharaoh in the morning as he is going out to the water, and station yourself to meet him on the bank of the Nile; and you shall take in your hand the staff that was turned into a serpent. **And you will say to him,** 'The Lord, the God of the Hebrews, sent me to you, saying, "Let My people go, that they may serve Me in the wilderness. But behold, you have not listened until now." Thus says the Lord, "By this you shall know that I am the Lord: behold, I will strike the water that is*

---

[2] Exodus 7:8–13.

in the Nile with the staff that is in my hand, and it shall be turned to blood. And the fish that are in the Nile will die, and the Nile will become foul; and the Egyptians will find difficulty in drinking water from the Nile."'" **Then the LORD said to Moses, "Say to Aaron,** *'Take your staff and stretch out your hand over the waters of Egypt, over their rivers, over their streams, and over their pools, and over all their reservoirs of water, that they may become blood; and there shall be blood throughout all the land of Egypt, both in {vessels of} wood and in {vessels of} stone.'"* **So Moses and Aaron did even as the LORD had commanded.** *And he lifted up the staff and struck the water that {was} in the Nile, in the sight of Pharaoh and in the sight of his servants, and all the water that {was} in the Nile was turned to blood.*
(Exodus 7:14–20)

This passage is instructive in that it says God spoke to Moses alone,[3] yet He obviously expected Aaron to carry out His instructions. Yet when Moses describes how the two of them followed God's directives, he doesn't say Aaron did what God had told Moses to tell him to do. He merely says, "he lifted up the staff and struck the water." Moses clearly assumes the reader will understand he is referring to Aaron because of what he has already written. That is tremendously valuable information in light of the fact that Moses often tells us God spoke to him, telling him what to say, yet it does not go on to mention that Aaron carried out God's instructions as Moses' agent.

From the above, we know that God designated Aaron as the one who was to speak to Pharaoh; and we also know that Aaron did that, but only as Moses' "prophet." Yet in the account of the deliverance of the sons of Israel from Egypt, the text invariably says "Moses said to him/Pharaoh."[4] Although Moses clearly expects his readers to understand that he always "spoke" to Pharaoh through his "prophet" Aaron, there is only

---

[3] The verbal and pronominal forms are all singular, which indicates God spoke to only one person—Moses.

[4] Exodus 8:9, 26, 29; 9:29; 10:9, 25, 29.

one indication in the biblical text that Aaron was actually the one speaking to Pharaoh:

> And **Moses and Aaron went to Pharaoh and said to him,** "Thus says the LORD, the God of the Hebrews, 'How long will you refuse to humble yourself before Me? Let My people go, that they may serve Me.'" (Exodus 10:3)

In that one statement alone does Moses state that both he and Aaron "spoke" to Pharaoh. But that indicates Aaron must have spoken to Pharaoh even in those cases where Moses tells us that he "spoke."[5] Moses confirms that is what he *meant* by what he writes later. At the end of his account, he makes it perfectly clear that, although God spoke only to him, both he and Aaron were involved in dealing with Pharaoh:

> Then the LORD said to Moses, "Pharaoh will not listen to you, so that My wonders will be multiplied in the land of Egypt." And **Moses and Aaron performed all these wonders before Pharaoh;** yet the LORD hardened Pharaoh's heart, and he did not let the sons of Israel go out of his land. (Exodus 11:9–10)

---

[5] Moses sometimes says "Aaron stretched out" his staff (Ex. 8:6, 17); at other times, he seems to say he did it himself (Ex. 9:23; 10:13, 22). But his tendency to say "Moses said" when in fact we know Aaron spoke as his "prophet" may apply to the staff as well. That would perhaps explain why he attributed the first few uses of the staff in the presence of Pharaoh to Aaron (cf. Ex. 4:30; 7:19–20; 8:5–6, 16–17) whereas he indicates the last several were his (Ex. 9:8–10, 22–23; 10:12–13, 21–22). We could assume that Moses would have us understand Aaron stretched out the staff in those cases as well, but that he did so as his agent. Actually, a case could be made for the fact that Aaron always wielded the staff for Moses in the same way that he always spoke for Moses. However, that conclusion is not warranted by the evidence.

Moses has told us specifically that Aaron would function as his "prophet." But he has never told us God appointed Aaron as his agent in regard to the staff. Since the biblical text does tell us God commissioned Moses to wield the staff (Ex. 4:17), and we are never explicitly told that Aaron was to wield it except in specific instances, we should not assume Aaron was Moses' agent in regard to the staff. On the contrary, the account of the people grumbling at Massah and Meribah (Ex. 17:1–7) argues against such a conclusion. In that case it is obvious God expected Moses to wield the staff.

Moses, Aaron, and the Sons of Israel

Moses clearly has a tendency to say that he said or did something when it is fairly obvious that Aaron was also involved—even if only as his "prophet." That proclivity has important bearing on how one should understand what Moses wrote. He has already stated specifically in Exodus 6:13 that "the LORD spoke to Moses and to Aaron, and gave them a charge to the sons of Israel and to Pharaoh king of Egypt." That indicates God intended the Prophet/Teacher relationship the two men had while dealing with Pharaoh to continue unchanged in their ministry to the sons of Israel as well. If that be so, there should be some indication of it in the biblical text, as indeed there is.

First of all, when Moses describes his ministry to the sons of Israel, he makes it clear that both he and Aaron were involved. For example, in the following passage, he says God told both of them to "speak to all the congregation of Israel":

*Now **the LORD said to Moses and Aaron** in the land of Egypt, "This month shall be the beginning of months for you; it is to be the first month of the year to you. **Speak to all the congregation of Israel,** saying, 'On the tenth of this month they are each one to take a lamb for themselves, according to their fathers' households, a lamb for each household.'"*
(Exodus 12:1–3)

The verb "speak" in verse 3 is plural, indicating God expected both men to be involved in "speaking" to the sons of Israel. That clearly indicates He expected them to continue the Prophet/Teacher relationship He had already established. But just as Moses did earlier, when he describes the two of them doing what God told them to do, he makes no mention of Aaron. He tells us that he "spoke" to the people:

*Then **Moses called for all the elders of Israel, and said to them,** "Go and take for yourselves lambs according to your families, and slay the Passover {lamb.}"*
(Exodus 12:21)

When God spoke to Moses and Aaron a second time, Moses again tells us God spoke to both of them. This time, however, he relates that they did exactly what God told them to do:

And the LORD said to Moses and Aaron, "*This is the ordinance of the Passover: no foreigner is to eat of it; but every man's slave purchased with money, after you have circumcised him, then he may eat of it. A sojourner or a hired servant shall not eat of it. It is to be eaten in a single house; you are not to bring forth any of the flesh outside of the house, nor are you to break any bone of it. All the congregation of Israel are to celebrate this. But if a stranger sojourns with you, and celebrates the Passover to the LORD, let all his males be circumcised, and then let him come near to celebrate it; and he shall be like a native of the land. But no uncircumcised person may eat of it. The same law shall apply to the native as to the stranger who sojourns among you." Then all the sons of Israel did {so;} **they did just as the LORD had commanded Moses and Aaron.** And it came about on that same day that the LORD brought the sons of Israel out of the land of Egypt by their hosts.*
(Exodus 12:43–51)

That passage indicates both Moses and Aaron were still working together as a team to deliver the sons of Israel from Egypt. It also confirms that Aaron must have been the one speaking even when Moses says he "spoke." What he *means* is, he "spoke" through his "mouth" Aaron. We can be certain of that because the statement "*they did* just as the LORD had commanded Moses and Aaron" is an echo of what Moses told us earlier when Moses is plainly describing them functioning in their Prophet/Teacher relationship:

So Moses and Aaron did {it;} just as the Lord commanded them, thus they did.
(Exodus 7:6)

From what we have seen so far, it is obvious that Moses and Aaron continued to minister jointly as God's "mouth" even after the focus of God's attention shifted away from Pharaoh to the sons of Israel. If that were not so, why would Moses tell us "the Lord said to Moses and Aaron" and "they did just as the Lord had commanded Moses and Aaron"? Why would he even mention Aaron if Aaron were not involved in some way? And why would anyone arbitrarily assume Aaron was involved in some way other than in his assigned role as the "prophet" of Moses?

After Moses describes *Corporate* Israel's observance of the Passover, he completely ignores Aaron's role as his "prophet." Time and again he relates what "God said to Moses"[6] and what "Moses said"[7] to the people. However, that is precisely what he did earlier when he described how he and Aaron worked together to deal with Pharaoh. In that case, it was clear that he was speaking to Pharaoh through Aaron, his "mouth;" yet he almost always says "Moses said to him" or "Moses said to Pharaoh." The lone exception is Exodus 10:3, where he says, "Moses and Aaron ... said."

Taking all of the above into account, it is obvious that Moses' silence regarding Aaron's role cannot be used as evidence that Aaron was not continuing to speak for him as his "mouth." Quite the contrary, one can be certain that Moses was still speaking to the sons of Israel through his "prophet" Aaron. And even after the people left Egypt, Moses and Aaron continued to work together in the same Prophet/ Teacher relationship that God had established. The following passage of Scripture makes that abundantly clear:

> *Then they set out from Elim, and all the congregation of the sons of Israel came to the wilderness of Sin, which is between Elim and Sinai, on the fifteenth day of the second month after their departure from the land of Egypt.* **And the whole congregation of the sons of Israel grumbled against Moses and Aaron in the wilderness. And the sons of Israel said to them,** *"Would that we had died by the LORD's hand in the land of Egypt, when we sat by the pots of meat, when we ate bread to the full; for you have brought us out into this wilderness to kill this whole assembly with hunger."* **Then the LORD said to Moses,**

---

[6] Exodus 13:1; 14:1, 15, 26.

[7] Exodus 13:3; 14:13.

"Behold, I will rain bread from heaven for you; and the people shall go out and gather a day's portion every day, that I may test them, whether or not they will walk in My instruction. And it will come about on the sixth day, when they prepare what they bring in, it will be twice as much as they gather daily." **So Moses and Aaron said to all the sons of Israel,** *"At evening you will know that the LORD has brought you out of the land of Egypt; and in the morning you will see the glory of the LORD, for He hears your grumblings against the LORD; and what are we, that you grumble against us?"* **And Moses said,** *"{This will happen} when the LORD gives you meat to eat in the evening, and bread to the full in the morning; for the LORD hears your grumblings which you grumble against Him. And what are we? Your grumblings are not against us but against the LORD."* **Then Moses said to Aaron, "Say to all the congregation of the sons of Israel,** *'Come near before the LORD, for He has heard your grumblings.'"* *And it came about as* **Aaron spoke to the whole congregation of the sons of Israel,** *that they looked toward the wilderness, and behold, the glory of the LORD appeared in the cloud.*
(Exodus 16:1–10)

In this passage, Moses graphically illustrates the ongoing Prophet/Teacher relationship that existed between him and his brother Aaron. First, he relates what the Lord said to him (v. 4). Next, he records what he and Aaron said to the sons of Israel (v. 6) and what he said (v. 8). Then, he says, "Moses said to Aaron, 'Say to all the congregation'" (v. 9). Finally, he states, "Aaron spoke to the whole congregation of the sons of Israel" (v. 10).

What Moses says in that passage confirms beyond all doubt that the Prophet/Teacher relationship God established between Moses and Aaron continued on after the sons of Israel left Egypt. God spoke to Moses, but Aaron was the one who spoke to the people. Moreover, when Moses says, "Moses and Aaron said to all the sons of Israel" (v. 6), he is merely echoing what he wrote concerning the two men speaking to Pharaoh:

And **Moses and Aaron went to Pharaoh and said to him,** *"Thus says the Lord, the God of the Hebrews, 'How long will you refuse to humble*

yourself before Me? Let My people go, that they may serve Me.'"
(Exodus 10:3)

In that verse, as in Exodus 16:6 above, Moses clearly *means* both men were involved in "speaking" because he was speaking to Aaron, and Aaron was speaking for him as his "prophet." That explains why the people were angry with both men: The two had been working together all along in communicating *The (oral) Teaching* to them. Therefore, the account of the sons of Israel grumbling against Moses and Aaron merely provides additional evidence that Aaron was continuing to speak as the "mouth" of Moses.

Did Moses and Aaron continue working together as a team throughout the entire wilderness wandering? The Hebrew text clearly indicates they did. But the key to gaining insight into the *meaning* of what Moses wrote lies in understanding his mind-set. He did not consider his brother Aaron to be anything more than his "mouth," that is, his "prophet." Therefore, he could say "the Lord said" or "Moses said" with full confidence the alert reader would understand he *meant* God spoke to him, he spoke to Aaron, and Aaron relayed the message to the people. In a few cases, he even gives subtle indicators that is his point of view.

In the following passage, Moses tells us "the Lord spoke to Moses and Aaron." Yet when God says, "Say to them," the imperative verb "say" is singular. That is, it requires a singular subject, which indicates God was speaking to only one person —Moses. Therefore, Moses obviously intends his reader to understand that, although he says God spoke to both him and Aaron, he actually *means* God spoke to him alone, delivering a message intended for both of them. He expects the reader to understand he then told Aaron what God had said and Aaron told the people. However, he also assumes the reader knows God held him alone responsible for ensuring the message was delivered:

And the LORD spoke to Moses and Aaron, saying, "How long {shall I bear} with this evil congregation who are grumbling against Me? I have heard the complaints of the sons of Israel, which they are making against Me. Say to them, 'As I live,' says the LORD, 'just as you have spoken in My hearing, so I will surely do to you; your corpses shall fall in this wilderness, even all your numbered men, according to your complete number from twenty years old and upward, who have grumbled against Me. Surely you shall not come into the land in which I swore to settle you, except Caleb the son of Jephunneh and Joshua the son of Nun.'"
(Numbers 14:26–30)

Later, when Moses describes the two men carrying out God's commands, he once again says "Moses spoke these words to all the sons of Israel":

*And when **Moses spoke these words to all the sons of Israel**, the people mourned greatly.*
(Numbers 14:39)

We have already seen that Moses did exactly the same thing when he described how he and Aaron "spoke" to Pharaoh. In that case, he said time and again, "Moses said to him" or "Moses said to Pharaoh." Yet he also makes it clear that God spoke to him, he spoke to Aaron, and Aaron spoke to the king of Egypt. Although Moses' mind-set may be difficult to understand, he is merely assuming the reader has already read and understood what he wrote concerning Aaron's role as his "prophet." He is the one speaking; Aaron merely mouths his words.

In yet another passage, Moses gives some rather obvious hints that he is intentionally subsuming Aaron's "prophetic" role into his every mention of God speaking to him:

*But on the next day **all the congregation of the sons of Israel grumbled against Moses and Aaron**, saying, "You are the ones who have caused the death of the LORD's people." It came about, however, when the congregation had assembled against Moses and Aaron, that they turned toward the tent of meeting, and behold, the cloud covered it and the glory of the LORD appeared. Then **Moses and Aaron came to the***

front of the tent of meeting, and the LORD spoke to Moses, saying,
"Get away from among this congregation, that I may consume them
instantly." Then they fell on their faces.
(Numbers 16:41–45)

Verse 41 clearly states that the people "grumbled against Moses and Aaron." That can only be because the two were ministering together, telling the people what God had "pointed out" to Moses. Moses even says "Moses and Aaron came to the front of the tent of meeting" (v. 43). But then he says, "the Lord spoke to Moses" and intentionally excludes Aaron. However, when he relates what the Lord said, he uses a plural form of the Hebrew verb "get away," which reveals that God *meant* "both of you get away." That discloses the Lord was indeed *delivering* a message intended for both Moses and Aaron. Lacking insight into the Prophet/Teacher relationship that God established between Moses and Aaron, however, the casual reader would naturally assume God was speaking to Moses alone.

Moses clearly has a distinct tendency to mention only himself rather than repeatedly bringing up the symbiotic relationship he had with his brother. He assumes his readers will read their unique relationship into every account. That is never more obvious than in the following passage:

*Then the sons of Israel, the whole congregation, came to the wilderness of Zin in the first month; and the people stayed at Kadesh. Now Miriam died there and was buried there. And **there was no water for the congregation; and they assembled themselves against Moses and Aaron. The people thus contended with Moses** and spoke, saying, "If only we had perished when our brothers perished before the LORD! Why then have you brought the LORD's assembly into this wilderness, for us and our beasts to die here? And why have you made us come up from Egypt, to bring us in to this wretched place? It is not a place of grain or figs or vines or pomegranates, nor is there water to drink." Then **Moses and Aaron came in from the presence of the assembly to the doorway of the tent of meeting, and fell on their faces. Then the glory of the LORD appeared to them; and the LORD spoke to Moses, saying, "Take the rod; and you and your brother Aaron assemble the congregation and*** *speak to the rock before their eyes, that it may yield its water.[8] You shall thus bring forth water for them out of the rock and let the congregation and their beasts drink." So Moses took the rod from before the LORD, just as He had commanded him; and Moses and Aaron gathered the assembly before the rock. And he said to them, "Listen now, you rebels; shall we bring forth water for you out of this rock?" Then Moses*

---

[8] It is somewhat amusing that God has used this passage of Scripture to confirm the unique relationship Moses had with his brother Aaron. If Moses wrote the Pentateuch, and there is no good reason to doubt that he did, he certainly did his best to downplay his brother's role. One can think of various reasons why he would have done that. The most likely is that by the time he recorded the scriptural account, he had come to regret having raised the issue of his lack of fluency in speaking and thereby having gotten himself into the Prophet/Teacher relationship he had with Aaron.

His attitude toward Aaron in several passages is uniformly negative. In the account of Israel's sin at Mt. Sinai, he lays the fault squarely at Aaron's feet (cf. Ex. 32:21–35). He states that "Moses saw that the people were out of control—for Aaron had let them get out of control" (v. 25) and later, "the Lord smote the people, because of what they did with the calf which Aaron had made" (v. 35). He even lets us know Aaron blatantly lied about his own role in the affair (v. 24). Had it not been for the unique role that Aaron played as Moses' "prophet," he probably would have been the first to be killed by the Levites on that occasion.

After God destroyed Nadab and Abihu because they "offered strange fire before the Lord" (Lev. 10:1–7), Moses angrily upbraided Aaron, contending he had failed to instill in his sons an appropriate attitude toward their responsibility as priests. He then records Aaron's response succinctly: "So Aaron, therefore, kept silent" (v. 3), indicating that Aaron probably would have voiced a contrary opinion had Moses not angrily pointed out his failing.

In his account of Aaron and Miriam rebelling against their brother Moses (Num. 12:1–15), Moses portrays the two in the worst possible light. God struck Miriam with leprosy, but spared Aaron. Again, that was probably because of his position as Moses' "prophet." Aaron, however, grovels before Moses, begging that Miriam be spared the indignity of her condition.

In these three instances, Aaron comes off as an individual with no personal commitment to the task for which God called Moses. That is apparently Moses' opinion of him. The fact that Aaron was also involved in the episode in which Moses struck the rock instead of speaking to it merely serves to sum up Moses' view of Aaron as one prone to rebellion. One would tend to suspect that Aaron was somehow responsible for the rebellion of Moses as well.

lifted up his hand and struck the rock twice with his rod; and water came forth abundantly, and the congregation and their beasts drank.
(Numbers 20:1–11)

Moses is again relating an incident in which the people were contending with him and Aaron. Again he says the Lord spoke only to him alone. But this time he provides enough information for the attentive reader to know what actually happened. When the Lord spoke to Moses, His primary focus was on what He wanted Moses to do. That is obvious because, when God told Moses to "take the rod," He used a singular form of the verb. However, when He said "speak to the rock," He used a plural form,[9] indicating that what He said included both Moses and Aaron.

Logic demands that only one of the two men could "take the rod." But if both were involved when it came time to "speak to the rock," Moses had to speak to Aaron and Aaron had to speak to the rock. That deduction is confirmed by Moses' question in verse 10: "Shall *we* bring forth water for you out of this rock?" But for some reason, Moses did not do what God told him to do.[10] He either refused to speak to Aaron, or Aaron refused to speak to the rock. He struck the rock instead; and God immediately pronounced judgment:

But the LORD said to Moses and Aaron, "Because you have not believed Me, to treat Me as holy in the sight of the sons of Israel, therefore you shall not bring this assembly into the land which I have given them."
(Numbers 20:12)

---

[9] The *significance* of the plural form in this case is too obvious to be overlooked. It is the only plural form in the entire set of instructions God gave Moses on this occasion. Knowing the roles these two men played in their joint ministry, one can hardly miss the point of God's statement. Moses is to speak what God wants said to the rock, but he is to do so through his "prophet" Aaron.

[10] It is one thing to be told you lack the fluency necessary to speak to the king of Egypt or to the sons of Israel. It is quite another to be told you are not fluent enough to speak to a rock. Perhaps in that rebuke lies the reason why Moses struck the rock rather than telling Aaron what to say to it.

In contrast to the preceding passage, the verbal forms in this passage are all plural. That indicates God was angry with both Aaron and Moses. But why would He have been angry with Aaron if Moses was the one who struck the rock? The answer lies in their unique Prophet/Teacher relationship. They had evidently come to a joint decision that they would not speak to the rock because the Scriptures leave no doubt that both were responsible:

> *Now when they set out from Kadesh, the sons of Israel, the whole con-*
> *gregation, came to Mount Hor. Then the LORD spoke to Moses and*
> *Aaron at Mount Hor by the border of the land of Edom, saying, "Aaron*
> *shall be gathered to his people; for he shall not enter the land which I*
> *have given to the sons of Israel, because **you rebelled against My com-***
> ***mand** at the waters of Meribah."*
> *(Numbers 20:22–24)*

The verbal form translated "you rebelled" in verse 24 is plural, clearly indicating both Moses and Aaron had rebelled. Therefore, they must have agreed on the approach they would use in bringing forth water from the rock. That is why God found them both guilty of rebellion.[11] The incident was a sad conclusion to their long and productive ministry for God.

Summary and Conclusion

In the last chapter, we ascertained that Moses *received oral Torah* before the sons of Israel arrived at Mt. Sinai. We also looked into when and how he obtained that insight. We found that God promised Moses He would "point out"[12] what Moses needed to know while Moses was speaking and also make it possible for him to tell others what God had "pointed out" to him.

---

[11] Mention of God's punishment of Moses can be found also in Deuteronomy 1:37; 3:23–29; 31:2 and 34:4–5.

[12] Exodus 4:12, 15–16.

In this chapter, we investigated Aaron's role as the first Teacher of Israel. Exodus 4:14–16 and 6:28–7:2 make it clear that God gave Aaron the specific role of relaying the words of Moses to both the king of Egypt and the sons of Israel. Those passages explain that Aaron spoke for Moses in the same way that a Prophet speaks for God. That *means* Aaron was the one teaching the people even though Moses, God's Prophet, was telling him what he needed to say.

There is no reason to assume the Prophet/Teacher relationship that God established between Moses and Aaron ever changed. On the contrary, unless one discounts the veracity of the biblical text, it is obvious that, when the text says God told Moses to "speak to the sons of Israel"[13] or some such thing, Moses accomplished that by speaking to Aaron. Aaron, in turn, told the sons of Israel what Moses had said.

The knowledge that Moses' "prophet" Aaron was speaking for God's Prophet Moses also provides insight into Moses' tendency to say, "Moses said to the people," when in fact Aaron was the one telling the people what Moses had said. He does exactly the same thing when he says, "Moses said to

---

[13] The majority of the time, the biblical text simply says God spoke to Moses and said something on the order of "Speak to the sons of Israel" (Ex. 14:1, 15; 19:3; 20:22; 25:1; 31:12; Lev. 1:1; 4:1; 7:28; 12:1; 18:1; 19:1; 20:1; 23:1, 9, 23, 33; 24:1; 25:1; 27:1; Num. 4:21; 5:1, 5, 11; 6:1; 9:9; 11:16; 15:1, 37; 16:23; 17:1; 28:1; 34:1 35:1). Other times, it says God spoke to Moses and Aaron and said, "Speak to the sons of Israel" (Ex. 12:1–3; Lev.11:1–2; 15:1–2).

The text sometimes indicates God gave instructions to Moses alone (Ex. 13:1; 14:26; 17:5, 14; 19:9–10; 24:1, 12; 33:1, 17; 34:1, 27; 40:1; Lev. 5:14; 6:1, 8, 19, 24; 8:1; 14:1; 16:2; 17:1; 21:1, 16; 22:1, 17, 26; 24:13; Num. 1:1; 3:5, 11, 14, 40, 44; 4:21; 6:22; 7:4, 11; 8:1, 5, 23; 9:1; 10:1; 11:16; 12:14; 13:1; 14:11; 15:35; 16:36, 44; 18:25; 21:8; 27:6, 12, 18; 31:1, 25). In other places, it says He gave instructions to both Moses and Aaron (Ex. 12:43; Lev. 13:1; 14:33; Num. 2:1; 4:1, 17; 14:26; 16:20; 19:1; 20:23).

On at least two occasions, the Scriptures say God spoke to Aaron directly (Lev. 10:8; Num. 18:1, 8, 20). On another occasion, He spoke to Moses, Aaron, and Miriam (Num. 12:4). As would be expected, after Aaron's death God gives instructions to Eleazar, the man who replaced Aaron (Num. 26:1).

Pharaoh"[14] even though he also tells us Aaron was the one who actually spoke to the Pharaoh. That indicates Pharaoh always dealt with both Moses and Aaron even when only Moses is mentioned.[15]

Aaron continued to speak for Moses as Moses' "prophet" until the time of his death at Mt. Hor. Yet Moses almost always says "Moses said" because, from his perspective, Aaron was nothing more than his "mouth" in the same way that he was God's "mouth." Moses was God's first Prophet. Aaron was His first Teacher/Priest. From Moses' perspective, the function of the Prophet was to teach the Priest. The function of the Priest was to teach the people. Future volumes in this series will demonstrate that fundamental relationship between the Prophets and the Teachers of Israel has never changed throughout the long history of Israel.

The reader should keep in mind the fact that the things explained in this chapter have far-reaching implications for any investigation into *The Mystery of Scripture*. If Aaron always spoke for Moses when God had something to say to the sons of Israel, that *means* Aaron was the one who was actually teaching the people. *He* was the Teacher; Moses was the Prophet. That bit of information explains several enigmatic circumstances related to the Priests' responsibility as the Teachers of Israel. To understand why that is, however, one must not lose sight of the fact that Aaron was not only the "mouth" of Moses, he was also *Corporate* Israel's first High Priest.

---

[14] Exodus 7:14–16; 8:1, 20, 29; 9:1, 13.

[15] Exodus 8:8, 25; 9:27; 10:8, 16, 24; 12:31.

CHAPTER 7:

THE JUDGES OF ISRAEL

All of the information provided to this point is necessary to your accurate understanding of how Moses taught the sons of Israel *The Mystery,* which the Prophets *parabolically* call *"The Way* of the Lord." In Chapter 1, I explained the *meaning* of the Hebrew term translated *"testimonies."* In Chapter 2, I did the same for the two terms translated *"statutes"* and *"judgments."* Then, in Chapters 3 and 4, I explained how these three terms relate to the two terms translated *"commandments"* and *"laws."*

In the last of those two chapters, I also explained how the Hebrew word **torah**—which is normally translated *"law"* but actually *means "teaching"*—relates to *The (oral) Teaching of Moses.* Then, in Chapters 5 and 6, I went on to show how the biblical text reveals that Aaron was the one who actually taught the sons of Israel because Moses lacked confidence in his own ability to speak. Aaron did so, however, only as the *parabolic* "prophet" of Moses. That is, God spoke to His Prophet Moses, who then told Aaron what God had said.

The unique Prophet/Teacher relationship that God established between Moses and Aaron continued until Aaron died. Therefore, the *significance* of Aaron teaching the sons of Israel as the *parabolic* "mouth" of Moses, who was himself the *parabolic* "mouth" of God, should not be ignored. An accurate understanding of specific events described in the Pentateuch depends on it. In this chapter and the next, I will explain some of those events.

The *meaning* and *significance* of the five terms *testimonies, statutes, judgments, commandments,* and **Torah** is yet another key to understanding the Truth of *The Mystery of Scripture.* That is so simply because Moses used these terms to make a careful separation between the different responsibilities held by the leaders of Israel prior to his death. That is, Moses (according to God's Own plan) used the distinction between the *statutes* and *judgments* as the basis on which he delegated specific responsibilities to others so that they might assist him in his ministry to the sons of Israel.

Moses assigned judges the responsibility for judging the sons of Israel according to the *judgments.* He assigned "the priests, the sons of Aaron" responsibility for teaching the sons of Israel *nonverbally* by conducting the *symbolic rituals* of the tabernacle cult that were governed by the *statutes.* All the while, he retained for himself the sole responsibility for teaching the sons of Israel *verbally* (through his "prophet" Aaron) the *oral* **Torah** (*The Teaching of Moses*) that explained the *meaning* and *significance* of all the *testimonies, commandments, statutes,* and *judgments.*

In this chapter, I will explain how Moses delegated to the judges of Israel responsibility for judging the sons of Israel according to the terms of the conditional *judgments.* In the next chapter, I will disclose how he made "the priests, the sons of Aaron" responsible for teaching Israel *nonverbally* by conducting the *symbolic rituals,* that is, the *parabolic pantomimes,* that were mandated by the *statutes.* That chapter will also show how he appointed still others—the entire tribe of Levi—to carry on his judging/teaching ministry after he died.

As an introduction to things I plan to explain later in the series, I will also explain the basic tribal organization of Israel in this chapter, including the "house," the "carriers," and the tribal council. That information is not all that important at this time, but it is essential for understanding things the Prophets recorded later.

Moses and the Judges of Israel

The Hebrew Scriptures indicate 600,000 military-aged men, not to mention women and children, left Egypt under the leadership of Moses.[1] Although God assigned Moses the sole responsibility for judging and teaching all those people, He certainly did not intend him to accomplish that herculean task by himself. Moses found it impossible to judge and teach even one-tenth of one percent (600) of the men. Consequently, he was forced to enlist many of his contemporaries as his assistants. The biblical text indicates their sole function was to help him *judge* Israel.

At first, Moses tried to *judge* and *teach* all of the sons of Israel by himself. He soon discovered that was impossible. So when his father-in-law saw that he was overly burdened with the task of not only *judging* the people according to God's *judgments* but also *teaching* the *oral **Torah*** that explained the *meaning* and *significance* of the *symbolic rituals* mandated by the *statutes*, he offered him some sage advice. Moses was more than willing to listen:

> And it came about the next day that Moses sat to judge the people, and the people stood about Moses from the morning until the evening. Now when Moses' father-in-law saw all that he was doing for the people, he said, "What is this thing that you are doing for the people? Why do you alone sit {as judge} and all the people stand about you from morning until evening?" And Moses said to his father-in-law, "Because **the people come to me**

---

[1] Exodus 12:37.

to inquire of God. When they have a dispute, it comes to me, and **I judge between a man and his neighbor, and make known the statutes of God and His laws**." *And Moses' father-in-law said to him, "The thing that you are doing is not good. You will surely wear out, both yourself and these people who are with you, for the task is too heavy for you; you cannot do it alone. Now listen to me: I shall give you counsel, and God be with you. You be the people's representative before God, and* **you bring the disputes to God, then teach**[2] **them the statutes and the laws, and make known to them the way in which they are to walk, and the work they are to do.** *Furthermore, you shall select out of all the people able men who fear God, men of truth, those who hate dishonest gain; and you shall place {these} over them, {as} leaders of thousands, of hundreds, of fifties and of tens. And let them judge the people at all times; and let it be that every major dispute they will bring to you, but every minor dispute they themselves will judge. So it will be easier for you, and they will bear {the burden} with you. If you do this thing and God {so} commands you,*

---

[2] The Hebrew verb translated "teach" in this passage (*hizhîr*) actually *means* "to enlighten, give light." It carries the nuance of "to warn" or "to enlighten concerning impending danger." It is used that way most of the time (2 Kings 6:10; 2 Chr. 19:10; Ezra 4:22; Ecc. 12:12; and Ez. 3:17, 18, 19, 20, 21; 33:3, 4–9). However, the most instructive use of the verb occurs in Daniel 12:3. The normal English translation of the verb in that verse since the publication of the King James Version (A.D. 1611) has been "shine"/"shine brightly":

And those who have insight will **shine brightly** *like the brightness of the expanse of heaven, and those who lead the many to righteousness, like the stars forever and ever.*
(Daniel 12:3)

That translation derives from the fact that the idiomatic use of the verb in this verse is part of a wordplay on the Hebrew noun *(zôhar)* translated "brightness." That noun is from the same root *(zhr)* as the verb *hizhîr*. A better translation of Daniel's statement would be "those who have insight will enlighten concerning impending danger," in the sense of warning others by providing them insight into the dangers inherent in their personal situation. Daniel is, of course, speaking concerning the impending wrath of God on the final generation of this Age.

then you will be able to endure, and all these people also will go to their place in peace."
(Exodus 18:13–23)

This passage illustrates how the role of the Teacher blended naturally with that of the judge. As Moses said, "I *judge* between a man and his neighbor, and *make known* the *statutes* of God and His *laws*."[3] It is logical that the person or persons responsible for judging according to the *judgments* would also be responsible for explaining ("making known") why God instituted them in the first place. Therefore, when the people came to Moses for him to resolve their disputes on the basis of God's *judgments,* Moses used the occasion to teach them the *meaning* and *significance* of the *judgments* as well as the *statutes.* He could do that because, as his expanded use of the term **torah** in the Book of Deuteronomy indicates, *The (oral) Teaching* that God had given him explained not only the *statutes* having to do with cultic ritual but also the conditional *judgments* of the civil/criminal code.

When Jethro realized Moses faced an impossible task in trying to judge and teach so many people, he suggested Moses delegate responsibility for judging to others so that he could devote himself completely to teaching. Moses tells us he immediately followed his father-in-law's advice:

So Moses listened to his father-in-law, and did all that he had said. And Moses chose able men out of all Israel, and made them heads over the people, leaders of thousands, of hundreds, of fifties and of tens. And they judged the people at all times; the difficult dispute they would bring to Moses, but every minor dispute they themselves would judge.
(Exodus 18:24–26)

As you can see, Moses delegated responsibility for judging Israel to the "heads" who were to assist him in *judging*

---

[3] The term **torah** has been translated "law."

according to the conditional *judgments* God had given. However, he did not also assign them responsibility for explaining *why* God had given *Corporate* Israel all those *judgments*. That is, he did not appoint these men to teach the *Torah—The (oral) Teaching*—associated with each *judgment*. That responsibility remained his alone, as he confirmed shortly before his death:

> *"See, **I have taught**[4] **you statutes and judgments** just as the LORD my God commanded me, that you should do thus in the land where you are entering to possess it."*
> *(Deuteronomy 4:5)*

In Chapter 6, I explained how Moses taught the sons of Israel by speaking through his "mouth" or "prophet" Aaron, who was High Priest of Israel during the wilderness wandering. In Chapter 8, I will explain the *significance* of that fact: Beginning with Aaron, the High Priest who taught the people as the "mouth" of the Prophet Moses, the priests of Israel

---

[4] The Hebrew verb translated "teach" in this passage is *limmed*. It is the only Hebrew verb used to describe the teaching ministry of Moses other than the two verbs used in Exodus 18:16, 20—which are the common verb *hôdî'a* ("to make known") and the relatively uncommon verb *hizhîr* ("to enlighten"). All three verbs indicate speaking was involved. However, the application of these three verbs to Moses' ministry is set out in stark relief by the fact that the verb *yarah* ("to point out") is never used in the Pentateuch with Moses as the subject. It is only used with reference to God (Ex. 4:12, 15; 15:25), Bezalel (Ex. 35:34), and the priests (Lev. 10:11; 14:57; Deut. 17:11; 24:8; 33:10). The verb *limmed* ("to teach") is never used in the Pentateuch outside the Book of Deuteronomy, where it describes the teaching activity of Moses (Deut. 4:1, 5, 14; 5:31; 6:1; 31:19, 22) and the sons of Israel in teaching their children (Deut. 4:10; 11:19). Moreover, it is never used to describe the activity of the priests.

The distinction the author made by his use of the various terms has to do with the way the instruction was carried out. The first three verbs (*limmed, hôdî'a*, and *hizhîr*) imply it was done via the spoken word. That is not necessarily the case with *yarah* ("to point out"). God provided non-verbal teaching to Moses by "pointing out" to Moses what Moses needed to say while he was speaking to Aaron. Bezalel taught by providing a non-verbal example from which others could learn. The priests did the same thing through the *symbolic rituals* of the tabernacle cult.

remained accountable to the Prophets. But that's getting a bit ahead of the story.

By organizing the people into military/judicial units of thousands, hundreds, fifties, and tens, Moses made the "head" of each unit responsible for judging and supervising only the men under his immediate command. If these numbers are intended to represent the actual number of men in each unit rather than just to designate various units—which is by no means certain—this arrangement also made sure each "head" was responsible for judging and supervising no more than the ten "heads" of the next smaller unit under his command.[5] However, even under this organizational scheme, Moses still had the unenviable task of supervising and judging the six hundred "heads" of the six hundred "thousands."

The biblical text indicates Moses found even this more simplified arrangement psychologically burdensome. In his final remarks to the sons of Israel, Moses refers back to the occasion on which he delegated authority to the heads of the military/judicial units of Israel. Read carefully what he says:

> *"The LORD our God spoke to us at Horeb, saying, 'You have stayed long enough at this mountain. Turn and set your journey, and go to the hill country of the Amorites, and to all their neighbors in the Arabah, in the hill country and in the lowland and in the Negev and by the seacoast, the land of the Canaanites, and Lebanon, as far as the great river, the river Euphrates. See, I have placed the land before you; go in and possess the land which the LORD swore to give to your fathers, to Abraham, to Isaac, and to Jacob, to them and their descendants after them.' And I spoke to you at that time, saying, 'I am not able to bear {the burden} of you alone. The LORD your God has multiplied you, and behold, you are this day as the stars of heaven for multitude. May the LORD, the God of your fathers, increase you a thousand-fold more than you are, and bless you, just*

---

[5] There is no valid reason not to assume the unit designations represent the actual number of men per unit.

as He has promised you! **How can I alone bear the load and burden of you and your strife***? Choose wise and discerning and experienced men from your tribes, and I will appoint them as your heads.' And you answered me and said, 'The thing which you have said to do is good.' So I took the heads of your tribes, wise and experienced men, and appointed them heads over you, leaders of thousands, and of hundreds, of fifties and of tens, and officers for your tribes. Then I charged your judges at that time, saying, 'Hear {the cases} between your fellow countrymen, and judge righteously between a man and his fellow countryman, or the alien who is with him. You shall not show partiality in judgment; you shall hear the small and the great alike. You shall not fear man, for the judgment is God's. And the case that is too hard for you, you shall bring to me, and I will hear it.' And I commanded you at that time all the things that you should do.* **Then we set out from Horeb***, and went through all that great and terrible wilderness which you saw, on the way to the hill country of the Amorites, just as the* LORD *our God had commanded us; and we came to Kadesh-barnea."*
(Deuteronomy 1:6–19)

Moses says he delegated responsibility for judging the sons of Israel to the heads of the various units because "I am not able to bear *the burden* of you alone. … How can I alone bear the load and burden of you and your strife?" He even indicates this happened before Israel left Mt. Sinai by saying "Then we set out from Horeb." So he is obviously referring to Exodus 18:18, where he delegated judicial authority to the heads of the military units. His statements confirm our understanding of the events described in Exodus 18, yet they also raise a new issue: What limits, if any, did Moses impose on the "heads" of the military/judicial units?

The first part of Moses' statement alludes to the occasion on which he received advice from his father-in-law, Jethro. However, his reference to his inability to deal with the impossible task of judging the sons of Israel in the face of their strife points to yet another passage of Scripture, where he made a strikingly similar statement. In this second instance, he specifically told God, "I alone am not able to carry all this people, because it is too burdensome for me."[6] A closer look at that account will shed additional light on the subject.

Moses and the Prophets of Israel

When Moses took Jethro's advice and organized the sons of Israel into units of thousands, hundreds, fifties, and tens, he

---

[6] Num. 11:10–30. That statement should raise questions in the mind of the alert reader. Moses must have delegated authority to the heads of the sons of Israel during the census taken in the second month of the second year after Israel left Egypt (Num. 1:1–4:49). To have done so earlier would have necessitated counting the people in violation of the regulations God gave regarding census-taking (Ex. 30:11–16). See *Not All Israel Is Israel*, pp. 124 ff.

The text of Exodus 18:24–26 seems to indicate Moses followed Jethro's advice immediately after he received it, which would mean the events described occurred shortly after the sons of Israel arrived at Mt. Sinai. That is certainly not the case. The Scriptures often place accounts together when they are related topically rather than temporally. You can see that clearly if you read Exodus 18 and then continue reading into the first two verses of Exodus 19. Exodus 18:5 tells you Jethro came to Moses at Mt. Sinai, yet if taken temporally, the first two verses of Exodus 19 seem to indicate Israel set out from Rephidim for Mt. Sinai after Jethro left to return to Midian.

The chronology of the wilderness wandering revolves around specific dates. Israel left Egypt after midnight on the night of the fifteenth day of the first month of their calendar year (Ex. 12), having just ratified a covenant with God by partaking of the Passover meal. They renewed their covenant with God three days later (Ex. 15:25–26). They reached Mt. Sinai in the third month of that year (Ex. 19:1), either on the first day of the month or on the Day of Pentecost, depending on what the phrase "that very day" is taken to *mean*. They renewed their covenant with God again at that time. They erected the tabernacle on the first day of the first month in the second year (Ex. 40:2, 17). They observed Passover beginning at twilight on the fourteenth day of the first month of the second year, and (presumably) some of them observed an alternate Passover beginning on the fourteenth day of the second month (Num. 9:1–14). They began taking a census of Israel on the first day of the second month in the second year (Num. 1:1) and set out from Mt. Sinai on the twentieth day of that same month (Num. 10:11).

gave the heads of these units responsibility for judging the sons of Israel. Although that arrangement alleviated most of his heavy workload, Moses was still left responsible for supervising the six hundred "heads of thousands" who reported directly to him. The problem was, he alone understood the *meaning* and *significance* of the civil/criminal *judgments* so as to be able to advise them in their supervision of the other judges of Israel. That left him with an insurmountable task.

The sons of Israel had already departed from Mt. Sinai and were on their way to Kadesh-barnea when some among them began complaining about the taste of the manna, which was all they had to eat. These troublemakers insisted that God give them meat to eat as well. Before long, the few in Israel who constantly complained had enticed all of the sons of Israel into sin. Eventually, many of the people began weeping openly, lamenting their lack of tasty food. Moses found the situation unbearable and complained to God:

> *Now Moses heard the people weeping throughout their families, each man at the doorway of his tent; and the anger of the LORD was kindled greatly, and Moses was displeased. So Moses said to the LORD, "Why hast Thou been so hard on Thy servant? And why have I not found favor in Thy sight, that Thou hast laid the burden of all this people on me? Was it I who conceived all this people? Was it I who brought them forth, that Thou shouldest say to me, 'Carry them in your bosom as a nurse carries a nursing infant, to the land which Thou didst swear to their fathers'? Where am I to get meat to give to all this people? For they weep before me, saying, 'Give us meat that we may eat!'* **I alone am not able to carry all this people, because it is too burdensome for me.** *So if Thou art going to deal thus with me, please kill me at once, if I have found favor in Thy sight, and do not let me see my wretchedness."*
> *(Numbers 11:10–15)*

God's immediate response was to arrange for the appointment of seventy other men as Prophets:

*The LORD therefore said to Moses, "Gather for Me seventy men from the elders of Israel, whom you know to be the elders of the people and their officers and bring them to the tent of meeting, and let them take their stand there with you. **Then I will come down and speak with you there, and I will take of the Spirit who is upon you, and will put {Him} upon them; and they shall bear the burden of the people with you, so that you shall not bear {it} all alone."***
(Numbers 11:16–17)

That passage specifically explains that God's purpose in appointing the seventy elders[7] as Prophets was to provide Moses assistance in governing the people. However, the passage immediately following it focuses on God's provision of *parabolic* "food" other than manna:

"And say to the people, 'Consecrate yourselves for tomorrow, and you shall eat meat; for you have wept in the ears of the LORD, saying, "Oh that someone would give us meat to eat! For we were well-off in Egypt." Therefore the LORD will give you meat and you shall eat. You shall eat, not one day, nor two days, nor five days, nor ten days, nor twenty days, but a whole month, until it comes out of your nostrils and becomes loathsome to you; because you have rejected the LORD who is among you and have wept before Him, saying, "Why did we ever leave Egypt?"'" But Moses said, "The people, among whom I am, are 600,000 on foot; yet Thou hast said, 'I will give them meat in order that they may eat

---

[7] The term *elder* (Hebrew: *zaqen*) is a generic term that simply *means* "old." The ancient Oriental cultures placed special emphasis on older people as the repository of wisdom. Therefore, the elders of Israel, whether or not they were in a specific position of authority, were looked to in situations where wise decisions were necessary. Hence, God sent Moses to the elders of Israel so they could decide whether the sons of Israel would do as He requested (Ex. 3:16). The elders also decided whether Israel should accept the terms of the covenant God offered (Ex. 19:7), and they were to be involved in deciding various criminal cases as well (Deut. 19:11–13; 21:1–9; 22:13–21; 25:5–10).

*for a whole month.' Should flocks and herds be slaughtered for
them, to be sufficient for them? Or should all the fish of the sea be
gathered together for them, to be sufficient for them?" And the
LORD said to Moses, "Is the LORD's power limited? Now you
shall see whether My word will come true for you or not."
(Numbers 11:18–23)*

That passage seems to indicate that the function of the
seventy elders/Prophets was strictly administrative in nature.
However, since Moses tells us God provided everything the
people needed in the wilderness,[8] the true function of the
elders/Prophets must lie elsewhere. The Truth resides in the
fact that the gathering of manna was a *statute* God had given
in order to test the people.[9] Therefore, God appointed the seventy elders/Prophets not because the people had transgressed
a conditional *judgment* but because they were rebelling
against His *statute*. Moses needed help in putting down their
insurrection and making sure the guilty were punished. So
God must have intended the elders/Prophets to bear responsibility for ensuring that the people adhered to all of the *commandments* of God rather than just the *judgments*. But notice
how God equipped the seventy elders for their task. He prepared them by making them Prophets:

*So Moses went out and told the people the words of the LORD.
Also, he gathered seventy men of the elders of the people, and
stationed them around the tent. Then the LORD came down
in the cloud and spoke to him; and He took of the Spirit who
was upon him and placed {Him} upon the seventy elders.
And it came about that when the Spirit rested upon them,
they prophesied. But they did not do {it} again. But two men
had remained in the camp; the name of one was Eldad and the
name of the other Medad. And the Spirit rested upon them (now
they were among those who had been registered, but had not gone*

---

[8] Deuteronomy 2:7; 8:4.
[9] Exodus 16:4.

out to the tent), and they prophesied in the camp. So a young man ran and told Moses and said, "Eldad and Medad are prophesying in the camp." Then Joshua the son of Nun, the attendant of Moses from his youth, answered and said, "Moses, my lord, restrain them." But Moses said to him, "Are you jealous for my sake? Would that all the LORD's people were prophets, that the LORD would put His Spirit upon them!" Then Moses returned to the camp, {both} he and the elders of Israel.
(Numbers 11:24–30)

The ordination of the seventy elders is separate from, and different than, the appointment of the heads of the various military/judicial units of Israel in Exodus 18:24–26. That is obvious because God's apportionment of His Spirit on the seventy elders occurred *after Corporate* Israel left Mt. Sinai, whereas Moses appointed the heads of the military units *before* they set out for Kadesh-Barnea. That presents an additional conundrum: If the former arrangement was intended to relieve Moses of the burden of judging Israel, why did he need an additional seventy elders? And what was the distribution of the Spirit of prophecy supposed to accomplish for these seventy?

The answers to these questions come from what the biblical text says next. Moses goes on to confirm that, in appointing the seventy elders/Prophets, God was concerned about the punishment of the guilty rather than the provision of food. He says God immediately destroyed those who had been demanding food other than manna:

*Now there went forth a wind from the LORD, and it brought quail from the sea, and let {them} fall beside the camp, about a day's journey on this side and a day's journey on the other side, all around the camp, and about two cubits {deep} on the surface of the ground. And the people spent all day and all night and all the next day, and gathered the quail (he who gathered least gathered ten homers) and they spread {them} out for themselves all around the camp. While the meat was still between their teeth, before it was chewed, **the***

*anger of the LORD was kindled against the people, and the
LORD struck the people with a very severe plague.
(Numbers 11:31–33)*

That reveals God had no intention of granting the people's
demand for any other food.[10] He was only interested in meting
out *judgment* on those who rebelled against any of His *commandments.* So His purpose in ordaining the seventy elders/
Prophets must have been to ensure that anyone found guilty
would be swiftly punished. Their function had to be related to
that of the heads of the military/judicial units. But how was it
related? And what were these men supposed to do? The text
continues to provide the details:

*Then Miriam and Aaron spoke against Moses because of the Cushite
woman whom he had married (for he had married a Cushite
woman); and they said,* **"Has the LORD indeed spoken only
through Moses? Has He not spoken through us as well?"** *And
the LORD heard it. (Now the man Moses was very humble, more
than any man who was on the face of the earth.) And suddenly the
LORD said to Moses and Aaron and to Miriam, "You three come out
to the tent of meeting." So the three of them came out. Then the
LORD came down in a pillar of cloud and stood at the doorway of the
tent, and He called Aaron and Miriam. When they had both come
forward, He said,*
"Hear now My words:
If there is a prophet among you,
I, the LORD, shall make Myself known to him in a vision.
I shall speak with him in a dream.
Not so, with My servant Moses,
He is faithful in all My household;
With him I speak mouth to mouth,

---

[10] In providing food for the guilty before He destroyed them, God was
rebuking Moses for even considering the people's request (v. 13). His
point: If someone questions the validity of one of God's *commandments,* he
is to be judged immediately, and punished without mercy.

Even openly, and not in dark sayings,
And he beholds the form of the LORD.
Why then were you not afraid
To speak against My servant, against Moses?"
So the anger of the LORD burned against them and He departed. But
when the cloud had withdrawn from over the tent, behold, Miriam
{was} leprous, as {white as} snow. As Aaron turned toward Mir-
iam, behold, she {was} leprous. Then Aaron said to Moses, "Oh, my
lord, I beg you, do not account {this} sin to us, in which we have
acted foolishly and in which we have sinned. Oh, do not let her be like
one dead, whose flesh is half eaten away when he comes from his
mother's womb!" And Moses cried out to the LORD, saying, "O
God, heal her, I pray!" But the LORD said to Moses, "If her father had
but spit in her face, would she not bear her shame for seven days? Let
her be shut up for seven days outside the camp, and afterward she
may be received again." So Miriam was shut up outside the camp for
seven days, and the people did not move on until Miriam was
received again.
(Numbers 12:1–15)

To understand why God appointed the seventy elders,
one must first understand the role of the Prophet in God's plan.
Christians erroneously believe the Prophets of Israel were primarily concerned with *predicting* future events. That is not true.
While the Prophets did predict, that was not the essence of
their ministry. They were concerned first and foremost with *the*
restoration and preservation of The Teaching of Moses. Their predic-
tions grew out of their supernaturally revealed knowledge of
The Mystery of God.

Miriam and Aaron challenged Moses' position as the foremost Prophet in Israel because they saw that he was no longer
the only Prophet in Israel. But what does that have to do with
the role of the seventy elders/Prophets? Everything. These two
rebels had just seen God take the prophetic Spirit that rested on
Moses and distribute it to seventy other men, making those

men Prophets as well. Aaron and Miriam then watched in awe as Eldad and Medad talked knowledgeably about the same things Moses had been teaching. Consequently, finding fault with Moses because he had taken a woman not to their liking, they immediately sought to elevate themselves to the status of Prophets with standing equal to him.[11]

God quickly squelched the aspirations of Miriam and Aaron, telling them that, among the Prophets of Israel, Moses stood head and shoulders above the rest because of his more direct relationship with God. He then emphasized His point by giving Miriam good reason to regret her actions. But what motivated Miriam and Aaron to question Moses' authority? To answer that, it is necessary to analyze the circumstances that prompted God to act.

First, Moses asked for help in dealing with Israel's rebellion. God responded by giving seventy elders exactly the same prophetic insight that Moses had because the people had rebelled against a *statute*. Their insight clearly made them equal to Moses in their knowledge of *The Teaching* because Joshua protested when he saw Eldad and Medad "prophesying" to the people in the same way that Moses had been "prophesying" to Aaron:

> So a young man ran and told Moses and said, "Eldad and Medad are prophesying in the camp." Then Joshua the son of Nun, the attendant of Moses from his youth, answered and said, "Moses, my lord, restrain them." But Moses said to him, "**Are you jealous for my sake**? Would that all the LORD's people were prophets, that the LORD would put His Spirit upon them!"
> (Numbers 11:27–29)

---

[11] The biblical text says God spoke to Aaron directly on two occasions (Lev. 10:8; Num. 18:1, 8, 20). The first of these happened before he and Miriam challenged Moses. That may have been what he had in mind as his claim to the title of Prophet. In the case of Miriam, the text of Scripture specifically calls her a "Prophetess" (Ex. 15:20).

Moses chided Joshua for trying to restrain the two Prophets by asking him, "Are you jealous for my sake?" If Eldad and Medad were not equal to Moses in some way, why would Joshua have any reason to be jealous? And if they did not understand and proclaim the same things as Moses, how could they have been Prophets? That reveals the seventy elders/Prophets were able to speak knowledgeably about the very same things Moses taught.

Second, the text says the seventy elders/Prophets prophesied only on that one occasion. However, the prophetic insight they *received* must have somehow equipped them to assist Moses in the overwhelming task of governing the sons of Israel. That is, after all, the reason why they were appointed. Therefore, their prophetic ministry could not have begun and ended with the brief "prophecy" they uttered in the presence of Moses. If that be so, what was their ministry as Prophets supposed to be? The answers begin to surface in the phrasing of Miriam and Aaron's challenge of Moses:

> *"And they said, "Has the LORD indeed spoken only through Moses? Has He not spoken through us as well?" And the LORD heard it.*
> *(Numbers 12:2)*

An accurate understanding of the challenge of Aaron and Miriam lies in the fact that Moses, as a Prophet of God, attained his knowledge of *The Mystery* directly from God through divine revelation.[12] He was not alone. The distinctive characteristic of all of God's Prophets was that they received their understanding of *The Mystery* the same way. Even Miriam had *received*

---

[12] Exodus 25:17–22; 33:7–11. Moses was unique in that he alone *received* divine revelation through face-to-face conversations with God across the veil in the Tent of Meeting (Ex. 33:11). At those times, God "made known" (Hebrew: *hôdî'a*) to Moses *verbally* the things He wanted him to understand as He did on the Mountain of God (Ex. 33:12–13) rather than just "pointing out" (Hebrew: *yarah*) things to him *mentally*.

divine insight on one occasion. That is why Moses calls her a "prophetess" in this passage:

> *For the horses of Pharaoh with his chariots and his horsemen went*
> *into the sea, and the LORD brought back the waters of the sea on*
> *them; but the sons of Israel walked on dry land through the midst*
> *of the sea. And* **Miriam the prophetess, Aaron's sister***, took the*
> *timbrel in her hand, and all the women went out after her with*
> *timbrels and with dancing. And Miriam answered them,*
> *"Sing to the LORD, for He is highly exalted;*
> *The horse and his rider He has hurled into the sea."*
> *(Exodus 15:19–21)*

Miriam obviously *received* divine revelation on at least that one occasion. However, until the appointment of the seventy elders as Prophets, Moses had been the only Prophet in Israel who was the recipient of *continuous* revelation. That is, God had been communicating an ongoing comprehensive understanding of *The Teaching* to him alone. But Moses had not been speaking to the people directly. He had been "prophesying" to Aaron, telling him what God said, and Aaron had been teaching the people, in effect making Aaron the Teacher. But after the ordination of the seventy elders/ Prophets, Moses was no longer the only possible source from which one could gain a knowledge of *The Teaching.*

When Eldad and Medad spoke to the people directly, that prompted Miriam and Aaron to act. Moses himself had not taught publicly. He had been speaking through Aaron. Therefore, when Moses refused to restrain these two as Joshua requested, Miriam and Aaron challenged Moses' authority as the only divinely appointed Teacher of Israel.

The biblical text says the seventy elders/Prophets prophesied only that one time. That *means* their responsibility could not have been to communicate an understanding of *The Teaching* that stood behind God's *commandments.* That is, God did not appoint them to "prophesy" publicly and thereby teach the people the *meaning* and *significance* of the *oral Torah* associated with all the *statutes* and *judgments*. Not at all.

The seventy elders/Prophets could not continue to prophesy to the people because even the Prophet Moses was not speaking to them directly. He was speaking only through his "prophet" Aaron. As long as Aaron was alive, he alone was allowed to explain *The Teaching* to the sons of Israel. You can see, therefore, why God would hardly have allowed these seventy Prophets to do something that even Moses could not do.

Exodus 18:13–26 makes it clear Moses started out with two major responsibilities: (1) to teach Israel and (2) to judge Israel. If the seventy elders/Prophets were not allowed to assist him by teaching anything related to *The Teaching*, their specific function must have been to supervise the heads of the various military/judicial units[13] just as Moses had previously. That *means* they must have been responsible for making sure that all the judges under the six hundred "thousands" judged with "righteous judgment."[14] To do that, they needed to know the *meaning* and *significance* of the *statutes* as well as the *judgments*.

Keep in mind the *context*: Moses had already admitted it was too time-consuming to teach the people (through his "prophet" Aaron) and judge them at the same time. Fairly soon after the sons of Israel set out from Mt. Sinai, he realized he could not teach the people while also supervising six hundred judges. Therefore, he asked for additional assistance, and God responded by appointing seventy elders as Prophets.

---

[13] The ratio of elders/Prophets to the heads of the six hundred "thousands" was just under one to ten, clearly in line with what would have been the already existing ratio of one head to ten heads of the next smaller unit.

[14] The concept of "righteous judgment" is a fundamental concept in *The Mystery*. The judges of Israel were expected to "judge righteously" (Deut. 1:16) and thereby carry out the requirements of the Mosaic legislation. Early Church Believers also understood they were to "judge righteously" the members of Israel—the Body of Jesus Christ (1 Cor. 5:9–13).

God took the Spirit of prophecy that was on Moses and distributed it to those seventy elders to give them a divinely revealed understanding of the *oral Torah* (*The Teaching*) that Moses understood. Thereafter, these seventy elders also understood the *meaning* and *significance* of the *statutes* and *judgments* God had given Israel. Their insight equipped them for the task of overseeing the six hundred "heads" who were the chief judges of Israel. That left Moses with only the task of teaching the people through his "prophet" Aaron. That was a task he could easily handle.

From this brief survey of the biblical evidence, one can be certain that the role of the seventy elders/Prophets was to supervise the judges who were heads of the military/judicial units. Their role was one of mediation. They *received* an understanding of *The Teaching* through divine revelation and sat as supervisors over judges who were also heads of the largest military units in Israel. To fulfill their responsibility, they relied on their own supernaturally revealed understanding of the *meaning* and *significance* of the *statutes* and *judgments* of God.

According to the judicial structure that Moses established, the "heads" of the military/judicial units of Israel sat as judges over the "heads" of the next smaller units under their command. That organizational structure continued down to the "heads" of the smallest military/judicial units—the "tens." The members of these smallest units were responsible only for supervising the conduct of their immediate family. Thus every member of Israel was responsible to someone who stood in relation to them as a "judge." But the complex organizational structure of *Corporate* Israel is not quite so easily explained.

Moses and the Council of Israel

The military/judicial structure that Moses established in Israel—the thousands, hundreds, fifties, and tens—was added to, without being totally integrated into, an already existing tribal structure. The coexistence of these two systems of organization, combined with the fluid terminology associated with *Corporate* Israel's original tribal structure, presents those who seek to translate and/or comment on the text of the Hebrew Scriptures with such a confusing array of statements that some have completely discounted the reliability of the biblical text.[15] Indeed, a great many liberal scholars today hold the Scriptures to be completely untrustworthy because the text appears to contradict itself on certain points. However, the fault is not in the text itself but in the confused mind of the scholar who seeks to impose his/her own categories of thought on the text.[16]

The following synopsis should reveal the sharp contrast between the fixed terminology Moses uses to refer to the military/judicial structure and the fluid terminology he uses to refer to *Corporate* Israel's previously existing tribal structure. It will also give you some idea of how Moses, at God's direction, merged the two structures into one. A detailed explanation of the *significance* of the way in which much of the terminology has been used in Scripture must be postponed until I can treat both topics more fully later on.

Israel's tribal structure stemmed from two main areas of concern to ancient Near Eastern peoples in general:

1. *Inheritance*
2. *Ancestor worship*

---

[15] The New American Standard Bible is one of the best translations available to the English reader who wants to get as close as possible to the text of the Hebrew/Greek Scriptures. However, the NASB translation of Moses' references to the tribal structure of Israel is particularly disappointing. Lack of insight into the tribal terminology Moses used has, in many cases, resulted in a translation through which the English reader cannot possibly discern the *meaning* of the original text.

[16] The change in the priesthood that occurred when Aaron died is a case in point. For well over a century, biblical scholars have taken the apparent contradiction between a priesthood confined to the sons of Aaron and a priesthood open to all Levites as an indication that the Book of Deuteronomy was written several centuries later than the rest of the Pentateuch.

God used these two concepts to *parabolically* explain the plan of salvation He planned to accomplish through the death and resurrection of Jesus Christ. However, I will not touch on that aspect of *The Mystery*[17] in this brief survey of ancient Near Eastern tribal terminology, since my only purpose is to provide a rudimentary explanation of Israel's organizational structure.

The basic ancient Near Eastern tribal unit was the "house." The sole prerequisite of a "house," whether large or small, was that it had been "built" by a "father" (living or deceased) who had engendered "seed," that is, male offspring (by one or more women). All living and deceased male descendants ("seed") of a "father" and all the women this man had "taken"[18] as wives, along with all his unmarried female offspring,[19] were members of the "house"[20] "built" by the father unless they had been "cut off from" it.[21]

---

[17] I will do that in future volumes of The Resurrection Theology Series.

[18] The idiom "take a woman" has particular *significance* in regard to the *fulfillment of the promise* God made to Abraham, as I have indicated in *Not All Israel Is Israel*, p. 88, fn. 3.

[19] See Genesis 38:11; Leviticus 22:13.

[20] The Hebrew idiom "build a house" will become much more *significant* later in connection with the Prophets' *parabolic* description of the death and resurrection of Jesus Christ. For now, it is sufficient to know that the idiom occurs in Genesis 16:2, Deuteronomy 25:9, Ruth 4:11, and 2 Samuel 7:13. For a superficial explanation of the *meaning* and *significance* of the idiom "build a house" in regard to the death and resurrection of Jesus Christ, see "Watching Ducks Sashaying 'Round the CornerStone," *The Voice of Elijah*, April 1993; "Time to Start Countin' (the Cost of Building the House)" *The Voice of Elijah Update*, May 1993; and "As Hot As Hell (and Every Bit as Certain)" *The Voice of Elijah Update*, September 1993.

[21] See *Not All Israel Is Israel* for an explanation of how God used the Hebrew idiom "cut off from" in connection with the *parabolic image* of *Corporate* Israel as the Firstborn Son of God. Jesus Christ is the *Heir* of God Who *inherited the promise* God made to Abraham and thereby became the *Heir* Who *inherited what was promised* when God *fulfilled the promise*. As the Apostle Paul explains in Galatians 3–4, that was possible only because God "cut off from" Israel all of the Jews except Jesus Christ before He ratified the New Covenant with Him as *Corporate* Israel.

Since Israel's society was patriarchal, that is, it had socio-logical norms based on males inheriting from their fathers, one often encounters the term *house* in the Hebrew Scriptures in the phrase *house of a father* (**beit**[22] *'ab*) or *house of fathers* (**beit *'abot*).[23] In these two constructs, the term *house* is always singular, indi-cating the singularity of the "house" unit. By contrast, the term *father* is sometimes singular, sometimes plural, depending on whether or not the "house" in view includes more than just the "house" of a single father. That is because the Hebrew term for *house* is a fluid term that can be used to designate the smallest unit in Israel—the single-father *family*,[24] or to refer to the larger multi-family *tribe*,[25] or even to point to the largest unit—the multi-tribe *people*[26] of Israel. That is evident since the indefinite "father" is often replaced with the name of a specific person, no

---

[22] The Hebrew term for "house," when used to *mean* "house of," is **beit**.

[23] The Hebrew term for "father" is *'ab*. The plural is *'abot*—"fathers."

[24] The Hebrew term for "family" is **mishpachah**.

[25] The English term *tribe* conceals the vivid mental imagery inherent in the ancient Oriental mind-set. Two Hebrew terms are normally translated as "tribe": **matteh** and **shebet**. Both are used to signify a "rod," "branch," or "staff." These two terms relate to yet another tribal concept. In the same way that the descendants of one individual were thought to be a "house," so also were they considered to be a "tree." The "father" of the "house" was the "trunk" or "root" of the "tree" (see Judg. 9:7 ff.; Is. 11:1; Ez. 17:1 ff.). First gener-ation descendants of the individual who founded a "house" were the main "branches" (tribes) off the "trunk" of the founder's "tree." Descendants of these "branches" (tribes) were considered to be smaller "shoots" on the same "tree" (cf. Is. 11:1; Jer. 23:5; Zech. 3:8; 6:12). This tree imagery stands behind the Hebrew idiom "cut off from" (see *Not All Israel Is Israel*, esp. pp. 196 ff.), and is an integral part of the Old Testament Gospel of Jesus Christ. (See "The Image of the King as a Tree," *The Voice of Elijah*, April 1991.) We still today retain the basic notion of a "family tree." However, we have reversed the image, making it a tree of ancestors rather than a tree of descendants.

[26] The Hebrew term for "people" is *'am*. Some of the implications of the Scriptures' use of this term are discussed in *Not All Israel Is Israel*. (See p. 9; p. 29, fn. 33; and pp. 85 ff.) The term implies the unity of "one people" attained by virtue of descent from a common ancestor or through (cove-nantal) intermarriage (cf. Gen. 11:6; 34:16).

matter whether the "house" is the smallest tribal unit, a *family* (*The House* of David),[27] or the much larger tribal unit, a *tribe* (*The House* of Judah),[28] or even the largest tribal unit, a *people* (*The House* of Israel).[29]

The "head" of the smallest tribal unit, the *family*, was the "father" of only those in his own "house," that is, of his own sons, his unmarried daughters, and his sons' women and children. But after his death, the "house" of a deceased father—for example, *The House* of Israel (the man Jacob) could potentially become larger and larger. As it grew, it would include the "houses" of many other "fathers." These "houses" would all be smaller than the totality of the "house" of the deceased "father," but still be part of it. Consequently, the growth of a "house of fathers" spawned the need for a tribal council[30] in which every

---

[27] 2 Samuel 3:1, 6.

[28] 2 Samuel 2:4, 11.

[29] 2 Samuel 1:12; 6:5.

[30] The Hebrew word for the governing council of Israel is *'edah*. The term is normally translated as either "assembly" or "congregation." Neither English word is sufficient to convey the full nuance of the Hebrew term. "Council" is a better term in most respects. Like the "house" from which it drew its members, the *'edah* varied in size depending on the total size of the "house"—that is, the "people." (See Numbers 16:1 ff. where those allied with Korah are repeatedly called "Korah's *'edah*" or "his *'edah*.")

A second term with which *'edah* is easily, and often, confused is the term *qahal*. The nuance of this last noun tends more to the *meaning* of "assembly." The verbal form of the noun *qahal means* specifically "to assemble" (both as a transitive and intransitive verb). Therefore, the two nouns are sometimes used together as a nominal construct with the *meaning* "the assembly of the council" (Ex. 12:6; Num. 14:5).

The *'edah* of Israel, because it included every male in Israel above the age of twenty, remained the council of Israel whether assembled or not. When assembled, however, the *'edah* became a *qahal*. Consequently, the term *qahal* is occasionally used where it appears to be a substitute for *'edah* (Num. 16:3). However, with few exceptions, the term *qahal* refers to the whole of Israel, including women, and children, and not just to the assembled *'edah*, that is, only to the assembly of those males above the age of twenty.

"house" in every *family, tribe,* and *people* was adequately represented.

The role of the tribal council was to resolve intertribal disputes and make decisions concerning matters that affected the welfare of the total *people.* Israel's tribal council was a representative form of government in which the larger "houses" had more council representatives than the smaller "houses." Since the "houses" within a "house of fathers" would always be of various sizes, the size of the council had to vary according to the size of the total "house" of Israel if the "council" was to be truly representative. To provide equitable representation, Israel's tribal council included every male from the age of twenty upward,[31] except for the members of the tribe of Levi.[32] However, the Hebrew text makes it clear that not all members of the council had equal standing in the council.

Those members of the council who held more authority were called collectively "the *heads* of the house of their *fathers,*" or, individually, "the *head* of the house of his *fathers.*" However, these "*heads* of the house of their *fathers*" did not all represent the same number of constituents. That is because the

---

[31] This is made clear from the account of the census in Numbers 1:1 ff. The purpose of the census was to count "all the *'edah* of the sons of Israel," yet those counted included only the men above the age of twenty:

> Then the LORD spoke to Moses in the wilderness of Sinai, in the tent of meeting, on the first of the second month, in the second year after they had come out of the land of Egypt, saying, **"Take a census of all the congregation** of the sons of Israel, by their families, by their fathers' households, according to the number of names, every male, head by head **from twenty years old and upward,** whoever {is able to} go out to war in Israel, you and Aaron shall number them by their armies."
> (Numbers 1:1–3)

[32] One interesting aspect of the way God used the tribal organization of Israel for His Own purposes is the exclusion of the tribe of Levi from the *'edah.* The fact that Levi was excluded is stated obliquely in Numbers 1:47–49 and specifically in Numbers 16:9. Although that holds potent *significance* for the one who seeks to understand *The Teaching,* an explanation of the *significance* of the exclusion of the Levites from the *'edah* must wait.

"houses" of "the *fathers*" of Israel were of various sizes. For example, the phrase "*heads* of the house of their *fathers*" sometimes refers to the twelve *heads* of the twelve *tribes* of the *people* of Israel.[33] At other times it refers to the *heads* of the individual *families* in a single *tribe* within the larger *people*.[34] Therefore, the phrase is nothing more than a general designation. The only prerequisite for its use was that the "house" which the "head" represented had to include more than just one "father." That is, the man was the "head" of more than a single-father "house." That is why the Hebrew term for *father* (*'ab*) is always plural.

The Carriers of the Names

The "*heads* of the house of their *fathers*"[35] were important members of the tribal council. However, even within this distinguished group of individuals there were some "heads"[36] who held an even more important position. These were the men who "carried" the "names" of the fathers.

---

[33] Numbers 1:4. See also verse 16 where the phrase is transmuted slightly to "heads of the tribes of their fathers."

[34] Exodus 6:14. Notice in this verse also that the term *family* (*mishpachah*) refers to the largest "house" below the level of tribe (*matteh*).

[35] On occasion the term *house* is omitted from the phrase "heads of the *house* of their fathers" so that it becomes "heads of their fathers." Nevertheless, the designation always retains the same referent: a "house" in Israel. The size of the house must be determined from the context. For example, in Numbers 36:1 the phrase "heads of the fathers" refers to just the heads of the *houses* within the *family* of Gilead, the son of Machir, the son of Manasseh. Yet in the same verse, the same phrase also refers to the heads of the much larger *tribes* within the *people* of Israel.

[36] Some of the heads of the "houses" of the tribes of Israel were also heads of the military/judicial units. However, the function of the "head" depended on the particular type of unit he headed. The military/judicial organization that Moses introduced was the legislative/judicial branch of the government. The older tribal organization was the executive branch. God brought the two together only in the person of the high priest, who wore the "breastpiece of judgment."

The ancient oriental peoples of whom Israel was a part were concerned about the continued existence of the "name" of an individual after his death. For reasons that are completely irrelevant to this discussion, they considered it important that a deceased "father" always have at least one living male descendant to "cause his name to be remembered."[37] Therefore, each "house" had one member whose primary distinction was that he "carried" the "name" of the deceased "builder" of the "house." They called that man a "carrier."[38]

---

[37] The burial of Absalom in 2 Samuel 18:16–18 is instructive in this regard. The text states Absalom erected a stone monument (*massebah*) during his lifetime because, he said, "I have no son to *cause my name to be remembered*" (translation and emphasis mine). Using the same Hebrew idiom, God enigmatically told the sons of Israel that He would come to them and bless them "in all the place" (*maqom*) "where *I will cause My name to be remembered*" (Ex. 20:24). He also warned them, "You must not *cause the name of other gods to be remembered*" (Ex. 23:13a). The statement following that admonition provides insight into what the idiom *means* when it refers to deity: "You must not cause it to be heard on your mouth" (v. 23:13b). There is a deeper *significance* to this verse than meets the eye, yet the Hebrew idiom "to cause a name to be remembered" clearly refers to children who "carry" the "name" of a god. That a human child could "carry" the "name" of a god was not a foreign concept to the ancients. For example, the name Abijah (1 Sam. 8:2; 1 Chr. 6:28) *means* "my father is Yahweh," whereas the name Abimelech (Gen. 20:1–18) *means* "my father is Malik." (Malik was a pagan god of Amorite origin.)

[38] The Hebrew word I have translated "carrier" is *nasi'*. It is a nominal form of the verb *nasa'* ("to carry"). Another Hebrew term with a form and verbal nuance parallel to *nasi'* is the term *qari'*. Although the nominal form *qari'* is usually translated as though it expressed a durative passive *meaning*, that is, "called" or "summoned," it actually has an active sense like the similar form *nabi'*—"prophet." It *means* something along the order of "caller." Not understanding the *significance* of what it *meant* for someone to be a "carrier" in ancient Israel, translators normally translate the word *nasi'* into English with a generic word like "leader." In Numbers 3:32 for example, Eleazar is said to be "the *carrier* of the *carriers* of the Levites" (translation mine), *meaning* he was the "carrier" who "carried" the "name" of Levi for the entire tribe of Levi, in which there were many other "carriers" of "names." Yet the English translation states generally that he was "chief of the leaders of Levi."

The "carriers" of the "names" of the "fathers" were automatically the "heads" of the "houses" "built" by the deceased men whose "names" they "carried." However, since every "carrier" was also a "head" over all the various-sized "houses" of which he was a member down to his own single-father "house," the "carriers" of the "names" of the "fathers" of the largest "houses" in Israel were singled out for particular distinction in the tribal council.[39]

The high priest, as part of the *parabolic pantomime*[40] conducted by the priests, wore the "breastpiece of judgment" on which the names of the twelve sons of Israel were inscribed. As the supreme authority in regard to cultic matters, he stood

---

[39] For example, there is a specific prohibition against cursing a "carrier" (*nasi'*) in Exodus 22:28. The fact that this warning is coupled with a prohibition against cursing God indicates the high regard accorded these individuals. In Korah's rebellion, 250 "carriers" (mainly from the tribes of Reuben and Levi) established their own tribal council (*'edah*) and challenged the authority of Moses (Num. 16:1 ff., 26:4–11), questioning the validity of his imposition of the Aaronic priesthood on what had previously been a strictly tribal priesthood (Ex. 19:22–24).

[40] The third volume of The Resurrection Theology Series—*House of Israel, Temple of God*—will explain this particular facet of *The Teaching*. Its *significance* relates to what the writer of the Book of Hebrews says concerning the High Priest Jesus Christ:

> *Therefore, holy brethren, partakers of a heavenly calling, consider Jesus, the Apostle and High Priest of our confession. He was faithful to Him who appointed Him, as Moses also was in all His house. For He has been counted worthy of more glory than Moses, by just so much as **the builder of the house has more honor than the house. For every house is built by someone, but the builder of all things is God.** Now Moses was faithful in all His house as a servant, for a testimony of those things which were to be spoken later; but **Christ** {**was faithful**} **as a Son over His house whose house we are**, if we hold fast our confidence and the boast of our hope firm until the end.*
> (Hebrews 3:1–6)

As you can see from this text, we have a long way to go before we can thoroughly understand what this writer took to be a matter of common knowledge in the Early Church. We'll get there. Eventually.

"before the Lord" in a *parabolic pantomime* as the "carrier" of the twelve "names" of the "fathers" of the twelve tribes of Israel. The stated purpose of the breastpiece was to provide a "memorial"—*literally*, a "remembrance"—of those twelve "names" before the Lord:

> "*And **Aaron shall carry the names of the sons of Israel in the breastpiece of judgment over his heart when he enters the holy place, for a memorial before the* LORD *continually.** And you shall put in the breastpiece of judgment the Urim and the Thummim, and they shall be over Aaron's heart when he goes in before the* LORD; *and Aaron shall carry the judgment of the sons of Israel over his heart before the* LORD *continually.*"
> (Exodus 28:29–30)

The *parabolic imagery* inherent in that *parabolic pantomime* has to do with the high priest "causing the names" of the twelve sons of Israel (Jacob) "to be remembered" before God. However, to understand the *meaning* and *significance* of the *parabolic pantomime*, one first needs to know that the high priest, as the "carrier" of the "names" of the twelve "fathers" of Israel, was also the "head" of *The House* of Israel and therefore stood as the "head" of the tribal council (the *'edah*). As such, he was THE CARRIER OF THE CARRIERS[41] of the sons of Israel. After the death of Joshua, the high priest became the recourse of last resort in

[41] The designation "carrier of the carriers" occurs in Numbers 3:32, where it says Eleazar, the son of Aaron, was "the *nasi'* of the *nesi'im*" (*nesi'im* is the plural of *nasi'*) of the Levites while his father was high priest. When Aaron died (Num. 20:22–29), Eleazar replaced him as high priest and wore the "breastpiece of judgment" as the "carrier" of the "names" of all the sons of Israel, not just as the "carrier" of the "names" of Levi. We know that Eleazar, as high priest, took an active part in the decision-making process as head of the *'edah*. (See Num. 27:2 ff.; 31:12–13, 26; and 32:2 ff., 28. But see also Numbers 36:1 where Eleazar is not mentioned specifically but may be included as just one among the many "heads of the fathers of the sons of Israel.") Eleazar continued in the role of high priest and "carrier" of the "names" of the sons of Israel under Joshua (Josh. 17:4; 21:1), and his son Phinehas followed him in that position (Josh. 22:13; Judg. 20:28).

situations where a *judgment* was required. In those cases where the members of the *'edah* found a decision too difficult for them to decide, the high priest used the "breastpiece of judgment" to ascertain the *judgment* of the Lord according to the procedure Moses established:

> So the LORD said to Moses, "Take Joshua the son of Nun, a man in whom is the Spirit, and lay your hand on him; and have him stand before Eleazar the priest and before all the congregation; and commission him in their sight. And you shall put some of your authority on him, in order that all the congregation of the sons of Israel may obey {him.} Moreover, he shall stand before **Eleazar the priest, who shall inquire for him by the judgment of the Urim before the LORD.** At his command they shall go out and at his command they shall come in, {both} he and the sons of Israel with him, even all the congregation."
> (Numbers 27:18–21)[42]

This passage raises some interesting questions concerning the authority structure that existed in Israel after the death of Moses. Joshua, who replaced Moses as the leader of *Corporate* Israel, is depicted as having a symbiotic relationship with the high priest "who shall inquire for him by the judgment of the Urim before the LORD." The reader must understand the nature of that relationship before he can understand the history of *Corporate* Israel as it is recounted in the biblical text. For now, it is only necessary to understand the basic organization of *Corporate* Israel and the separate roles of Prophet, priest, and judge during the wilderness wandering.

Conclusion

In the wilderness, the judges of Israel, that is, the "heads" of the various military units under the supervision of the sev-

---

[42] See also Judges 1:1 and 20:27–28 where the "breastpiece of judgment" is not mentioned but was almost certainly used.

enty elders/Prophets, were responsible for judging the sons of Israel according to the conditional *judgments*. The purpose of this organizational structure was to make sure that the sons of Israel adhered to the *statutes* and the civil/criminal *judgments* God had given. Alongside the newer military/judicial structure, however, *Corporate* Israel retained an older tribal structure. The basic unit of that structure was the "house," with each "house" having its own "head." It should come as no surprise that those two authority structures soon came into conflict. That is obvious on at least one occasion when God Himself stepped in to mandate the penalty for infringement of His *commandments*:

> *While Israel remained at Shittim, the people began to play the harlot with the daughters of Moab. For they invited the people to the sacrifices of their gods, and the people ate and bowed down to their gods. So Israel joined themselves to Baal of Peor, and the LORD was angry against Israel. And the LORD said to Moses, "Take all **the leaders of the people** and execute them in broad daylight before the LORD, so that the fierce anger of the LORD may turn away from Israel." So* **Moses said to the judges of Israel***, "Each of you slay his men who have joined themselves to Baal of Peor."*
> *(Numbers 25:1–5)*[43]

---

[43] The military/judicial system that Moses introduced clearly stands in direct conflict with the older tribal system here. To understand why that is, one must first understand that the focus of this passage revolves around the practice of ritual prostitution (by a woman called a "*zonah*"), which was common in the ancient Near East. However, there is a much deeper *significance* to the events of Baal Peor. The purpose of ritual prostitution was to engender a "name" (a male child) who could "carry the name" of the "father of the house." That was a primary concern of the tribal "heads of the house of the fathers" under the original tribal structure of Israel, but the practice had been outlawed by the Mosaic Covenant (cf. Deut. 12:3). So the "heads of the fathers" were trying to produce a "carrier" of a "name" according to a tribal methodology God had specifically condemned. For a more in-depth explanation, see articles in *The Voice of Elijah* and forthcoming volumes in The Resurrection Theology Series.

On this occasion, the sin of the sons of Israel was so great that God told Moses to make sure the penalty for breaking His *commandments* was dispensed quickly. Moses appealed immediately to the heads of the military/judicial system he had established. That is, he passed the order along to the judges, probably through the elders/Prophets immediately under him in the chain of command. The text indicates he expected the judges to investigate the matter and determine who among the "heads of the house of the fathers" had been engaging in the sacred prostitution ritual. One can safely conclude, therefore, that each judge was responsible only for judging the behavior of those "heads of the house of their fathers" under his jurisdiction. Under those circumstances, those judges who did not take appropriate action to execute the guilty would become guilty themselves.

To understand the *significance* of this passage, one needs to know that the Hebrew word (**roshim**) translated "leaders" here is the same word that has been translated "heads" in Exodus 18:25. There it refers to the "heads" of the various military/judicial units. In this case, however, it refers to the "heads" of the tribal "houses" of Israel rather than to the "heads" of the military/judicial units.

The above example demonstrates how God expected the proper observance of the civil/criminal *judgments* to be carried out. However, one area of *The Law of Moses* remained completely beyond the purview of the elders/Prophets and the judges of Israel. That was teaching the **Torah**—the *meaning* and *significance* of the *judgments* and the *symbolic rituals* of the tabernacle cult that were governed by the *statutes*. The responsibility for "pointing out" the *meaning* and *significance* of God's **Torah** lay with the priests alone from the time of Moses until the Pharisees usurped that priestly role at the time of Antiochus Epiphanes.

As far as God was concerned, the basic roles of the Prophet and the priest never changed throughout the history of Israel up to and including *the Prophet and High Priest*, Jesus Christ. The Prophet was responsible for ensuring the purity of *The Teaching*; the priest was responsible for teaching the people and making sure the *symbolic rituals* were conducted in accordance with the divine intent. The difference between the Prophet and the priest lay primarily in the way in which they *received* insight into *The Teaching*.

The Prophets of Israel *received* their understanding of *The Teaching* directly from God through divine revelation. By contrast, God expected the priests to *receive The Teaching* from the previous generation of priests and *deliver* it unchanged to the next generation, teaching it just as they had been taught. In other words, the priests were supposed to gain an accurate understanding of *The Teaching* from those who were priests before them. That *meant* God would find it necessary to send a Prophet only when the priests' understanding of *The Teaching* stood in need of correction.

In the eyes of God, the Prophet and the priest had exactly the same responsiblity. Both were responsible for making sure the sons of Israel were accurately taught *The Teaching of Moses*, not only *verbally* but also *nonverbally*—that is, through the *symbolic rituals* of the sacrificial cult. Although the relationship between Prophet and priest never changed, it was one of constant conflict throughout Israel's pre-exilic history, and with good reason.

The Hebrew Scriptures tell us the priests failed miserably at their assigned task of *handing down The Teaching of Moses*. Consequently, God found it necessary to send His Prophets to Israel time and time again to *restore The Teaching*. However, the Prophets often found it impossible to turn the priests back to *The Teaching of Moses*. They nonetheless succeeded admirably in their allotted task, but only because they produced a coherently written explanation of *The Teaching*, well hidden in the *parabolic statements* of the prophetic texts. It will be necessary for us to look into the writings of the Prophets later on in this series. For now, it is enough to continue on and investigate the responsibility Moses assigned the priests.

Chapter 8:

The Teachers of Israel

In Chapter 7, I explained how Moses, by taking Jethro's advice, delegated responsibility for judging the sons of Israel to the "heads" of the military/judicial units so that he could devote himself fully to the task of teaching the *oral Torah* that explained the *meaning* and *significance* of the *statutes* and *judgments*. The sole responsibility of these "heads" was to judge Israel according to the *judgments* God had given through Moses. They had no responsibility for teaching the *oral Torah* that explained the *meaning* and *significance* of the *statutes* and *judgments*.

When Moses found this initial arrangement unduly burdensome, God had him select an additional seventy elders/ Prophets who had responsibility for overseeing the judges who judged Israel. Although God also gave these seventy Prophets a supernatural understanding of *The Mystery* He had already revealed to Moses, He did not allow them to prophesy and thereby teach Israel. Their insight into *The Teaching of Moses* was strictly for the purpose of equipping them for the task of overseeing the judges of Israel.

In this chapter, I will explain who was responsible for teaching the sons of Israel the *oral Torah* after Moses died. For those who prefer to read the conclusion first, it was the entire tribe of Levi. Moses explains that in the Book of Deuteronomy.

Moses clearly understood God had appointed him the first Teacher of Israel. Shortly before he died, he told the sons of Israel, "I have *taught you* statutes and judgments just as the Lord my God commanded me."[1] That indicates he had been *orally* teaching the sons of Israel (through his "prophet" Aaron) the *meaning* and *significance* of both the *statutes* and the *judgments* in the wilderness.[2] However, Moses also tells us God intended him to be but the first in a long line of divinely ordained Teachers of Israel. That fact is further confirmed by the beliefs of the Jews. They insist Moses *received oral **Torah*** at Mt. Sinai—which is true; he did. But they also claim their ancestors *handed down* that *oral Torah* from one generation to the next[3] as God commanded until it was finally recorded in the Mishnah around A.D. 200—which is not true; they did not *hand* it *down*. Instead, they lost it—not once or twice, but repeatedly.

---

[1] Deuteronomy 4:5.

[2] Several other verses also indicate Moses understood he was supposed to teach the sons of Israel the *meaning* of the Covenant Code during the wilderness wandering. See Deuteronomy 4:14; 5:31; 6:1.

[3] Jewish tradition also says God expected them to *hand down* the *oral tradition* Moses *received* on Mt. Sinai through the process of discipling:

> Moses received Torah from Sinai and delivered it to Joshua, and Joshua to the Elders, and the Elders to the Prophets, and the Prophets delivered it to the Men of the Great Synagogue. These said three things; Be deliberate in judging, and raise up many disciples, and make a hedge for the Torah.
> R. Travers Herford, The Ethics of the Talmud: Sayings of the Fathers (New York: Schocken Books, 1962), p. 19.

That statement implies the Prophets were responsible for *handing down* The Teaching of Moses. That is not so. God entrusted that responsibility to the priests. Therefore, it will eventually be necessary to explain why Jewish tradition would claim otherwise. The answer lies in Jesus' assertion that the scribes and Pharisees had "*seated themselves* in the chair of Moses" (Matt. 23:2). He knew the Pharisees had illegitimately claimed for themselves the priests' authority as the Teachers of Israel after the Maccabbean revolt (ca. 167 B.C.). At that time, they appealed to a higher (prophetic) authority in order to legitimate their usurpation of the priestly role.

What the Jews believe concerning *The Teaching of Moses* is not normally considered at all important by Christians. But it should be. It is part and parcel of the Jewish heritage the Early Church gained from Jesus Christ and the Apostles.[4] Jesus Christ *handed down The Teaching* to His disciples and told them they were to *hand* it *down* from generation to generation just as Moses had told the sons of Israel so long before.[5] Moreover, the evidence indicates Early Church leaders did what they were supposed to do. That is, they obediently "walked in *The Way*" until Pretenders, by touting the benefits of Greek philosophy, convinced them to "turn aside from *The Way*," and thereby carried them off into theological speculation.[6]

Later on in this series, when we expose the ugly truth concerning Judaism's false claim concerning the *oral tradition* of the Pharisees, it will be essential that you understand who God held responsible for teaching the sons of Israel *The Teaching of Moses*. Therefore, it is absolutely essential that we ask, and answer, a few questions now: *Who* were the divinely ordained Teachers of Israel? *What* were they expected to teach? And *how* were they expected to teach it?

In this chapter, you will discover that different people had responsibility for teaching different things in different ways at different times. Initially—during the wilderness wandering—Moses taught Israel *verbally*, but he accomplished

---

[4] Christians have long had a tendency to treat the Hebrew Scriptures as a hated stepchild that must be taken into account, but primarily ignored until it's needed to carry some particularly heavy theological load. They lavish the vast majority of their attention on the New Testament, never stopping to consider that the Apostles who wrote those divinely inspired autographs did so on the basis of their detailed, *supernaturally revealed* understanding of the Hebrew Scriptures. Those are the facts. The King's Ball has long since ended, and everything has turned back into mice and pumpkins—except for that one stray slipper. And it won't fit anyone but that stepchild.

[5] Matthew 28:18–20.

[6] See my ongoing commentary on the Apostolic and Early Church literature in *The Voice of Elijah Update*.

that by speaking through his "prophet" Aaron. Hence, Aaron the high priest was actually the first *priestly* Teacher of Israel. Aaron and his sons—"the priests, the sons of Aaron"—also held the priesthood as their exclusive domain during the wilderness wandering. This Aaronic priesthood taught the people *nonverbally* by conducting the *symbolic rituals* of the tabernacle cult according to the *statutes* that governed them.

Moses charged the "heads" of the military/judicial units with responsibility for judging the sons of Israel according to God's civil/criminal legislation—the conditional *judgments*—during the wilderness wandering. Seventy elders/Prophets stood as supervisors over the judges. But these Prophets were responsible only for ensuring that the judges meted out "righteous judgment" in accordance with the divine intent of the *judgments*. They were not allowed to explain the *meaning* or *significance* of the *statutes* or *judgments*. That prerogative was Moses' alone, because he stood as supervisor over the seventy elder/Prophets and the priests.

After Aaron's death, Moses admitted the entire tribe of Levi to the priesthood. Thereafter, all the Levites—not just Aaron and his sons—were priests. Since teaching the people *nonverbally* by conducting the *symbolic rituals* of the tabernacle cult as *parabolic pantomime* had been the exclusive domain of the priesthood all along, this expanded priesthood—the *Levitical* priests—became responsible for continuing those rituals. From that point on "the *Levitical* priests," not just "the priests, the sons of Aaron," had responsibility for teaching *nonverbally* by conducting the *symbolic rituals* mandated by the *statutes*.

When Moses admitted the entire tribe of Levi to the priesthood just prior to *Corporate* Israel's entry into the Promised Land, he also placed the judges of Israel directly under their supervision. That *meant* the responsibility of the *Levitical* priests for teaching the people *nonverbally* suddenly came to include more than just the *symbolic rituals* mandated by the *statutes*. It now encompassed the entire legal system of Israel—that is, the *testimonies, commandments, statutes,* and *judgments.* Accordingly, Moses made the *Levitical* priests responsible for teaching the people *nonverbally* the *meaning* and *significance* of all the *symbolic rituals* of Israel, even those demanded by the *judgments.*

Moses instituted one final change to the organizational structure of *Corporate* Israel shortly before his death. Since he had already *handed down* to the *Levitical* priests the entirety of the *oral Torah* he *received,* he made them responsible for *handing down* that *oral Torah* to the next generation *verbally,* just as he had done by speaking through his "prophet" Aaron. He also included instructions that the *Levitical* priesthood continue *handing down* that *oral Torah* to all future generations.

In effect, Moses made the *Levitical* priests the respository of *The Teaching.* They thereby became accountable for three things: (1) making sure the judges of Israel judged Israel with "righteous judgment" according to the *judgments,* (2) teaching *The Teaching nonverbally* by conducting the symbolic rituals of the tabernacle according to the *statutes,* and (3) *verbally handing down* the *oral Torah—The Teaching of Moses—*just as Moses had done through his "prophet" Aaron. That *oral Torah* explained the *meaning* and *significance* of all "the *commandments,*" that is, the *meaning* and *significance* of all the *testimonies, statutes,* and *judgments.*

Moses instituted all of these changes shortly before his death, while the sons of Israel were still camped beyond the Jordan, preparing to enter the Promised Land. Yet in all of the organizational changes he made, he left one tremendously *significant* thing unchanged—the Prophet's responsibility to supervise the priests. Therefore, throughout *Corporate* Israel's long history in the land, the Prophet remained responsible for correcting the priestly Teachers of Israel, to try to make sure the priests accurately taught the Truth of *The Teaching of Moses,* and to ensure that they made sure the judges of Israel judged with "righteous judgment." Seldom did the Prophets succeed, but not for lack of trying.

A careful study of the Hebrew Scriptures will confirm that Moses made the changes I have described, but my explanation may get a bit detailed. So just remember the main point: After Moses died, who was responsible for *handing down* the oral **Torah** Moses **received** at Mt. Sinai?

The Priests: The Sons of Aaron

Moses repeatedly states that only Aaron and his sons were priests during the wilderness wandering. They alone were qualified to minister in the tabernacle, where they conducted the *symbolic rituals* of the sacrificial cult. The following passages emphasize that point:

> *"**Then bring near to yourself Aaron your brother, and his sons with him, from among the sons of Israel, to minister as priest to Me**—Aaron, Nadab and Abihu, Eleazar and Ithamar, Aaron's sons. And you shall make holy garments for Aaron your brother, for glory and for beauty."*
> *(Exodus 28:1–2)*

> *"And for Aaron's sons you shall make tunics; you shall also make sashes for them, and you shall make caps for them, for glory and for beauty. And **you shall put them on Aaron your brother and on his sons with him; and you shall anoint them and ordain them and consecrate them, that they may serve Me as priests**. And you shall make for them linen breeches to cover {their} bare flesh; they shall reach from the loins even to the thighs. And they shall be on Aaron and on his sons when they enter the tent of meeting, or when they approach the altar to minister in the holy place, so that they do not incur guilt and die. It {shall be} a statute forever to him and to his descendants after him. **Now this is what you shall do to them to consecrate them to minister as priests to Me:** take one young bull and two rams without blemish, and unleavened bread and unleavened cakes mixed with oil, and unleavened wafers spread with oil; you shall make them of fine wheat flour. And you shall put them in one basket, and present them in the basket along*

with the bull and the two rams. Then you shall bring Aaron and his sons to the doorway of the tent of meeting, and wash them with water. And you shall take the garments, and put on Aaron the tunic and the robe of the ephod and the ephod and the breastpiece, and gird him with the skillfully woven band of the ephod; and you shall set the turban on his head, and put the holy crown on the turban. Then you shall take the anointing oil, and pour it on his head and anoint him. And you shall bring his sons and put tunics on them. **And you shall gird them with sashes, Aaron and his sons, and bind caps on them, and they shall have the priesthood by a perpetual statute. So you shall ordain Aaron and his sons."**
(Exodus 28:40–29:9)

"It shall be a continual burnt offering throughout your generations at the doorway of the tent of meeting before the LORD, where I will meet with you, to speak to you there. And I will meet there with the sons of Israel, and it shall be consecrated by My glory. And I will consecrate the tent of meeting and the altar; **I will also consecrate Aaron and his sons to minister as priests to Me**. *And I will dwell among the sons of Israel and will be their God. And they shall know that I am the LORD their God who brought them out of the land of Egypt, that I might dwell among them; I am the LORD their God."*
(Exodus 29:42–46)

"And you shall anoint Aaron and his sons, and consecrate them, that they may minister as priests to Me."
(Exodus 30:30)

"Then you shall bring Aaron and his sons to the doorway of the tent of meeting and wash them with water. *And you shall put the holy garments on Aaron and anoint him and consecrate him, that he may minister as a priest to Me. And you shall bring his sons and put tunics on them; and you shall anoint them even as you have anointed their father, that they may minister as priests to Me; and* **their anointing shall qualify them for a perpetual priesthood throughout their generations."**
(Exodus 40:12–15)

Since only Aaron and his sons had been consecrated as the priests of Israel, they alone were divinely ordained to minister in the Tabernacle—during the wilderness wandering. Their role was to teach Israel *nonverbally* by conducting the *symbolic rituals* of the tabernacle cult. But that was possible only because the purpose of the *symbolic rituals* God established was to teach *nonverbally* through *parabolic pantomime.*[7] God confirms that in what He says about the leprosy *torah*:

> ... *to teach* when they are unclean, and when they are clean. This is the LAW[8] of leprosy.
> (Leviticus 14:57)

This verse explicitly states that teaching was the purpose of the *symbolic ritual* the priests were supposed to follow in detecting and cleansing lepers. It is common knowledge that the priests alone had the solemn duty of conducting this and the other *symbolic rituals* of the tabernacle cult. But it is not common knowledge that they did so as *parabolic pantomime* with the specific purpose[9] of "pointing out"[10] the *meaning* and

---

[7] The cultic rituals were actually *sacred drama*, which is the terminology that scholars working in the field of ancient religion use. *Parabolic pantomime* more accurately describes how God used them.

[8] Keep in mind *torah* has here been translated "law."

[9] The purpose of the *parabolic pantomimes* of the Prophets and priests of Israel has long been misunderstood by Jews and Christians alike. I have explained that purpose somewhat on other occasions. See "The Parabolic Pantomimes of Jesus Christ," *The Voice of Elijah*, January 1991; "The Passover Parable," *The Voice of Elijah*, July 1991; and "They've Put God in a Box! (Or So They Think)" *The Voice of Elijah*, January 1993. In future volumes of The Resurrection Theology Series I will explain it more fully.

[10] Moses makes a clear distinction between the verbs *yarah* ("to point out"), *limmed* ("to teach/cause to learn"), and *hôdî'a* ("make known to"). The verb *yarah* describes the activity of the priests, but never the activity of Moses. That verb does not necessarily denote verbal teaching, but rather implies teaching by example—by "pointing out" what should be done. The other two describe the activity of Moses. See above, p. 159, fn. 16 and below, p. 252, fn. 32.

significance of the *oral **Torah*** that God was "making known" through His Prophet Moses. That is, "the priests, the sons of Aaron" were to cause the sons of Israel to remember the *meaning* and *significance* of the *statutes*. They did so not only through *symbolic rituals*, but also through their personal conduct:

> *The LORD then spoke to Aaron, saying, "Do not drink wine or strong drink, neither you nor your sons with you, when you come into the tent of meeting, so that you may not die—it is a perpetual statute throughout your generations—and so as to make a distinction between the holy and the profane, and between the unclean and the clean, and **so as to teach**[11] **the sons of Israel all the statutes** which the LORD has spoken to them through Moses."*
> *(Leviticus 10:8–11)*

The point of this passage is fairly obvious: The priests were to teach by example. What is not so obvious, however, is the fact that their sacred obligation, as the silent teachers of the sons of Israel, was to teach *nonverbally*—through *parabolic pantomime*—the same things that Moses taught when he "spoke" through his "prophet" Aaron. Yet one of the *symbolic rituals* that "the priests, the sons of Aaron" conducted at the tabernacle did involve a short verbal statement. The priests were to bless the sons of Israel by invoking *The Name* of the Lord on them:

> *Then the LORD spoke to Moses, saying, "Speak to Aaron and to his sons, saying, 'Thus you shall bless the sons of Israel. You shall say to them:*
> *The LORD bless you, and keep you;*
> *The LORD make His face shine on you,*
> *And be gracious to you;*
> *The LORD lift up His countenance on you,*
> *And give you peace.'*

---

[11] The verb translated "teach" in this passage is *yarah* ("to point out").

So they shall invoke My name on the sons of Israel, [12]
and I then will bless them."
(Numbers 6:22–27)

It will become clear later on in this chapter that Moses assigned the entire tribe of Levi responsibility for teaching Israel just as he had taught Israel—*verbally*. From that point on, the *Levitical* priests were expected to teach *The Teaching of Moses* both *verbally*—as Moses did through Aaron, the high priest— and *nonverbally*, through *parabolic pantomime*—just as "the priests, the sons of Aaron" did in the wilderness. Unfortunately, the *Levitical* priests failed to do what Moses appointed them to do. Evidence of that is Ezekiel's indictment of the priests for failing to teach the people the *meaning* and *significance* of the *symbolic rituals* of the sacrificial cult:

> *"Her priests have done violence to **My law**[13] and have profaned My holy things; they have made no distinction between the holy and the profane, and **they have not taught the difference between the unclean and the clean; and they hide their eyes from My sabbaths**, and I am profaned among them."*
> *(Ezekiel 22:26)*

Ezekiel's charge is but a preview of coming attractions. In the next volume of this series, we will take a closer look at the

---

[12] Even in blessing the people the priests were conducting *parabolic pantomime*. The point of the *pantomime* is to remind Israel the "name of the Lord" is also the "blessing of the Lord." It is just another part of *The Mystery* that revolves around Jesus Christ as *The Name* of God Who "built *the House*" of God and thereby "raised up a seed" for David. I've already explained some of the *parabolic imagery* in **The Voice of Elijah** and **The Voice of Elijah Update**. I'll explain it all more fully in the second and third volumes of The Resurrection Theology Series.

[13] Although the *meaning* of the term **torah** in this statement retains the same referent as the **torah** of the priesthood in the wilderness (the *symbolic ritual* of the cultic worship), the term **torah** had long since taken on the much broader *meaning* assigned it by Moses in the Book of Deuteronomy, that is, the totality of the Covenant Law. (See above, pp. 138 ff.)

accusations the Prophets brought against the priests of Israel because of their failure to teach *The Teaching*. However, it is not possible to understand the Prophets' sarcastic statements if one does not first understand the *Levitical* priests had responsibility for teaching the sons of Israel the *meaning* and *significance* of all God's *commandments*—the *judgments* as well as the *statutes*.

As you will see, shortly before Moses died, he changed the arrangement that existed in the wilderness and made both *verbal* and *nonverbal* teaching the domain of the *Levitical* priests. Later on in this chapter, I will show how these changes to Israel's governmental structure occurred. But first, you must understand the firm distinction that God made between "the priests, the sons of Aaron" and the rest of the Levites during the wilderness wandering. That is, you must understand the subservient role the Levites played in the *parabolic pantomime* that Moses and Aaron conducted in the wilderness.

The Levites: Servants of the Priests

As I have already explained, only Aaron and his sons were consecrated to minister in the Tabernacle as priests during the wilderness wandering. The priesthood remained their exclusive domain until shortly after Aaron died,[14] at which time all of the other Levites became priests.[15] Prior to that time, the Levites were expressly prohibited from joining Aaron and his sons in their priestly duty. In contrast to Aaron and his sons, the Levites (who were all the members of the tribe of Levi other than Moses, Aaron, and the sons of Aaron) were "given" to the priests as servants to assist them in the work associated with the tabernacle:

> *Then the LORD spoke to Moses, saying, "Bring the tribe of Levi near and set them before Aaron the priest, that they may serve him. And they shall perform the duties for him and for the whole congregation*

---

[14] Numbers 20:22–29.
[15] Deuteronomy 10:6–9.

before the tent of meeting, to do the service of the tabernacle. They shall also keep all the furnishings of the tent of meeting, along with the duties of the sons of Israel, to do the service of the tabernacle. **You shall thus give the Levites to Aaron and to his sons;** *they are wholly given to him from among the sons of Israel. So you shall appoint Aaron and his sons that they may keep their priesthood, but the layman who comes near shall be put to death."*
(Numbers 3:5–10)

"Thus you shall separate the Levites from among the sons of Israel, and the Levites shall be Mine. Then after that the Levites may go in to serve the tent of meeting. But you shall cleanse them and present them as a wave offering; for they are wholly given to Me from among the sons of Israel. I have taken them for Myself instead of every first issue of the womb, the first-born of all the sons of Israel. For every first-born among the sons of Israel is Mine, among the men and among the animals; on the day that I struck down all the first-born in the land of Egypt I sanctified them for Myself. But I have taken the Levites instead of every first-born among the sons of Israel. And **I have given the Levites as a gift to Aaron and to his sons** *from among the sons of Israel, to perform the service of the sons of Israel at the tent of meeting, and to make atonement on behalf of the sons of Israel, that there may be no plague among the sons of Israel by their coming near to the sanctuary."*
(Numbers 8:14–19)

If the Levites were not priests, but merely priestly servants during Israel's wilderness wandering, what then was their specific function? The answer resides in the account of the first census of *Corporate* Israel. When Moses numbered Israel at Mt. Sinai,[16] God gave him specific orders as to how to take a census of the tribe of Levi. He told him the Levites were not to be counted along with the other sons of Israel; they were to be counted separately because their military duties were not the general military duties assigned to the twelve tribes of Israel.

---

[16] Numbers 1:1 ff.

Their duty was specifically restricted to the disassembly, portage, guarding, and assembly of the tabernacle:[17]

The Levites, however, were not numbered among them by their fathers' tribe.[18] For the LORD had spoken to Moses, saying, "Only the tribe of Levi you shall not number, nor shall you take their census among the sons of Israel. But you shall appoint the Levites over the tabernacle of the testimony, and over all its furnishings and over all that belongs to it. They shall carry the tabernacle and all its furnishings, and they shall take care of it; they shall also camp around the tabernacle. So when the tabernacle is to set out, the Levites shall take it down; and when the tabernacle encamps, the Levites shall set it up. But the layman who comes near shall be

---

[17] In the following explanation concerning the Levites' role in the wilderness, I am drawing primarily from the work of Jacob Milgrom, especially his *Studies in Levitic Terminology* and his commentary on the Book of Numbers, *The JPS Torah Commentary: Numbers.*

[18] The account of the census of Israel in Numbers 1:1–4:49 makes it clear that the Levites were barred from the priesthood. They were restricted to the disassembly, portage, assembly, and guarding of the tabernacle (cf. Num. 3:1–4:49). The distinction between the priests and Levites has been discussed in some detail by Jacob Milgrom in various works, especially his *Studies in Levitical Terminology, 1: The Encroacher and the Levite, The Term 'Aboda* (University of California Publications, Near Eastern Studies: Berkeley, 1970) and his commentary on the Book of Numbers, *The JPS Torah Commentary: Numbers* (The Jewish Publication Society: Philadelphia, 1990), pp. 423–24. His various works contain numerous instances of marvelous insight into the *meaning* of the text of the Scriptures.

Perhaps the most insightful contribution Milgrom has made is his explanation of the two Hebrew terms *'abodah* and **mishmeret**. His argument is well-founded: *'abodah* means "transportation work," whereas **mishmeret** means "guard duty." However, because he adheres to the basic tenets of the Documentary Hypothesis first propounded by Julius Welhausen well over a century ago, Milgrom has failed to grasp many of the ramifications of his own conclusions. Not the least of these is the fact that the groundwork he has laid provides the basis for understanding that the Levites became priests immediately after the death of Moses, just as Israel was preparing to enter the Promised Land. At that time all the Levites were accorded the rights previously reserved for the sons of Aaron alone (cf. Deut. 10:6–9). That fact has enormous *significance* for our investigation into *The Mystery.*

put to death. And the sons of Israel shall camp, each man by his own camp, and each man by his own standard, according to their armies. But **the Levites shall camp around the tabernacle of the testimony,** *that there may be no wrath on the congregation of the sons of Israel. So* **the Levites shall keep charge of the tabernacle of the testimony."** *Thus the sons of Israel did; according to all which the LORD had commanded Moses, so they did.*
(Numbers 1:47–54)

At God's direction, Moses numbered the three families of the tribe of Levi separately from the other tribes of Israel. He assigned each Levite family specific duties related to the transportation work and guard duty associated with the tabernacle. First, He gave the Kohathites responsibility for carrying and guarding all of the tabernacle furniture, including the altar and the Ark of the Covenant, while the tabernacle was in transit:

Then the LORD spoke to Moses and to Aaron, saying, "Take a census of the descendants of Kohath from among the sons of Levi, by their families, by their fathers' households, from thirty years and upward, even to fifty years old, all who enter the service to do the work in the tent of meeting. **This is the work of the descendants of Kohath in the tent of meeting, {concerning} the most holy things.** *When the camp sets out, Aaron and his sons shall go in and they shall take down the veil of the screen and cover the ark of the testimony with it; and they shall lay a covering of porpoise skin on it, and shall spread over {it} a cloth of pure blue, and shall insert its poles. Over the table of the bread of the Presence they shall also spread a cloth of blue and put on it the dishes and the pans and the sacrificial bowls and the jars for the libation, and the continual bread shall be on it. And they shall spread over them a cloth of scarlet {material,} and cover the same with a covering of porpoise skin, and they shall insert its poles. Then they shall take a blue cloth and cover the lampstand for the light, along with its lamps and its snuffers, and its trays and all its oil vessels, by which they serve it; and they shall put it and all its utensils in a covering of porpoise skin, and shall put it on the carrying bars.*

And over the golden altar they shall spread a blue cloth and cover it with a covering of porpoise skin, and shall insert its poles; and they shall take all the utensils of service, with which they serve in the sanctuary, and put them in a blue cloth and cover them with a covering of porpoise skin, and put them on the carrying bars. Then they shall take away the ashes from the altar, and spread a purple cloth over it. They shall also put on it all its utensils by which they serve in connection with it: the firepans, the forks and shovels and the basins, all the utensils of the altar; and they shall spread a cover of porpoise skin over it and insert its poles. And **when Aaron and his sons have finished covering the holy {objects} and all the furnishings of the sanctuary, when the camp is to set out, after that the sons of Kohath shall come to carry {them,} so that they may not touch the holy {objects} and die.** *These are the things in the tent of meeting which the sons of Kohath are to carry. And the responsibility of Eleazar the son of Aaron the priest is the oil for the light and the fragrant incense and the continual grain offering and the anointing oil—the responsibility of all the Tabernacle and of all that is in it, with the sanctuary and its furnishings."*
(Numbers 4:1–16)

The admonition concerning the danger the Kothathites faced in touching the holy furniture before it was covered is followed immediately by a stern warning as to the dangers of allowing the Kohathites to catch even a glimpse of it. The two together merely serve to emphasize the fact that the Levites were in no way priests:

Then the LORD spoke to Moses and to Aaron, saying, **"Do not let the tribe of the families of the Kohathites be cut off from among the Levites. But do this to them that they may live and not die when they approach the most holy {objects:} Aaron and his sons shall go in and assign each of them to his work and to his load; but they shall not go in to see the holy {objects} even for a moment, lest they die."**
(Numbers 4:17–20)

God next explained the task of the Gershonites to Moses. In contrast to the Kohathites, the Gershonites could approach the tabernacle to remove and prepare its outer coverings for transit only after the danger posed by the holy furnishings had been removed:

> Then the LORD spoke to Moses, saying, "Take a census of the sons of Gershon also, by their fathers' households, by their families; from thirty years and upward to fifty years old, you shall number them; all who enter to perform the service to do the work in the tent of meeting. **This is the service of the families of the Gershonites, in serving and in carrying: they shall carry the curtains of the Tabernacle and the tent of meeting** {with} its covering and the covering of porpoise skin that is on top of it, and the screen for the doorway of the tent of meeting, and the hangings of the court, and the screen for the doorway of the gate of the court which is around the Tabernacle and the altar, and their cords and all the equipment for their service; and all that is to be done, they shall perform. All the service of the sons of the Gershonites, in all their loads and in all their work, shall be {performed} at the command of Aaron and his sons; and you shall assign to them as a duty all their loads. This is the service of the families of the sons of the Gershonites in the tent of meeting, and their duties {shall be} under the direction of Ithamar the son of Aaron the priest." (Numbers 4:21–28)

There is no mention of any danger related to the work of the Gershonites. That stands in stark contrast to the work of the Kohathites. That lack of mention merely shows that, by removing the sacred furniture immediately after it had been covered by the priests, the Kohathites had removed the source of the danger the tabernacle precinct posed to laymen.

Finally, God described the task of the Merarites. He explained that their responsibility involved the disassembly, transport, and reassembly of the various bars, pillars, cords, and pegs that comprised the infrastructure of the tabernacle:

"{*As for*} *the sons of Merari, you shall number them by their families, by their fathers' households; from thirty years and upward even to fifty years old, you shall number them, everyone who enters the service to do the work of the tent of meeting.* **Now this is the duty of their loads, for all their service in the tent of meeting: the boards of the Tabernacle and its bars and its pillars and its sockets, and the pillars around the court and their sockets and their pegs and their cords, with all their equipment and with all their service;** *and you shall assign {each man} by name the items he is to carry. This is the service of the families of the sons of Merari, according to all their service in the tent of meeting, under the direction of Ithamar the son of Aaron the priest.*"
(*Numbers 4:29–33*)

The four passages just quoted tell us God considered the distinction between priest and Levite to be absolute. The priests had a solemn responsibility for conducting the *symbolic rituals* of the tabernacle cult as *parabolic pantomime*, and the Levites were nothing more than servants of the priests. They were assigned to Aaron and his sons, the priests, to assist them in transporting and guarding the tabernacle during the wilderness wandering. Moreover, they carried out their assigned tasks under the direct supervision of Eleazar and Ithamar, "the priests, the sons of Aaron." In sum, they were little more than laymen and could not so much as catch a glimpse of the sacred furniture inside the sanctuary lest God destroy them. That stands in sharp contrast to "the priests, the sons of Aaron," who ministered daily in the sanctuary, viewing and handling the sacred objects as part of their normal priestly duties.

The Korahite Rebellion

In the wilderness, Moses taught the sons of Israel *verbally* (speaking through Aaron) what "the priests, the sons of Aaron" taught them *nonverbally* through both their personal conduct and the *symbolic rituals* of the tabernacle. The Levites were bit players in the *parabolic pantomime* conducted by the priests. Even in that, they were supervised by Eleazar and Ithamar, the sons of Aaron.[19]

Shortly after Israel set out from Mt. Sinai, an arrogant Kohathite named Korah decided to challenge not only God's restriction of the priesthood to "the priests, the sons of Aaron" but also His restriction of verbal instruction to Moses alone. The account of Korah's insurrection provides specific information that is crucial to an understanding of exactly whom God held responsible for teaching Israel after Moses died. Korah's challenge was direct and to the point:

> *Now Korah the son of Izhar, the son of Kohath, the son of Levi, with Dathan and Abiram, the sons of Eliab, and On the son of Peleth, sons of Reuben, took {action,} and they rose up before Moses, together with some of the sons of Israel, two hundred and fifty leaders of the congregation, chosen in the assembly, men of renown. And they assembled together against Moses and Aaron, and said to them, "You have gone far enough, for all the congregation are holy, every one of them, and the LORD is in their midst; so **why do you exalt yourselves above the assembly of the LORD?**"*
> *(Numbers 16:1–3)*

Korah's accusation that Moses and Aaron were exalting themselves above everyone else in Israel's tribal council has to do with the fact that he knew only Moses, Aaron, and the sons of Aaron could enter the tabernacle. However, it also stems directly from the fact that Moses (at God's behest) repeatedly reminded the people that all Israel was holy:

> *Then the LORD spoke to Moses, saying, "Speak to all the congregation of the sons of Israel and say to them, 'You shall be holy, for I the LORD your God am holy.'"*
> *(Leviticus 19:1–2)*[20]

---

[19] Numbers 3:32; 4:16, 28, 33.
[20] See also Leviticus 11:44–45; 20:7, 26.

That explains why Korah said, "all the congregation are holy, every one of them, and the LORD is in their midst." However, Korah did not understand that God established gradations of holiness,[21] not to mention the further distinction between what was clean and unclean.[22] Had he stopped to think about it, he could have seen the grades of holiness in the fact that laymen could enter only the court of the tabernacle; the priests could enter only the court and the outer sanctuary of the tabernacle; but Aaron, the high priest, could enter the Holy of Holies, even if only on the Day of Atonement.[23]

Korah's ignorance in regard to the graduated holiness of Israel is not as easily explained as his rebellion: He was puffed up with pride because he was a Kohathite, one of the Levites God had assigned responsibility for carrying the Ark of the Covenant, the most holy piece of tabernacle furniture. In his pride at having such a privileged assignment, he decided to challenge Moses' declaration concerning who was, and who was not, qualified to be priest. Since Korah's challenge dealt with the issue of who was qualified to minister as priest, Moses immediately selected the offering of incense—a strictly priestly function—as the test for determining the one whom God had selected to be high priest:

> *When Moses heard {this,} he fell on his face; and he spoke to Korah and all his company, saying, "Tomorrow morning the LORD will show who is His, and who is holy, and will bring {him} near to Himself; even the one whom He will choose, He will bring near to Himself.* **Do this: take censers for yourselves, Korah and all your company, and put fire in them, and lay incense upon them in the presence of the LORD tomorrow; and the man whom the LORD chooses {shall be} the one who is holy.** *You*

---

[21] See, for example, M. Haran, "The Priestly Image of the Tabernacle," *Hebrew Union College Annual* 36 (1965), pp. 191–226.

[22] Leviticus 11.

[23] Leviticus 16.

have gone far enough, you sons of Levi!"
(Numbers 16:4–7)

Moses was well aware of the danger incurred by anyone other than an ordained priest offering incense to the Lord. He knew God had already destroyed two fully qualified priests— Nadab and Abihu, the sons of Aaron—just because they failed to follow the prescribed ritual for offering incense. These two perfectly acceptable priests had done nothing more untoward than offer incense with "strange fire."[24] So Moses definitely knew Korah's fate was sealed if he proved arrogant enough to proceed with his challenge. However, Moses had also perceived the real motive in Korah's challenge—his aspiration to the priesthood. That's why he asked him whether it was so:

*Then Moses said to Korah, "Hear now, you sons of Levi, is it not enough for you that the God of Israel has separated you from the {rest of} the congregation of Israel, to bring you near to Himself, to do the service of the Tabernacle of the LORD, and to stand before the congregation to minister to them; and that He has brought you near, {Korah,} and all your brothers, sons of Levi, with you? And **are you seeking for the priesthood also**? Therefore you and all your company are gathered together against the LORD;*

---

[24] Leviticus 10:1–7. The point of the destruction of Nadab and Abihu is not difficult to determine. The first sacrifice Aaron offered on the newly constructed altar (Lev. 9:8–21) after his consecration and ordination by Moses (Lev. 9:1–7) had just been consumed by the "fire of the Lord"—"the glory of the Lord"—that came out of the cloud that overshadowed the tabernacle (Lev. 9:22–24). That event describes the supernatural ignition of the fire that burned on the brazen altar, a fire that was to be kept burning continually (Lev. 6:12–13) as a visible part of the fire that God is (Deut. 4:24). The incineration of Nadab and Abihu emphasized that point: The supernatural fire of God is not like the fire of this Earth, but is in the category of the fire of the sun and stars. It is, as the ancient Greeks and Phoenicians believed, a "creative" fire that does not so much destroy as it transforms. Apparently, the Liar is going to duplicate the same awe-inspiring ignition of the fire on the altar when he reestablishes the Temple cult in Jerusalem (Rev. 13:13).

but as for Aaron, who is he that you grumble against him?"
(Numbers 16:8–11)

Korah paid for his folly with his own life and the lives of all those who ignorantly chose to stand with him in his arrogance. The next morning God destroyed his entire company immediately after confirming that Aaron and his sons were His choice for the priesthood. But God went one step further. He ordered that the bronze censers of Korah and his band be made into plating for the altar. The reason given for that action confirms beyond any shadow of a doubt that the Levites were not priests, at least not during the wilderness wandering:

*Then the LORD spoke to Moses, saying, "Say to Eleazar, the son of Aaron the priest, that he shall take up the censers out of the midst of the blaze, for they are holy; and you scatter the burning coals abroad. As for the censers of these men who have sinned at the cost of their lives, let them be made into hammered sheets for a plating of the altar, since they did present them before the LORD and they are holy; and they shall be for a sign to the sons of Israel." **So Eleazar the priest took the bronze censers which the men who were burned had offered; and they hammered them out as a plating for the altar, as a reminder to the sons of Israel that no layman who is not of the descendants of Aaron should come near to burn incense before the LORD;** that he might not become like Korah and his company—just as the LORD had spoken to him through Moses.*
(Numbers 16:36–40)

There is one more not-so-obvious consequence of Korah's action. Prior to Korah's rebellion, the Kohathites carried all of the tabernacle furniture. But the following passage of Scripture reveals that, because of Korah's rebellion, the Kohathites lost the privilege of carrying the two most holy pieces of tabernacle furniture—the sacrificial altar and the Ark of the Covenant. God transferred responsibility for carrying those two items to "the priests, the sons of Aaron," immediately after the Kohathite rebellion:

> So the LORD said to Aaron, "You and your sons and your father's household with you shall bear the guilt in connection with the sanctuary; and you and your sons with you shall bear the guilt in connection with your priesthood. But bring with you also your brothers, the tribe of Levi, the tribe of your father, that they may be joined with you and serve you, while you and your sons with you are before the tent of the testimony. And they shall thus attend to your obligation and the obligation of all the tent, but they shall not come near to the furnishings of the sanctuary and the altar, lest both they and you die. And they shall be joined with you and attend to the obligations of the tent of meeting, for all the service of the tent; but an outsider may not come near you. So you shall attend to the obligations of the sanctuary and the obligations of the altar, that there may no longer be wrath on the sons of Israel. And behold, I Myself have taken your fellow Levites from among the sons of Israel; they are a gift to you, dedicated to the LORD, to perform the service for the tent of meeting. But **you and your sons with you shall attend to your priesthood for everything concerning the altar and inside the veil, and you are to perform service.** I am giving you the priesthood as a bestowed service, but the outsider who comes near shall be put to death."
> (Numbers 18:1–7)

Unfortunately, the translator's general translation of Numbers 18:7, "you are to perform service," is much too ambiguous to provide the reader of the English version any insight at all into what God actually told Aaron about the new duties assigned to the priests. The key to understanding what God said to Aaron resides in the Hebrew word *'abodah* (which *means* "transportation work"). The *meaning* and *significance* of this term has been completely overlooked by translators and commentators alike. It indicates that God transferred responsibility for transporting the Ark of the Covenant from the Kohathites to "the priests, the sons of Aaron" as a direct result of Korah's rebellion.

A more specific (and better) translation of Numbers 18:7 would be "you [plural, *meaning* 'the priests'] must do transportation work."[25] From that, one can at least see that God was assigning "the priests, the sons of Aaron" responsibility for carrying "everything concerning the altar and inside the veil." That is, they now had responsibility for carrying the altar and the Ark of the Covenant (the only piece of furniture inside the veil).

The Levitical Priesthood

The above discussion reveals that, during the wilderness wandering:

1) The Levites were not priests; they were servants of the priests.

2) As priestly servants, the Levites' responsibility included the work associated with transporting the tabernacle.[26]

3) Responsibility for transporting the Ark of the Covenant was initially assigned to the Kohathites, but because of Korah's rebellion, that responsibility was later restricted to the priests.

---

[25] J. Milgrom is the commentator coming closest to the Truth concerning the *significance* of Numbers 18:6–7. See his discussion in *The JPS Torah Commentary: Numbers* (pp. 148, 343–344). He has explained the term *'abodah* as having the specific *meaning* "transportation work" in that work and in his *Studies in Levitical Terminology*. However, even he fails to understand what Numbers 18:7 *means* when it says the sons of Aaron were responsible for the "transportation work" (*'abodah*) of "the altar and inside the veil." Prior to Korah's rebellion, the priests had no responsibility for any *'abodah* related to the tabernacle. That was the responsibility of the Levites alone. The *'abodah* of the two items in question ("everything concerning the altar and inside the veil") was specifically the responsibility of the Kohathites.

[26] The Levites also guarded the tabernacle. However, since that part of their responsibility is not pertinent here, I will discuss it on another occasion.

If God was not averse to changing the administrative structure of *Corporate* Israel in response to the sinful actions of Korah and his friends, why would anyone assume He would hesitate to change that same structure later on when it suited His unique purposes? Moses tells us He did just that near the end of the wilderness wandering. Immediately after Aaron died, Moses began the process by bestowing all the privileges of the priesthood on the entire tribe of Levi. That included the responsibility for them once again to carry the Ark of the Covenant. Moses explains that in his account of the death of Aaron:

> *(Now the sons of Israel set out from Beeroth Bene-jaakan to Moserah. There Aaron died and there he was buried and Eleazar his son ministered as priest in his place. From there they set out to Gudgodah; and from Gudgodah to Jotbathah, a land of brooks of water.* **At that time the LORD set apart the tribe of Levi to carry the ark of the covenant of the LORD, to stand before the LORD to serve Him and to bless in His name until this day.** *Therefore, Levi does not have a portion or inheritance with his brothers; the LORD is his inheritance, just as the LORD your God spoke to him.)*
> *(Deuteronomy 10:6–9)*

Moses plainly says "the LORD set apart the tribe of Levi" after the death of Aaron and bestowed on them three prerogatives that had previously been the exclusive domain of "the priests, the sons of Aaron." Those were the right to:

1) Carry the Ark of the Covenant of the Lord.
2) Stand before the Lord to serve Him.
3) Bless in His Name.

One could easily miss the point of this passage if he were not already aware that:

1) Responsibility for transporting the Ark of the Covenant had been taken away from the Kohathites and given to "the priests, the sons of Aaron" after the rebellion of Korah.

2) Only "the priests, the sons of Aaron" could "stand before the Lord[27] to serve Him."

3) Only "the priests, the sons of Aaron" could "bless in His Name."

In the wilderness, "the priests, the sons of Aaron" carried the Ark of the Covenant, stood "before the Lord to serve Him," and blessed the people "in His Name." Therefore, Moses clearly made a fundamental change in the priesthood shortly after Aaron's death.[28] One should ask why such an alteration was necessary. The Truth in this regard, as in so many others, is crucial to an accurate understanding of the Scriptures.

With Aaron's death, the sons of Israel began a transition from the seminomadic circumstances of the wilderness wan-

---

[27] The expression "before the Lord" refers to a specific location inside the court of the tabernacle, in front of the tent of meeting. Only the priests could "serve" the Lord in that location.

[28] There is actually a fourth indication in Deuteronomy 10:6–9 that all the Levites became priests when Aaron died. It becomes evident from God's statement to Aaron when He assigned the transportation of the altar and the Ark of the Covenant to the priests. The biblical text makes a clear distinction between the inheritance of the priests and that of the Levites:

> Then the LORD said to Aaron, **"You shall have no inheritance in their land, nor own any portion among them; I am your portion and your inheritance among the sons of Israel.** And to the sons of Levi, behold, I have given all the tithe in Israel for an inheritance, in return for their service which they perform, the service of the tent of meeting."
> (Numbers 18:20–21)

In the wilderness, the inheritance of the priests was the Lord, whereas the inheritance of the Levites was the tithe of the sons of Israel. From that, it is clear that Deuteronomy 10:9 is saying all the Levites had obtained the inheritance of the priests:

> (At that time the LORD set apart the tribe of Levi to carry the ark of the covenant of the LORD, to stand before the LORD to serve Him and to bless in His name until this day. **Therefore, Levi does not have a portion or inheritance with his brothers; the LORD is his inheritance**, just as the LORD your God spoke to him.)
> (Deuteronomy 10:8–9)

dering to the settled agrarian existence they took up after their conquest of the Promised Land. In the wilderness, God met all of Israel's needs, providing both food and clothing.[29] The sole responsibility of the sons of Israel was to learn *The Teaching of Moses.* So Moses (speaking through his "prophet" Aaron) taught the people *The Teaching* while "the priests, the sons of Aaron" carried out the *nonverbal* instruction of all Israel by means of *parabolic pantomime.*

The Levites other than the family of Aaron had no priestly duties during the wilderness wandering. Their responsibility was transporting and guarding the tabernacle. However, the passage quoted above[30] reveals Moses elevated all of the Levites to the status of priests when Aaron died. Why did he do that? And how did he fit all these new priests into the responsibilities of the priesthood? To answer those questions, one must look more closely at the responsibilities Moses assigned the Levites.

As Deuteronomy 10:8 indicates, Moses gave the *Levitical* priests the responsibility for pronouncing blessing on the people. We already know that responsibility had previously belonged to "the priests, the sons of Aaron":

*"Then **the priests, the sons of Levi, shall come near, for the LORD your God has chosen them to serve Him and to bless in the name of the LORD**; and every dispute and every assault shall be settled by them."*
(Deuteronomy 21:5)

Moses also gave the *Levitical* priests responsibility for conducting the *nonverbal symbolic rituals*—the *parabolic pantomimes*—of the tabernacle cult. That is made clear by what Moses says about the *torah* that pertains to "leprosy":

*"Be careful against an infection of leprosy, that you diligently observe and **do according to all that the Levitical priests shall***

---

[29] Deuteronomy 2:7.
[30] Deuteronomy 10:6–9.

teach you; as I have commanded them, so you shall be careful to do. Remember what the LORD your God did to Miriam on the way as you came out of Egypt."
(Deuteronomy 24:8–9)

Moses has already told us "the priests, the sons of Aaron" conducted this *symbolic ritual* during the wilderness wandering, where its purpose was to teach ("point out") *nonverbally* through *parabolic pantomime*:

… to teach when they are unclean, and when they are clean. This is the law of leprosy.
(Leviticus 14:57)

Moses also discloses that he not only gave the *Levitical* priests responsibility for conducting the *symbolic rituals* mandated by the cultic *statutes*, he also assigned them the ultimate responsibility for overseeing the judges of Israel. He first told the people they should appoint judges in the various settlements where they lived:

"You shall appoint for yourself judges and officers in all your towns which the LORD your God is giving you, according to your tribes, and they shall judge the people with righteous judgment. You shall not distort justice; you shall not be partial, and you shall not take a bribe, for a bribe blinds the eyes of the wise and perverts the words of the righteous. Justice, {and only} justice, you shall pursue, that you may live and possess the land which the LORD your God is giving you."
(Deuteronomy 16:18–20)

Moses then outlined the procedure the judges of Israel should follow whenever a case was "too difficult" for them to decide. They were to take it to the *Levitical* priests:

"If any case is too difficult for you to decide, between one kind of homicide or another, between one kind of lawsuit or another, and between one kind of assault or another, being cases of dispute in your courts, then you shall arise and go up to the place which the

LORD *your God chooses.* **So you shall come to the Levitical priest or the judge who is {in office} in those days, and you shall inquire {of them,} and they will declare to you the verdict in the** CASE. *And you shall do according to the terms of the verdict which they declare to you from that place which the* LORD *chooses; and* **you shall be careful to observe according to all that they teach you. According to the terms of the** LAW *which* **they teach you, and according to the** VERDICT *which they tell* **you**, *you shall do; you shall not turn aside from the word which they declare to you, to the right or the left. And the man who acts presumptuously by not listening to the priest who stands there to serve the* LORD *your God, nor to the judge, that man shall die; thus you shall purge the evil from Israel. Then all the people will hear and be afraid, and will not act presumptuously again."*
(Deuteronomy 17:8–13)[31]

The adjudication procedure described in that passage is strikingly similar to what Moses established at Mt. Sinai. Compare the following passage with the one above:

So Moses listened to his father-in-law, and did all that he had said. And Moses chose able men out of all Israel, and made them heads over the people, leaders of thousands, of hundreds, of fifties and of tens. **And they judged the people at all times; the difficult dispute they would bring to Moses, but every minor dispute they themselves would judge.**
(Exodus 18:24–26)

It is clear from a careful reading of Deuteronomy 17 that Moses did not change the role of the judges of Israel. They

---

[31] In this passage, "case" and "verdict" are translations of the Hebrew term *mishpat*, the term normally translated "judgment." "Law" is the normal translation of *torah*. The *judgments* are expressly called *torah* in this passage because Moses is assigning the *Levitical* priests responsibility for "pointing out" the *significance* of the *judgments* in the same way they were to "point out" the *significance* of the *statutes*. They were to do so through the *symbolic ritual* of overseeing the judges of Israel.

had no responsibility for teaching anything in the wilderness, and they gained none when their supervision was transferred to the *Levitical* priests. The *Levitical* priests merely replaced Moses and the elders/Prophets as the ones with knowledge of the *meaning* and *significance* of the conditional *judgments*. That is because Moses had already finished *handing down* the oral **Torah** to the *Levitical* priests. They had no further need of supernatural revelation. They knew the Truth.

The passages above indirectly reveal why Moses elevated the *judgments* to the status of *nonverbal* **Torah**—that is, why he made them *parabolic pantomime*. He was merging the teaching and judging responsibilities he had separated on the advice of Jethro. After combining the two, he assigned the oversight of both to the *Levitical* priests. That makes it clear he intended for the *Levitical* priests to assume responsibility for teaching an *oral* **Torah** that encompassed an explanation of the *meaning* and *significance* of both *statutes* and *judgments*. The following passage confirms that conclusion:

> *So Moses wrote **this** LAW and gave it to **the priests, the sons of Levi** who carried the ark of the covenant of the LORD, and to all the elders of Israel. Then Moses commanded them, saying, "At the end of {every} seven years, at the time of the year of remission of debts, at the Feast of Booths, when all Israel comes to appear before the LORD your God at the place which He will choose, **you shall read this** LAW **in front of all Israel in their hearing. Assemble the people, the men and the women and children and the alien who is in your town, in order that they may hear and learn and fear the LORD your God, and be careful to observe all the words of this** LAW. And their children, who have not known, will hear and learn to fear the LORD your God, as long as you live on the land which you are about to cross the Jordan to possess."*
> *(Deuteronomy 31:9–13)*

After Moses changed *Corporate* Israel's organizational structure, the three mantles previously worn by Moses, the elders/Prophets, and "the priests, the sons of Aaron" fell to the entire tribe of Levi—that is, "the *Levitical* priests." After Moses died, the Levites were supposed to minister as God's Teachers, priests, and judicial supervisors. They failed at all three tasks. But the key to understanding the Prophets' indictment of *Corporate* Israel lies in knowing that Moses expanded the priesthood to include the Levites and included the civil/criminal *judgments* under the oversight of the priests. That, in turn, explains *why* he expanded his use of the word **torah** to include not only God's *statutes* but also all of His other *commandments*.

During the wilderness wandering, the priests had only the responsibility for "pointing out" *nonverbally* the *meaning* and *significance* of the *oral* **Torah** through the *symbolic rituals*— the *parabolic pantomimes*—mandated by the *statutes*. When Moses redefined the priestly role and gave "the *Levitical* priests" responsibility for teaching Israel *verbally* the *meaning* and *significance* of all the *commandments* of God—*statutes* as well as *judgments*—he indicated the priests would continue to do what Aaron, the high priest, had always done. They would teach the *oral* **Torah** Moses had *received* from God. However, Moses made sure the Levites understood that **Torah** now included *parabolic pantomimes* related to the civil/criminal *judgments* as well as those related to the cultic *statutes*. In short, he told the sons of Israel that all the *commandments* of God mandated *symbolic rituals* with specific *meaning*.

When Moses blessed Israel shortly before his death, he described the responsibility of the *Levitical* priests this way:

> *"They shall teach Thine ordinances to Jacob,*
> *And Thy law to Israel.*
> *They shall put incense before Thee,*
> *And whole burnt offerings on Thine altar."*
> *(Deuteronomy 33:10)*[32]

---

[32] *Teach* is a translation of the Hebrew verb **yarah** ("point out"); *law* is a translation of **torah**. *Ordinances* is a translation of **mishpatim**—*judgments*.

The poetry in this verse is a good example of Hebrew parallelism: The thought of the first line is continued in the second; the thought of the third is continued in the fourth. Moreover, the last two lines explain how "the Levitical priests" were supposed to accomplish their responsibility as stated in the first two lines. They were to "point out" the *meaning* and *significance* of the *oral Torah* related to the *statutes* by conducting the *symbolic rituals* of the tabernacle cult as *parabolic pantomime*.

Teach the Children Well ...

In the wilderness, Moses spoke to the people—in *parabolic pantomime*—through his "mouth," the high priest Aaron. "The priests, the sons of Aaron" were not allowed to teach *verbally*, because that prerogative remained Moses' alone until shortly before his death.[33] Instead, "the priests, the sons of Aaron" taught the sons of Israel *nonverbally* by conducting the *symbolic rituals* of the tabernacle cult as *parabolic pantomime*. The prohibition against anyone other than Moses teaching *verbally* was so absolute that, even after God gave the seventy elders/Prophets insight into the *meaning* and *significance* of the civil/criminal *judgments* by which the judges judged, they were not allowed to prophesy so as to explain anything they understood.

The priests were also limited in the scope of what they could teach *nonverbally* during the wilderness wandering. They could only "point out" *nonverbally* the things that Moses taught *verbally* concerning the *meaning* and *significance* of the *statutes* that governed the *symbolic rituals* of the tabernacle cult. They could not "point out" anything at all about the *meaning* or *significance* of the civil/criminal *judgments* because those fell under the jurisdiction of the seventy elder/Prophets who supervised the heads of Israel's military/judicial units.

When Moses changed the administrative structure of *Corporate* Israel after the death of Aaron, his changes resulted in a

---

[33] Deuteronomy 4:4–14.

fundamental reorganization of the upper echelons of Israel's government. That consisted of three essential changes:

1) All the Levites became priests.

2) The Levitical priests assumed responsibility for teaching Israel as Moses had taught Israel.

3) The Levitical priests replaced the elders/Prophets as those whom God held responsible for supervising the judges of Israel.

Although Moses gave "the *Levitical* priests" responsibility for *handing down* the *oral Torah* he had *received* from God, he did not make them responsible for the instruction of every member of Israel. They only replaced Moses and the elders/Prophets as the ultimate repository of the knowledge of *The Teaching*. Although their primary priestly responsibility was to see that *The Teaching* was *handed down* from generation to generation, Moses made every "head" of a "house" in Israel responsible for the education of the members of his own "house."

As I explained above in connection with the Feast of Unleavened Bread, God intended laymen to explain to their children the *meaning* and *significance* of the *symbolic rituals* the sons of Israel were supposed to conduct:[34]

> "For seven days you shall eat unleavened bread, and on the seventh day there shall be a feast to the LORD. Unleavened bread shall be eaten throughout the seven days; and nothing leavened shall be seen among you, nor shall any leaven be seen among you in all your borders. **And you shall tell your son on that day, saying, 'It is because of what the LORD did for me when I came out of Egypt.' And it shall serve as a sign to you on your hand, and as a reminder on your forehead, that the law of the LORD may be in your mouth;** for with a powerful hand the LORD brought you out of Egypt. Therefore, you shall keep this ordinance at its appointed time from year to year."
> (Exodus 13:6–10)

---

[34] See above, pp. 131–132.

It is not difficult to see that even during the wilderness wandering, every "head" of every "house" was supposed to teach the members of his immediate family. That arrangement remained unchanged even after Moses placed the judges under the supervision of the Levites and expanded the scope of *nonverbal Torah* to include the *judgments* of God. The biblical text clearly indicates that was the case. In the following passage, Moses states God had given him responsibility for teaching the sons of Israel so they could teach their children:

> *"Only give heed to yourself and keep your soul diligently, lest you forget the things which your eyes have seen, and lest they depart from your heart all the days of your life; but make them known to your sons and your grandsons. {Remember} the day you stood before the LORD your God at Horeb, when the LORD said to me, 'Assemble the people to Me, that I may let them hear My words so they may learn to fear Me all the days they live on the earth, and **that they may teach their children.'** And you came near and stood at the foot of the mountain, and the mountain burned with fire to the {very} heart of the heavens: darkness, cloud and thick gloom. Then the LORD spoke to you from the midst of the fire; you heard the sound of words, but you saw no form—only a voice. So He declared to you His covenant which He commanded you to perform, {that is,} the Ten Commandments; and He wrote them on two tablets of stone. And **the LORD commanded me at that time to teach you statutes and judgments**, that you might perform them in the land where you are going over to possess it."*
> (Deuteronomy 4:9–14)

Moses clearly understood God held him responsible for teaching the sons of Israel. But he emphasized again and again that God held each "head" of a "house" responsible for teaching his children the *meaning* and *significance* of the various stipulations of the legal code:

> *"Now **this is the commandment, the statutes and the judgments which the LORD your God has commanded {me} to***

teach you, *that you might do {them} in the land where you are going over to possess it, so that you and your son and your grandson might fear the* LORD *your God, to keep all His statutes and His commandments, which I command you, all the days of your life, and that your days may be prolonged. O Israel, you should listen and be careful to do {it,} that it may be well with you and that you may multiply greatly, just as the* LORD, *the God of your fathers, has promised you, {in} a land flowing with milk and honey. Hear, O Israel! The* LORD *is our God, the* LORD *is one! And you shall love the* LORD *your God with all your heart and with all your soul and with all your might. And these words, which I am commanding you today, shall be on your heart; and **you shall teach them diligently to your sons** and shall talk of them when you sit in your house and when you walk by the way and when you lie down and when you rise up. And you shall bind them as a sign on your hand and they shall be as frontals on your forehead. And you shall write them on the doorposts of your house and on your gates."*
(Deuteronomy 6:1–9)

As that passage discloses, God expected every one of the sons of Israel to *hand down The Teaching* to the next generation just as he had *received* it from the previous generation. On another occasion Moses states exactly the same thing:

*"**You shall therefore impress these words of mine on your heart and on your soul; and you shall bind them as a sign on your hand, and they shall be as frontals on your forehead. And you shall teach them to your sons**, talking of them when you sit in your house and when you walk along the road and when you lie down and when you rise up. And you shall write them on the doorposts of your house and on your gates, so that your days and the days of your sons may be multiplied on the land which the* LORD *swore to your fathers to give them, as long as the heavens {remain} above the earth."*
(Deuteronomy 11:18–21)

In addition to placing a strong emphasis on the individual's responsibility for teaching the children of each new generation, Moses also made provision for the public reading of "this *Torah*" every seven years:

> So Moses wrote this law and gave it to the priests, the sons of Levi who carried the ark of the covenant of the LORD, and to all the elders of Israel. Then Moses commanded them, saying, **"At the end of {every} seven years**, at the time of the year of remission of debts, at the Feast of Booths, when all Israel comes to appear before the LORD your God at the place which He will choose, you shall read this law in front of all Israel in their hearing. **Assemble the people**, the men and the women and children and the alien who is in your town, in order **that they may hear and learn and fear the LORD your God**, and be careful to observe all the words of this law. And **their children, who have not known, will hear and learn to fear the LORD your God**, as long as you live on the land which you are about to cross the Jordan to possess."
> (Deuteronomy 31:9–13)

By publicly reading the scroll that Moses had written, "the *Levitical* priests" included young children in the public instruction of Israel. That *symbolic ritual* was intended to remind the sons of Israel of the importance of *handing down* to their children the *oral tradition* God had established in Israel. With that final admonition, Moses turned responsibility for teaching the sons of Israel over to "the *Levitical* priests":

> And it came about, when Moses finished writing the words of **this** LAW in a book until they were complete, that Moses commanded the Levites who carried the ark of the covenant of the LORD, saying, "Take **this book of the** LAW and place it beside the ark of the covenant of the LORD your God, that it may remain there as a witness against you."
> (Deuteronomy 31:24–26)

After the Levites deposited the "scroll of the *Torah*" in the sanctuary, they alone were responsible for "pointing out"— both *verbally* and *nonverbally*—the *meaning* and *significance* of *The Teaching* Moses had hidden in it. Unfortunately, they failed to do as they had been instructed. Consequently, the sons of Israel soon lost *The Teaching*. In his final words, Moses clearly states he knew they would fail. He told them they would all too soon "turn (aside) from *The Way*." That is, they would do just as their fathers had done while he was still on the Mountain of God:

> *"For I know your rebellion and your stubbornness; behold, while I am still alive with you today, you have been rebellious against the* LORD; *how much more, then, after my death? Assemble to me all the elders of your tribes and your officers, that I may speak these words in their hearing and call the heavens and the earth to witness against them.* **For I know that after my death you will act corruptly and turn from the way which I have commanded you;** *and evil will befall you in the latter days, for you will do that which is evil in the sight of the* LORD, *provoking Him to anger with the work of your hands."*
> *(Deuteronomy 31:27–29)*

Summary

This concludes our inquiry into who was responsible for teaching Israel after Moses died. It also completes our survey of the history of *The Mystery* up to the death of Moses. However, it is just the beginning of our survey of the evidence that pertains to *Corporate* Israel's knowledge of *The Mystery*. The next volume will continue this investigation by looking into things the Prophets say concerning Israel's loss of *The Teaching*.

In this chapter, I showed you how Moses merged the responsibilities for teaching and judging the sons of Israel and entrusted the newly combined responsibility to "the *Levitical* priests." He began by allowing the entire tribe of Levi to serve as priests. Then he charged them with oversight of the judges of Israel. It thereby became their responsibility to *hand down The Teaching of Moses* from one generation of priests to the next after he died. That was a drastic change.

During the wilderness wandering, the priesthood had been restricted to "the priests, the sons of Aaron." As priests, they conducted the *symbolic rituals* of the tabernacle as a *parabolic pantomime* whose purpose was to "point out" the *meaning* and *significance* of the *Torah* related to the cultic *statutes.* Moses assigned the rest of the tribe of Levi to the priests as priestly servants to help them in the disassembly, transportation, guarding, and assembly of the tabernacle. In the wilderness, the Levites were no better than laymen. They could not so much as catch a glimpse of the sacred furniture of the tabernacle before the priests covered it for transport.

Shortly after the sons of Israel set out from Mt. Sinai, however, a Kohathite named Korah challenged the established order, seeking to become a priest. Consequently, God relieved the Kohathites of the responsibility for carrying the sacrificial altar and the Ark of the Covenant, giving it instead to the Aaronic priesthood. Thereafter, "the priests, the sons of Aaron" carried these two pieces of tabernacle furniture.

When Moses admitted the entire tribe of Levi to the priesthood shortly after Aaron died, "the *Levitical* priests" became responsible for conducting the *symbolic rituals* of the tabernacle as *parabolic pantomime*. But right before his own death, Moses expanded the scope of *Torah* to include not only the cultic *statutes* but also the civil/criminal *judgments.* At that time, he assigned "the *Levitical* priests" responsibility for overseeing the judges of Israel who were charged with judging the sons of Israel according to those *judgments.*

As one of his final acts, Moses exhorted the sons of Israel to be careful to *hand down* their knowledge of *The Teaching* to their children by taking every opportunity to teach them the *meaning* and *significance* of the *symbolic rituals* God had given them to observe. He then wrote the **Torah** (*The Teaching*) God had given him on a scroll and gave that scroll to the *Levitical* priests to put in the sanctuary as a "witness" against the sons of Israel. Moses also told them to take the scroll out of the sanctuary every seventh year for public reading.

Moses concluded his remarks by warning "the *Levitical* priests" that he already knew they would "turn aside from *The Way.*" Anyone who knows the *meaning* of the Hebrew idioms "walk in *The Way*" and "turn aside from *The Way*" can be sure he is referring to their loss of *The (oral) Teaching of Moses* that God *delivered* to Moses in the wilderness.

CHAPTER 9:

THE TESTIMONY OF THE SCRIPTURES

If the information presented in the preceding chapters is true, the Church today clearly lacks an accurate understanding of the sacred Scriptures to which so many "Christians" cling so dearly. That anomalous situation will prove deadly for most. Why would the guilty hold tightly to a "witness" that cogently testifies against them? Only because they have taken refuge in Satan's lie. Like their mother Eve, they have been deceived by yet another of the Liar's half-truths. But one need not feel sorry for them. They place great confidence in the lies they believe because those lies allow them to do as they please without any concern at all for the God Who is.

On various occasions, I have openly stated that God called me to restore *The Apostolic Teaching* in these Last Days for the benefit of those who will "return to *The Way* of the Lord." My sole responsibility is to make the Truth of *The Teaching* available for those who choose to believe it. My calling is not at all concerned with those who reject what I teach and my claim that God called me to teach it. That is their choice. But for those who still do not want to believe the Truth after reading what I have written, I offer the following information to absolve myself completely of any responsibility for their abject ignorance.

When it came time for Moses to die, he brought Joshua to the entrance of the tent of meeting so that God could transfer Moses' authority to him. During that meeting, God told the two men He already knew the sons of Israel would be unfaithful to the terms of the Mosaic Covenant.[1] For that reason, He ordered Moses to write a song and teach it to the people. The stated purpose of that song, *The Song of Moses*,[2] was to be a "witness" against Israel:

> *"Now therefore, write this song for yourselves, and teach it to the sons of Israel; put it on their lips, in order **that this song may be a witness for Me against the sons of Israel.**"*
> *(Deuteronomy 31:19)*

The biblical text goes on to tell us Moses did exactly what God commanded. He wrote the song and "taught" it to the sons of Israel. That is, he explained the *meaning* and *significance* of the song to them. Then he gave "the *Levitical* priests" "the Book of the Law" he had written, and they placed it in the sanctuary:

> **So Moses wrote this song the same day, and taught it to the sons of Israel.** *Then He commissioned Joshua the son of Nun, and said, "Be strong and courageous, for you shall bring the sons of Israel into the*

---

[1] The usual mental response of "Christians" to the unfaithfulness of the sons of Israel is to envision them refusing to adhere to a legalistic "do this, don't do that." That is only because the Church has accepted the interpretation of the Hebrew Scriptures put forward by her unfaithful sister, the Jews, who were "cut off from" Israel long ago. The Pharisees believed legalism was all that God required of them, and they *handed down* that mistaken belief to the Jews who rejected their Messiah, Jesus Christ. Nothing could be further from the Truth. *The Mystery of Scripture* inheres in but one single truism: God gave Moses an *oral Torah* by which, if one believes the Truth of that *Teaching*, one can be saved. If that sounds remarkably like the Protestant doctrine of salvation by faith, that is because *The Teaching of Moses* is the origin of that Protestant doctrine. The conundrum facing the Protestant Church today lies in the fact that one cannot have saving faith (belief) without a definite *content*; and if the *content* of one's faith is not true, that person will not be saved.

[2] Deuteronomy 32:1–43.

land which I swore to them, and I will be with you." And it came about,
when Moses finished writing the words of this law in a book until they
were complete, that Moses commanded the Levites who carried the ark
of the covenant of the LORD, saying, "Take this book of the law and place
it beside the ark of the covenant of the LORD your God, that it may
remain there as a witness against you."
(Deuteronomy 31:22–26)

By doing as God commanded, Moses completed his ministry as the first Prophet/Teacher of Israel.[3] His final words to a people who had been fully instructed in *The Teaching* come immediately after *The Song of Moses*.[4] It would be a good idea for you to carefully study what Moses said. In it one can find the Truth regarding God's purpose in giving these ancient people an *oral Torah* they were to *hand down* to their descendants:

Then Moses came and spoke all the words of this song in the hearing of
the people, he, with Joshua the son of Nun. When Moses had finished
speaking all these words to all Israel, he said to them, "Take to your
heart all the words with which I am warning you today, which

---

[3] The Scriptures tell us Moses did two other things before he went up Mt. Nebo to die. He first spoke the words of *The Song of Moses* in the hearing of the people; then he blessed "all Israel." The second action has *significance* in regard to our understanding of *the promise*.

In *Not All Israel Is Israel*, I did not go into detail regarding the second covenant God made with the sons of Israel at Mt. Sinai (*Not All Israel Is Israel*, p. 134, fn. 4). I will outline it briefly here. At Mt. Sinai, God "cut off from" Israel all the sons of Israel except Moses because of their sin in worshiping Aaron's calf. As the only remaining member (singular) of Israel, Moses was *Corporate* Israel—the sole *heir of the promise* just as Jesus Christ was in His Own day (*Not All Israel Is Israel*, pp. 187 ff.). The sons of Israel were allowed to participate in the second covenant ratified at Mt. Sinai only because Moses insisted (Ex. 32:32). They did so, however, by being all "baptized into Moses," as the Apostle Paul put it (1 Cor. 10:2). Therefore, as the sole *heir of the promise*, Moses transferred *the promise* to all Israel via his *blessing* at his death. As explained in *Not All Israel Is Israel*, that is the same way the Patriarchs transferred *the promise* to the son they had chosen to *inherit the promise*. (See *Not All Israel Is Israel*, pp. 14 ff.)

[4] Deuteronomy 32:1–43.

you shall command your sons to observe carefully, {even} all the
words of this law. For it is not an idle word for you; indeed it is
your life. And by this word you shall prolong your days in the land,
which you are about to cross the Jordan to possess."
(Deuteronomy 32:44–47)

That admonition is a concisely stated summary of the
importance God attached to *The Teaching of Moses*. The *oral*
Torah He *delivered* to the sons of Israel through Moses nearly
3500 years ago would have provided eternal life to countless
millions over the centuries had it not been repeatedly lost. That
would never have happened had it not been for the idiocy of
those who have no interest in the Truth. It was, as Moses
affirmed earlier, an easy task that God set before the sons of
Israel. They had only to hear the Truth and believe it:

"For this commandment which I command you today is not too difficult
for you, nor is it out of reach. It is not in heaven, that you should say,
'Who will go up to heaven for us to get it for us and make us hear it,
that we may observe it?' Nor is it beyond the sea, that you should say,
'Who will cross the sea for us to get it for us and make us hear it, that
*we may observe it?' But **the word is very near you, in your mouth***
***and in your heart, that you may observe it**."*
(Deuteronomy 30:11–14)

Ancient Israel failed to do what God intended. Contrary
to Jewish claims concerning the legalistic fabrication of the
Pharisees that was ultimately recorded in the Mishnah, their
forefathers did not *hand down* the *oral* **Torah** that God *delivered*
to Moses. The two remaining volumes in this series will provide more than ample evidence of that. However, those volumes will also disclose the Church failed at that same task.
Therefore, the Church today stands in no greater favor with
God than do the Jews. Both failed to do what God demanded.
However, their sin is made all the more heinous by the fact
that, just as the Apostle Paul wrote so long ago, a firm belief in
The Teaching is not a difficult thing to maintain:

But the righteousness based on faith speaks thus, "DO NOT SAY IN YOUR
HEART, 'WHO WILL ASCEND INTO HEAVEN?' (that is, to bring Christ

down), or 'WHO WILL DESCEND INTO THE ABYSS?' (that is, to bring Christ up from the dead)." But what does it say? "THE WORD IS NEAR YOU, IN YOUR MOUTH AND IN YOUR HEART"—that is, the word of faith which we are preaching, that if you confess with your mouth Jesus {as} Lord, and believe in your heart that God raised Him from the dead, you shall be saved; for with the heart man believes, resulting in righteousness, and with the mouth he confesses, resulting in salvation. For the Scripture says, "WHOEVER BELIEVES IN HIM WILL NOT BE DISAPPOINTED."
(Romans 10:6–11)

The alert reader will immediately realize Paul is quoting the words of Moses from Deuteronomy 30:11–14. Paul did that because he knew God's purpose in *The Teaching* has never changed. It has only gained a greater historical perspective. The two remaining volumes of this series will provide insight into that perspective.

In the next volume, I will continue to lay out the history of *The Teaching of Moses* by showing you what the sons of Israel did with *The Teaching* immediately after the death of Joshua. I will also confirm the *meaning* of various idioms related to *The Way*— *The Teaching of Moses*—and show you how the sons of Israel quickly "turned aside from *The Way*."[5] That will explain why the Prophets affirm that *Corporate* Israel's essential sin was to continually "turn aside from *The Way*."[6]

Over the course of the next several years, I plan to complete the remaining volumes in this series and in The Resurrection Theology Series. In that series, I will explain the things you need to know in order to understand *The Teaching of Moses* for yourself. In the meantime, I remind you that both the **Torah** Moses wrote on the scroll he gave to the Levites for safekeeping and the *testimonies* written on the tablets of stone that Moses placed in the Ark of the Covenant were intended to function as *witnesses* that testified against *Corporate* Israel should the people ever "turn aside from *The Way*." How did

---

[5] Judges 2:17.

[6] Isaiah 53:6; 56:11; Jeremiah 2:17; 3:21; 18:15.

they provide *testimony*? By verifying that the sons of Israel had lost *The Teaching* God had given them.

The Song of Moses

"The two tablets of the *testimonies*" have long since gotten lost. That is certainly not the case with the contents of the scroll on which Moses wrote *The Song of Moses*. That scroll contained at least the Book of Deuteronomy, if not the entire Pentateuch. It was, therefore, the first edition of the Hebrew Scriptures. The information the other Prophets of Israel added to the Scriptures after the time of Moses merely contributes additional evidence as to *Corporate* Israel's sin.

The Church—the *parabolic* Body of Jesus Christ, *The Man* Who now is *Corporate* Israel—no longer understands the things Moses wrote in the Pentateuch. Therefore, that scroll—the Hebrew Scriptures—still stands as a silent *witness*, providing *testimony* concerning the Church's great sin in losing *The Apostolic Teaching*. That is something every Christian Believer must (and will) deal with in his or her own way. However, since *The Song of Moses* was included in that first edition of the Hebrew Scriptures, I will conclude this volume with that song. In it you will find a succinct summary of *The Teaching of Moses*:

> *Then Moses spoke in the hearing of all the assembly of Israel the words*
> *of this song, until they were complete:*
> *"Give ear, O heavens, and let me speak;*
> *And let the earth hear the words of my mouth.*
> *Let my teaching drop as the rain,*
> *My speech distill as the dew,*
> *As the droplets on the fresh grass*
> *And as the showers on the herb.*
> *For I proclaim the name of the* LORD;
> *Ascribe greatness to our God!*
> *The Rock! His work is perfect,*
> *For all His ways are just;*
> *A God of faithfulness and without injustice,*

Righteous and upright is He.
They have acted corruptly toward Him,
{They are} not His children, because of their defect;
{But are} a perverse and crooked generation.
Do you thus repay the LORD,
O foolish and unwise people?
Is not He your Father who has bought you?
He has made you and established you.
Remember the days of old,
Consider the years of all generations.
Ask your father, and he will inform you,
Your elders, and they will tell you.
When the Most High gave the nations their inheritance,
When He separated the sons of man,
He set the boundaries of the peoples
According to the number of the sons of Israel.
For the LORD'S portion is His people;
Jacob is the allotment of His inheritance.
He found him in a desert land,
And in the howling waste of a wilderness;
He encircled him, He cared for him,
He guarded him as the pupil of His eye.
Like an eagle that stirs up its nest,
That hovers over its young,
He spread His wings and caught them,
He carried them on His pinions.
The LORD alone guided him,
And there was no foreign god with him.
He made him ride on the high places of the earth,
And he ate the produce of the field;
And He made him suck honey from the rock,
And oil from the flinty rock,
Curds of cows, and milk of the flock,
With fat of lambs,
And rams, the breed of Bashan, and goats,
With the finest of the wheat—
And of the blood of grapes you drank wine.
But Jeshurun grew fat and kicked—

You are grown fat, thick, and sleek—
Then he forsook God who made him,
And scorned the Rock of his salvation.
They made Him jealous with strange {gods;}
With abominations they provoked Him to anger.
They sacrificed to demons who were not God,
To gods whom they have not known,
New {gods} who came lately,
Whom your fathers did not dread.
You neglected the Rock who begot you,
And forgot the God who gave you birth.
And the LORD saw {this,} and spurned {them}
Because of the provocation of His sons and daughters.
Then He said, 'I will hide My face from them,
I will see what their end {shall be;}
For they are a perverse generation,
Sons in whom is no faithfulness.
They have made Me jealous with {what} is not God;
They have provoked Me to anger with their idols.
So I will make them jealous with {those who} are not a people;
I will provoke them to anger with a foolish nation,
For a fire is kindled in My anger,
And burns to the lowest part of Sheol,
And consumes the earth with its yield,
And sets on fire the foundations of the mountains.
I will heap misfortunes on them;
I will use My arrows on them.
{They shall be} wasted by famine, and consumed by plague
And bitter destruction;
And the teeth of beasts I will send upon them,
With the venom of crawling things of the dust.
Outside the sword shall bereave,
And inside terror—
Both young man and virgin,
The nursling with the man of gray hair.
I would have said, "I will cut them to pieces,
I will remove the memory of them from men,"
Had I not feared the provocation by the enemy,

Lest their adversaries should misjudge,
Lest they should say, "Our hand is triumphant,
And the LORD has not done all this."'
For they are a nation lacking in counsel,
And there is no understanding in them.
Would that they were wise, that they understood this,
That they would discern their future!
How could one chase a thousand,
And two put ten thousand to flight,
Unless their Rock had sold them,
And the LORD had given them up?
Indeed their rock is not like our Rock,
Even our enemies themselves judge this.
For their vine is from the vine of Sodom,
And from the fields of Gomorrah;
Their grapes are grapes of poison,
Their clusters, bitter.
Their wine is the venom of serpents,
And the deadly poison of cobras.
Is it not laid up in store with Me,
Sealed up in My treasuries?
'Vengeance is Mine, and retribution,
In due time their foot will slip;
For the day of their calamity is near,
And the impending things are hastening upon them.'
For the LORD will vindicate His people,
And will have compassion on His servants;
When He sees that {their} strength is gone,
And there is none {remaining,} bond or free.
And He will say, 'Where are their gods,
The rock in which they sought refuge?
Who ate the fat of their sacrifices,
{And} drank the wine of their libation?
Let them rise up and help you,
Let them be your hiding place!
See now that I, I am He,
And there is no god besides Me;
It is I who put to death and give life.

I have wounded, and it is I who heal;
And there is no one who can deliver from My hand.
Indeed, I lift up My hand to heaven,
And say, as I live forever,
If I sharpen My flashing sword,
And My hand takes hold on justice,
I will render vengeance on My adversaries,
And I will repay those who hate Me.
I will make My arrows drunk with blood,
And My sword shall devour flesh,
With the blood of the slain and the captives,
From the long-haired leaders of the enemy.'
Rejoice, O nations, {with} His people;
For He will avenge the blood of His servants,
And will render vengeance on His adversaries,
And will atone for His land {and} His people."
(Deuteronomy 31:30–32:43)

If you do not understand the *parabolic imagery* that Moses used in his song, you obviously do not understand *The Teaching of Moses*. The Apostles understood that *parabolic imagery*, as did the Early Church Fathers. Later on in this series, I will show you evidence that the Apostles taught the *parabolic imagery* of *The Teaching* to the Apostolic Church as *The Way*. However, the Church "turned aside from *The Way*" some 1800 years ago just as the sons of Israel had done so many times before.

The question is, Are you willing to return to *The Way*? Only you can answer that question, and answer it you will—one way or the other. Having read what I have written, you will either believe it, or you will reject it. It is impossible for you not to do one or the other. One cannot simply sit on the fence. But no matter what you decide to believe, I will stand absolved of any guilt in your regard. By the time I have written all the things I plan to write, I will have accomplished what God called me to do. I will have *restored "The Way* of the Lord" so that those who desire to can return to the Lord.

I merely remind you that, should you decide not to believe "*The Way*," the witness of *The Song of Moses* provides an incredibly detailed testimony as to your sin; and it will testify against you on that Great Day. So, believe it if you care to; disbelieve it if you dare to; it makes no difference to me one way or the other. I'm just doing what God called me to do.

INDEX